The Cosmo Girl's Guide
to
The New Etiquette

The Cosmo Girl's Guide
to
The New Etiquette

Cosmopolitan Books   New York

Acknowledgments

Many writers contributed to *The Cosmo Girl's Guide to the New Etiquette* and we are grateful to all of them. The authors of specific chapters appear chronologically on the contents pages. In addition, we wish to thank the following for permission to reprint articles which appeared originally in COSMOPOLITAN MAGAZINE:

Junius Adams, "Mixing Drinks for Men," © Hearst Corp. 1967; Jean Baer, "Travel Broadens Male Horizons," from the book *Follow Me* (Macmillan), © 1965 Jean Baer; "Intelligent Woman's Guide to the Cocktail Party," © Hearst Corp. 1965; Nan Brody, "Hazards of Houseguesting," © Hearst Corp. 1970; Ellen Cohn, "The Care and Handling of Cleaning Women," © Hearst Corp. 1970; Marguerite Cullman, "How to Entertain Foreign Visitors Without Panic," © Hearst Corp. 1965; Laura Cunningham, "Why I Wear My False Eyelashes to Bed," © Hearst Corp. 1968; Nora Ephron, "How to Start a Conversation," Copyright © Hearst Corp. 1968, reprinted by permission of Nora Ephron c/o International Famous Agency; Marquita O. Fisher, "How to Write That Love Letter," © Hearst Corp. 1966; Jani Gardner, "Things to Do with Your Hands That Men Like," © Hearst Corp. 1970; Veronica Geng, "Street Compliments," © Hearst Corp. 1970; "A Little Bit of Class," © Hearst Corp. 1970; Gael Greene, "How Sexually Generous Should a Girl Be?" © Hearst Corp. 1968; Joyce Greller, "How-To-Do-It Greeting Guide," © Hearst Corp. 1968; Margo Hammack, "Boating Behavior for the Uninitiated," © Hearst Corp. 1967; Nora Johnson, "The Art of Apology," Copyright © Nora Johnson, 1969, reprinted by permission of The Sterling Lord Agency; Diane Judge, "What I Would Tell a Career Girl about Dressing Well," © Hearst Corp. 1969; Dorothy Kalins, "Yes, You *Can* Sound Like a Rich Girl," © Hearst Corp. 1969; Anne-Marie Lamanda, "You Look Great! How Do You Sound?" © Hearst Corp. 1968; Paula Mattlin, "How to Order in an Italian Restaurant," © Hearst Corp. 1971; "If You Don't Know Your Crepes from Your Coquilles Or . . . How to Order from a French Menu," © Hearst Corp. 1969; Deedee Moore, "An Airplane Kind of Love," © Hearst Corp. 1968; Paige Rense, "Is That the Right Fork?" © Hearst Corp. 1968; Jeannie Sakol, "39 Ways to be a Great Date," © Hearst Corp. 1968; "Guide for Party Girls," © Hearst Corp. 1970; Jill Schary, "Generosity in All Things," © Hearst Corp. 1968; "How I Turn a Man On," © Hearst Corp. 1968; "The Gentle Art of Selective Honesty," © Hearst Corp. 1970; Mary Lyle Weeks, "Tact," © Hearst Corp. 1967.

Cosmopolitan Books

Editorial Director   Helen Gurley Brown

Editor-in-Chief   Jeanette Sarkisian Wagner
Assistant Editor   Veronica Geng
Copy Editors   Marjorie Kalter, Ellen Tabak

Contents

Foreword: Helen Gurley Brown

Part One: The Private You

1. *Your Beautiful Body, 5*
   Gael Greene

2. *Take Care of Your Teeth and Gums, Baby, 13*

3. *Dress and Undress, 16*
   Gael Greene

4. *Fashion Cues, 21*
   Diane Judge

5. *Why I Wear My False Eyelashes to Bed, 26*
   Laura Cunningham

Part Two: The Public You

1. *How to Have a Little Bit of Class, 35*
   Veronica Geng

2. *The New Language*, 42
    Gael Greene

3. *How-to-Do-It Greeting Guide*, 44
    Joyce Greller

4. *You Look Great! How Do You Sound?*, 48
    Anne-Marie Lamanda, Dorothy Kalins

5. *Starting a Conversation*, 57
    Nora Ephron

6. *How to Remember Names*, 62

7. *Never Amiss Again*, 64
    Gael Greene

8. *How to Write That Love Letter*, 65
    Marquita O. Fisher

9. *The Use and Abuse of Friends*, 70
    Gael Greene

10. *Twenty Tips on Making Friends in the Big City*, 73

11. *Scorn Not the Street Compliment!*, 75
    Veronica Geng

12. *The Perfect Tactician*, 80
    Mary Lyle Weeks

13. *The Gentle Art of Selective Honesty*, 86
    Jill Schary

14. *Dating Expertise*, 95
    Gael Greene, Jeannie Sakol

15. *Eating Out in French and Italian, 102*
    Paula Mattlin

16. *Meeting His Mother, 117*

17. *Office Romance, 119*
    Gael Greene

18. *Caviar and Catnip: Inspired Gifting, 122*
    Gael Greene

19. *Being a Hostess, 129*
    Gael Greene, Junius Adams, Marguerite Cullmann,
    Ellen Cohn

20. *Being a Guest, 156*
    Nan Brody, Jeannie Sakol, Jean Baer

21. *Two for the Road, 168*
    Gael Greene, Deedee Moore, Margo Hammack,
    Jean Baer

22. *Money, Of Course, 193*
    Gael Greene

23. *Generosity in All Things, 205*
    Jill Schary

24. *The Art of Apology, 210*
    Nora Johnson

25. *Coexisting with Women's Lib, 215*
    Gael Greene

26. *A Quickie Etiquette Quiz, 217*
    Paige Rense

Part Three: The Libidinal You

1. *How to Be a Virgin with Style and Grace,* 223
   Gael Greene

2. *Sexual Expertise and How to Get It,* 226
   Gael Greene

3. *How I Turn a Man On,* 227
   Jill Schary

4. *How Sexually Generous a Girl Should Be,* 229
   Gael Greene

5. *How to Communicate in Bed,* 235
   Gael Greene

6. *Twenty-five Thoughtful Things to Do for a Man in the Bedroom,* 238
   Gael Greene

7. *Things to Do with Your Hands That Men Like,* 241
   Jani Gardner

8. *A Philosophy of Considerate Adultery,* 243
   Gael Greene

9. *The Etiquette of Not Getting Pregnant,* 246
   Gael Greene

10. *Accidental Pregnancy Countdown,* 249
    Gael Greene

11. *Illicit Togetherness,* 253
    Gael Greene

Foreword

What does etiquette mean today to a girl like you? Well, etiquette has *always* meant good manners and courtesy, but now it means even more. Etiquette could be defined as intuition, empathy, thoughtfulness, as well as self-confidence and poise. It's knowing what to do with your roommate (male) when your mother comes to visit, as well as knowing how to defend yourself—*yes*, even now, with all that sexual freedom—against men who want *you* more than you want *them*. Etiquette is knowing when to honor traditional social rules and when to ignore them.

Etiquette can never *be* a static style of behavior . . . the same year after year. It evolves. Alas, many arbiters of manners just don't seem to *acknowledge* the changes or keep pace with what people—especially a girl like you—really *do*. Nobody tells you where to hang your fall in a strange man's bedroom or what *not* to wear under your see-through blouse. This book does! To find out correct procedures for the formal ceremonies of life—who escorts the mother of the bride down the aisle or where to put the butter knife—we would recommend the very excellent Amy Vanderbilt or Emily Post etiquette books. For more personal situations . . . well, there is *this* book of etiquette compiled *especially* for you, That Cosmopolitan Girl. We have tried honestly—and with good taste—to confront hundreds of *contemporary* subjects—the etiquette of living with a man, how to survive infidelity, what to do when you get pregnant but didn't *mean* to. Some of the advice is surprisingly old-fashioned, but I don't think you'll find any of it stuffy or square. In a sense we are sensualists and have taken *that* approach to solutions—the advice is designed to make you confident *and* lovable. "Love is the willingness to assume the responsibility for someone else's happiness," a brilliant lawyer-scientist once said. Our approach to etiquette is love-oriented in that way.

So here you are—the private you, the public you, and the libidinal you . . . female, oh so female, and yet absolutely a first-class woman. "A gentleman," said H. L. Mencken, "is one who never strikes a woman without provocation." A lady, no doubt, is one who never supplies

1

the provocation! "The gentleman," said Oscar Wilde, "is one who never hurts anyone's feelings unintentionally." A lady melts her enemies with kindness. The final test of manners, an unknown Englishman once wrote, "is respect for those who can be of no possible service to you." Right on!

As to who needs manners today, possibly a great beauty or an heiress can manage to flaunt all the rules of courtesy, but no one will really *like* her or want to be with her. Yet simply being *correct* isn't the answer *either*. Etiquette must be dispensed with warmth and sincerity. There is *no* rigid code . . . more and more *you* must judge the situation on its merits and decide what would be the *kindest* thing to do . . . send off the least sparks . . . cause the least trauma . . . where is honesty cruel and a small lie the gift of love.

Here then are some guidelines, compiled lovingly just for you. If generosity and compassion are figuratively tattooed right inside your heart, you can never go too far wrong.

Helen Gurley Brown
EDITOR-IN-CHIEF, COSMOPOLITAN

PART ONE
The Private You

1. YOUR BEAUTIFUL BODY

Beauty is visual attractiveness. Beauty is also polite. Perhaps it simply never occurs to you that the twenty-seven minutes you spend in front of your multibulb makeup mirror applying all those perfumed balms and paints is not vanity but a reflection of good manners. Perhaps you consider beauty care as competition or mere survival, and good health as too mundane and boring to think about. Well, when Dame Margot Fonteyn was interviewed on the eve of her fiftieth birthday about her still-incredible youth and stamina, the seemingly ageless ballerina mused, "I suppose I should get a face-lift. It would be much *kinder* to my friends." Yes, her friends!

Your vitality and good looks indeed are a reflection of your kindness to the world. The way you move and stand, your rosy, scrubbed-clean face artfully ablush says *you care.* You have pride in yourself . . . you are, therefore, *worth caring about.* Nothing is a clearer giveaway of severe depression than an abandoned body—the face ignored, the hair asnarl, shapeless, soiled clothes. Loretta Young, with her ramrod posture and perfectionism, would no more think of appearing on the street face-naked than body-naked. "I owe it to the public," she says.

You may not be a raving beauty. Accept yourself and improve what you are. To abandon the project because you'll never pass for Raquel Welch no matter how hard you try is a cop-out. (Raquel didn't look that way when *she* started either!) Invest in plain-girl power: inner dazzle, verbal dazzle, cerebral dazzle, libidinal dazzle. *Work* at it.

Listen to Jeanne Moreau, that most womanly of liberated women: "Sex appeal comes from within. Be conscious of your figure and take care of it—it's like being clean. And if you're intelligent, why not show it? There's nothing frightening about intelligence."

And anyway . . . little flaws can be devastatingly attractive! Look what Brigitte Bardot did with a too-full lower lip and slightly buck

5

teeth. Do you think Sophia Loren spends hours brooding because her bosom is unfashionably ample? See how far Twiggy went with that ironing-board build. The imperfect nose. Remember Barbra Streisand. Freckles, slightly generous derrière. Myopia . . . think how handsome Grace Kelly looks in her glasses, and perhaps some of Monica Vitti's appealing sultriness has to do with her nearsightedness.

The late Coco Chanel kept a pot of rouge at her bedside. "Think of the man who sleeps beside you," Chanel said. "Does he want to wake up to a pale face? Whatever time you go out in the morning or at night, put on your makeup and perfume exactly as if you were going to meet the man of your life."

Good grooming *is* good manners. The priceless dividend of looking smashing—and *knowing* you do—is that once you're put together, you can direct your attention outward. When you see the well-turned-out beauty in your three-way mirror, you then *relax* and concern yourself with everything else around you.

Fussiness

It's a bore to be constantly fussing and pulling and adjusting something about yourself. Make sure you are well-glued before you leave home. Is your wig anchored . . . are your eyelashes intact? If the eyelashes are tacky, buy new ones or patch these. If the wig rides or slips, don't wear it. Stop hunting for real or imaginary wrinkles. *Never* talk about your beauty rituals in public. You only call attention to flaws by apologizing for them. Men are not the *least* bit interested in your contact lenses, skin problems, upper thigh woes, and nervous twitches.

Of course you will not perish or be stoned if caught without your face on, but try and avoid it. Worse than no grooming at all is compulsive anxiety. If you are stranded on a desert island with Omar Sharif and a deck of bridge cards, but minus your white camouflage stick and your moisturizer, life will go on. He's a bridge freak and there are *other* games. You can even survive without toothpaste . . . nibble some parsley or a bit of watercress, suck a lemon or lime. Salt water is perfect.

You, Without Clothing

Love your body and everyone else will too. A loved body is well-tended, clean, and healthy. Regular medical checkups and twice a year visits to the dentist . . . vitamins and a balanced diet . . . enough sleep . . . the ability to relax . . . all these are your allies. Use them.

Study body language. You can buy books on the subject—kinesis—or watch others whose grace you admire. Learn to convey your message by your movements: I am female. I love being me. I am lovable.

Perfect posture is one of your most positive statements. Slumping has never been known to excite or attract anybody. *That* body language says: I hate me. I'm hiding. Standing tall takes inches off your waistline, elongates your entire frame, gives you a good breast profile. Consider a posture class, exercise gym, or Yoga lessons to teach you how to control your body movements. Why do some girls look so graceful and happy standing around at cocktail parties while other poor unfortunates look lost, lumpy, and forlorn?

Nobody said it was *easy*. Exercise is a *drag* . . . a *bore* . . . a *terrible chore*. As Lauren Bacall confides: "I force myself to go to the gym." And Lauren is in far better shape than most girls her age. *Force* yourself.

Hair: Enough, Too Much, and Alas

Hair is a glorious camouflage. The squashiest nothing little face can be transformed into sultry sensuality by great gobs of beautiful shining hair, preferably your own. Rich-girl hair, a shiny, silky mane that cascades from a smooth forehead to below the shoulders, is better than money-in-the-bank. It requires washing, setting, and conditioners two or three times a week, but gives you unquenchable confidence. Tangled, dirty, frizzy hair can sabotage even a born-beauty. I cannot imagine what life was like *before* hairpieces. Impossible. Invest in one, *after* you've considered many alternative styles.

Hair is a negative when it's stubble on your legs (men know you shave, but they hate to see the evidence or the act), silky black on your upper lip, lacquered into a gluey solidity on your head, or so perfect you panic if the wind blows and make your man put the top up on his convertible—carry a scarf, put it over your head and be carefree. And a curse on the girl who says: "George, don't! You're messing my hair and I just had it done!"

How to Behave at the Hairdresser's

Mothers are marvelous, but a good hairdresser is a girl's best silent friend. Hunt for one who makes you feel comfortable and look super . . . adore him, court him, tip him, gift him, bury him in compliments and homemade cookies. Be loyal. Don't devastate him with your comments or become hysterical when he approaches with a scissors . . . communicate.

If the hairdo really isn't *quite* what you wanted, don't destroy it before his very eyes. Tame it a bit at home . . . explain better next time.

Make an appointment, don't just pop in: Be on time! Or a little early. Don't always ask to be worked in around other appointments and then scream when you run twenty minutes overtime.

7

Keep track of time so you don't get burned to a crisp under the dryer. If you like, scrub your face before going in and give yourself a creamy lubrication or light facial massage under the dryer. A beauty salon is a great place to read and write letters, but not for social phone calls. Tip generously (see money chapter) and remember all your pets at Christmas (see gift chapter). Be courteous to *everyone* . . . say please when you ask for a cup of coffee, and be extravagant with your "thank you"s.

The Well-Tempered Epidermis

Clean skin . . . scrub it really clean . . . often . . . let it breathe. Give it steam and a *little* bit of sun. Sun, courted *prudently,* can be your skin's best flatterer, according to New York dermatological genius Dr. Norman Orentreich, but sun also can be your *worst* enemy. *Never* allow yourself to burn. If you're so busy tanning now, don't be surprised to see a leathery prune in your mirror by the time you are thirty-five. Learn all about sun screeners and sun tanners.

For a serious skin problem, nothing will do but a good dermatologist and discipline. Find one; follow his regimen. There's something to be said for faith, too. If you *really* believe raw apples or tomato slices are magic on your skin . . . then a raw apple or tomato facial is for you. I have a friend who swears by a yogurt mask.

Mirror, Mirror, Tell Me True!

Well, of course, we all know Doris Day has twenty-two makeup men assigned to do her face, and when Lynda Bird Johnson wanted to know what to do with herself, George Masters (then Saks Fifth Avenue's hair and makeup expert in Los Angeles) was *instantly* available. But what about you? Where do you find help?

Read your favorite magazine, Cosmopolitan and *Harper's Bazaar,* and others. Some of their beauty advice may not be exactly right for you . . . much is exaggerated to make a point. *Get* the point . . . then buy yourself a range of cosmetic colors and experiment. Ask the consultants who work at cosmetic counters. Work in front of a brutally well-lit mirror. Squint . . . see where white shadow helps to widen eyes or bring out cheekbones . . . see where deeper tones will give you cheekbones you weren't born with. Try again. When a makeup wizard visits your town to do department store demonstrations . . . go . . . be a guinea pig. Evaluate the results. Do you look and feel better?

Remember day makeup and night makeup are two different animals. Colors will appear different under dazzling sunlight than under fluorescent lights in an office. Basically, fluorescents drain color from your face, taking away pinks and reds, and leaving grays and blues. You will have to remember to use more blusher, true reds, warmer colors to look pretty while you are at your desk. The kindest lights are Mr. Edison's good light bulb (preferably with pink hue) and romantic candles. Remember both when you are decorating a bedroom or living room. (In your kitchen and bathroom you'd better be able to see *very clearly!*)

Men say they *hate* false eyelashes . . . that means your false eyelashes shouldn't *look* false. Avoid a gummy glue line or exaggerated spikes. Apply liner carefully to bridge any gap between the real lash and the fake.

Beauty-to-Go

Bibi is a model who works out at my gym and cleverly carries the ingredients of her fresh, "natural" beauty in a gigantic fishing-tackle box. For portable grooming, you need a carrier too—something more practical, I hope. Keep one of every beauty aid you need in your office and a second, smaller, survival kit in a zipper vinyl cosmetic bag you carry in your purse. I keep a third one-of-everything packed in an overnight case for out-of-town trips. If you have to pack quickly, you're liable to forget *something*.

Your At-Home Survival Kit

MOUTH
toothpaste • two toothbrushes (alternate) • dental floss • two new toothbrushes (for guests) • Water Pik, if you can afford one

FACE—SKIN
moisturizer • astringent • face peel/facial mask • gleamers • blushers • lipsticks and brush • matte-finish makeup • eyelashes, glue • eye shadows, liner, mascara • makeup brushes • makeup remover • body creams • body powder • depilatory • deodorant • pumice stone/cream • tweezers • perfume/cologne • Chap Stick • sun filter/screener creams

HAIR
hair spray (light) • shampoo • hair dryer • combs • hairbrushes (two) • hair conditioners • tints, rinses, frostings • hair bleach

NAILS
nail files • polish remover • polish/base coat/top coat

MISCELLANEOUS
Band-Aids (assorted) • Kleenex • cotton pads • vaginal douche • sunglasses • ski goggles • razor (electric is safer on the skin) • rubber gloves (wear them when doing dishes, other water chores) • scale • three-way makeup mirror • a leotard (to see yourself as you really are)

Your Office Survival Kit

toothbrush/toothpaste (tiny size) • makeup remover • makeup kit (small plastic refills from your large at-home size) • deodorant • spray perfume/cologne • hair spray • hairbrush • purse-size spray mouthwash • nail file • polish remover/cotton pads • Band-Aids • Kleenex • spare pairs of pantyhose (one beige, one black)

Your Travel Survival Kit

toothpaste/brush • makeup remover • makeup • body cream • deodorant • depilatory or razor • tweezers • spray perfume/cologne • sun lotions • shampoo/conditioner • hairbrush • nail file • Band-Aids • sunglasses

Hands

Your hands speak for you. Unless you're going to walk around the rest of your life in a knee-length poncho, you just can't hide ragged cuticles, split nails, chipped polish, chewed stubs and nicotine stains. Think about what you *do* with your hands—the gestures (gentle, restrained, nondistracting), the movements (holding a champagne glass, pouring a cup of soothing Earl Grey tea), the loving touches. Hands ought to be silky soft, groomed, and move with feminine grace. You need a good hand cream or body moisturizer applied daily. Wear rubber gloves when doing dishes or washing his car.

All the Perfumes of Arabia

You *do* smell good. You take a long, hot relaxing bath, or a quick freshening shower, daily—or both! You really lather your body with a good soap, brush your teeth, even carry a tiny spray flacon of mouthwash in your purse for garlic crises at lunch. An obsession with bodily odors is a type of hysterical puritanism, but smelling clean is *wholesome*. Our macrobiotic-organic-hippie friends talk about being "natural"—no deodorants or scent—but it doesn't take more than a few days before even *they* can't stand being in the same room together.

Perfume conveys a message . . . are you woodsy, slinky, petulant, sophisticated, a tigress or a pussycat? Don't use a particular perfume just because the name appeals or you love the packaging. Sniff the samples at cosmetic counters. Apply them. Find the scent that is *you*. Make it your signal, so a man smelling that scent in a crowded room when you are *not* there will think of you. Use it at pulse points. Spray all over your body and hair. Try Helen Gurley Brown's favorite scentism—douse a bit of cotton, place a second cotton in front to protect your clothes and tuck it into your bra . . . it lasts and lasts. In these braless times, you may have to tape it to your chestbone.

Does He Smell Good Too?

If your man is a primitive and doesn't always smell as sweet as lemon or sandalwood, it's not easy to let him know. You might give him a giant gift set of male grooming aids and say, "I just love the way these things smell," . . . or "Once I met Joe Namath and he smelled like this." Other ploys: Ask him to take a shower with you. Soap each other all over. Start leaving a deodorant soap in the shower. Tell him how marvelous he smells after he showers. Set an example. One girl I know occasionally shakes her lover, puts on a big smile and says: "Honey, don't you want to brush your teeth?" He does.

If his sneakers have that last year air, toss them into the washing machine. "They needed it desperately," you tell him. If he wears shirts a day more than he should, start snitching them and send them to the laundry. "Oh, you wouldn't have wanted to wear that shirt again," you say. Or wash it yourself. Yes, yourself.

"You ate garlic for lunch, wow . . ." you say, leaning against the wall, a bit faint. That might perplex him a bit at first. "What can I do?" he'll ask. Tell him. Or show him "His Survival Kit" list below. Or leave it lying around. Perhaps he'll get the message.

His Survival Kit

FACE—SKIN
beard softener • after-shave lotion • blemish medication • good razor • moustache scissors, comb and brush (if he has a moustache or beard) • septic stick • toothbrushes (two) • toothpaste • mouthwash spray • sun tanners and screens • bronze gel • Chap Stick • Water Pik • deodorant • deodorant soap • cologne • hand cream

HAIR
brushes • combs • conditioner • shampoo (not yours!) • a great barber

MISCELLANEOUS
Band-Aids • nail clippers for hands/feet • ski goggles • sunglasses • travel case for holding shaving equipment, shoe-shine essentials, etc.

ABOVE ALL
You

THINGS THAT ARE TACKY

Chewing on your hair.
Biting at your cuticle.

Sitting legs apart or awkwardly arranged.

Climbing into taxis in the rump-up position.

Chewing gum.

Smoking on the street.

Dangling a cigarette from your lip while talking.

Dirty back of neck, inside ears—who are you fooling?

Making everyone else feel guilty because they can eat eclairs and you're consigned to a tangerine.

Munching fingernails.

Pawing at your face.

Squinting because you like to pretend you can see without your glasses.

Asking your friend in a loud voice: "Is that a wig?" Maybe she likes to pretend it's all her.

Dirty comb and brush.

Making up at the dining table.

Curlers in public . . . no excuse unless you're on your way to the photographer for a sitting.

Chipped nail polish . . . or one naked nail.

Pointed claws . . . or the nails of one hand twice as long as the other.

Mask makeup.

A dramatic line where your makeup ends and the real you begins.

Scraggly split ends.

The real-you hair growing in—don't tint hair unless you vow to touch-up with obsessive devotion.

Talking about your internal eccentricities: operations, neuroses, allergies, diet.

2. TAKE CARE OF YOUR TEETH AND GUMS, BABY

Girls often neglect their gums, which is a shame since your mouth (right over your gums) is where you get *kissed*, and the whole area *ought* to be one of the nicest parts of you. Toothpaste and mouthwash *help* keep breath fresh, but a girl's mouth is never really kissably sweet unless *gums* are pink and healthy. Besides, neglect can mean more than a not-nice smell (bad enough!). If you don't do right by your gums, you're likely to lose your *teeth!*

Gum damage is *the* most common cause of tooth loss among adults. (Too many people just don't realize that teeth are potential goners when gum tissue begins to break down.) So be grateful if your dentist bullies you a little about your gums—that means he's doing his job.

Healthy gums are firm, pink, and tight against tooth and bone. Reddened, inflamed, puffy gums are *sick*, and when inflammation is allowed to persist, the fleshy tissue becomes loosened, flaplike, and pockets of infection (dentists call them abscesses) set in. Infection undermines bone structure beneath the gums, and this leads to eventual loss of teeth.

How do you avoid gum inflammation? First, take care of your *general* health. Tension, overwork, temporary illness, and vitamin shortage (particularly vitamin C) are all possible causes of inflamed gums.

Next, take care of your teeth. Neglect your teeth, and gums *automatically* suffer. Tooth care starts with a conscientious twice-a-day brushing. This helps rid teeth of tartar and plaque—a soft, clinging, skinlike film made of saliva, bacteria, and starchy food material. (The bacteria, which can cause tooth decay, are also a source of gum irritation and infection.) Tartar is a hard coating, built up from calcium deposits, that doesn't *hurt* your teeth (though it's usually stained and unattractive *looking*), but irritates the gums by cutting into them.

13

How you brush is important. You should brush *all* the surfaces of your teeth—cheek, top, and back sides. (Hidden surfaces are *just* as likely to accumulate bacteria and tartar.) Use an up-and-down or *circular* motion; horizontal side-to-side brushing can abrade your teeth. If you are too lazy to brush properly, get an electric toothbrush, which gives an energetic circular cleaning *automatically.*

Brush and *stimulate* your gums; they were *designed* to take a certain amount of abrasive action, probably because primitive man had such a tough, fibrous diet. Modern foods are finely milled, and gums long for the stimulation they *used* to get from hard, fresh vegetables and fruits, and from chewy meats.

The rubber tip on the handle end of your toothbrush is also good for stimulating gums; when you brush, finish up by working the tip around the edges of your teeth. Stim-U-Dents (toothpick-size wooden slivers that wedge in and massage spaces between teeth) help keep gums firm and pink as a cavewoman's, too.

By far the *best* way to stimulate gums (and have a kissable mouth generally) is to use a Water Pik oral irrigating device after every meal. Dentists *rave* about it, and there are also other makes on the market now. The Water Pik works electrically, shooting a fine, pulsating (twenty pulses per second) stream of water into the mouth and between teeth. This *feels* wonderful and just about *guarantees* improved gum health. The Water Pik also helps keep between-teeth spaces free of crammed-in food particles. (When food bits remain in the interstices between teeth, bacteria multiply and toxins are released that irritate gums and threaten teeth with decay.) Fill the Water Pik up to the top with warm water, use it regularly, and *know* you're doing the best thing for your pretty mouth. Other ways to keep between-teeth spaces clean: use dental tape (flatter than floss) or Pick-A-Dents (cleverly hooked, reusable plastic toothpicks) to get between and behind teeth.

Now that you know *what* you need for gum care, and why these procedures are necessary, here is a working-girl program designed by one dentist (he loves working girls to have kissable mouths):

1. After breakfast: Brush thoroughly, work gums over with the rubber tip on toothbrush; irrigate gums with your new Water Pik.

2. After lunch: Presumably you're at the office and can't conveniently brush or irrigate; skip down to the ladies' room (or just wait for a minute alone) and, with the dental tape or a Pick-A-Dent, get rid of leftover lunch-bits between teeth. Rinse mouth thoroughly with salt water if you can.

3. After dinner: Brush and use Water Pik if you're dining at home; otherwise, work at between-teeth spaces with Pick-A-Dent or dental tape. (No—*not* at the table!)

4. Before bed: Give gums a real treat! You've brushed after dinner; now use Water Pik again or at least a Stim-U-Dent. Massaging gums with your *fingers* helps, too.

14

Follow this schedule (or something similar) and your dentist will go into *raptures* over the state of your gums next time he sees you. *Don't* skip seeing him. No matter how conscientious you've been, you need a cavity check, and he can polish and scrape off tartar and plaque that brushing can't banish. For some girls, even twice-yearly visits aren't enough to keep gums pink and lovely. (*My* teeth require tartar-scraping about every three months.) Smoking—which leads to grubbier, heavier deposits of plaque—may *also* make it necessary for you to visit the dentist oftener. Smokers, especially, can benefit from a once-a-week brushing with plain old baking soda.

Now one more word about the horrors awaiting you if you *don't* care for teeth and gums! Periodontitis, the medical name for gum inflammation (laymen usually call it pyorrhea), may develop after a time of neglect. Trench mouth and gingivitis are two of the commonest types of periodontitis. (Trench mouth is not, contrary to popular notion, particularly contagious among adults. The bacteria that cause the infection are present in practically every grown-up mouth, but become active only when gums have been neglected, or when resistance is lowered by illness, too much dating and drinking, not enough sleep.)

First thing to do if periodontitis crops up is see your dentist, naturally! He'll instantly remove all gum irritants, like build-ups of tartar and plaque, as well as the rough edges of teeth and fillings. If necessary, he'll also scrape off dead or dying gum tissue. In an *acute* case of periodontitis, he may prescribe antibiotics. Next he'll remind you to do all the things we've been talking about—gum massage, keeping tooth spaces clear, etc., etc. If you take *care* of your gums, of course, you'll probably never *get* periodontitis. That's what you want, because every time gum inflammation occurs, it causes *some* degree of damage to the bone structure that holds your precious teeth in place. Recurrent bouts of inflamed gums have a cumulative bad effect—even if you *do* remedy the trouble promptly each time.

Be *good* to your gums! This isn't one more take-it-or-leave-it self-improvement piece of advice; this is your *mouth!* With or *without* kisses—and we hope *with*—you want it healthy and happy.

3. DRESS AND UNDRESS

Talk about liberation! Suddenly all the old rules of dress have been suspended. Unisex, the Great Pants Revolution, ten million boots marching across the nation, and the great unleashing of bras have swept a century of fuss and fogginess into the junk heap.

Once the strictures were clear as springwater, hats for church and town, gloves always, no bare legs on nice girls—ever, girdles an absolute must, pants strictly for the country, and still only for the young. Now nurses and bank tellers wear pantsuits, patrician matrons dine in transparent pajamas and women of "a certain age" boldly appear in black bodystockings and ammunition belts. Alas, it's easy to fall flat on your Carmen Miranda dirndl. There is still one rule: propriety. That means wear what's *right* for you and what's *right* for what you are going to do. Everything you put on should polish your assets like sterling and blur your flaws like camouflage.

"Look for the woman in the dress," was a favorite theme of the late Coco Chanel. "If there is no woman, there is no dress." And . . . "In love, what counts is to please a man," Coco liked to say. "If it pleases him, paint yourself green."

Dress to please the man in your life. But don't overdo it. Dressing for a man *doesn't* mean dragging him to your favorite stores to make him choose what he likes on you. It means you wear what makes you look appealing and avoid the chaff. Men can be drearily conservative. They resist change and need to be lured to a new look or a new length, slowly and gradually. Stay aware and try.

The man who falls all over the giggly brunette with the pop-up bosom or the naked tummy or the shortest shorts in the room will want to fade into the wallpaper if you—his adored—appear in the same costume. Be careful . . . even if you happen to be in better trim than Miss Pop-Up Bosom.

16

Go with fashion, but don't sell yourself into fashion slavery. Twelve girls at the same cinema-festival opening in velvet knickers, identical bullet belts, and fringed boots are pathetic. You, in the same panne velvet knickers but with a suede belt locked by an old art-nouveau buckle, are infinitely more interesting. Style is individual. It's what *you* do with fashion to make it yours alone! When everyone in your crowd is rigged up like a strolling Gypsy or Moroccan princess, do not underestimate the pow of sleek black simplicity.

Men hate the midi, they think. But men *adore* tightly laced boots and tiny waistlines and flashes of thigh, and you can have all that with the midi. And I have yet to meet a man who objected to a midi cut up the side or front to reveal short shorts underneath. Not every midi will suit you, but somewhere there is a proportion cut just for you. Impossible, you say: Aha. You're in serious trouble and need to shed twenty pounds. Quick.

Designer Anne Klein said it: "Far-out fashion can be fun, but I can't bear to see a girl who isn't relaxed and easy with these clothes. Watching someone yank at a hemline or endlessly fuss with her fall drives me crazy . . . find a look that's right and comfortable." I said it before. I repeat: Pull yourself together, then *forget* about it.

A dress you can't move or cuddle in without worrying about moulting feathers or splitting a seam is a disaster . . . no matter how divine it looked in *Vogue*. Give it away and never buy another with similar faults. You're going to be a grouch all evening if those groovy grommets dig into your rib cage with every breath.

Nothing can ruin your day more efficiently than a shoe that pinches, abrades, and digs. You can read the pain plain as yogurt on your face. If the *glass slipper* doesn't slip on easily in midafternoon when your feet are most vulnerable . . . forget it. You can't break in a shoe . . . it only breaks you with pain and wasted dollars.

Avoid the Grooming Gloom

1. A close fit is no fit at all. A good alteration lady is your third best friend (after Mother and the hairdresser).

2. Clean underwear *every day*.

3. If you hate to wash and iron, don't buy clothes that need it. (I didn't own an iron until a friend—considering me a poverty case—passed one along three months ago. I haven't used it yet.) But you will need a large budget for cleaning bills. If you don't have money, learn to wash and iron and avoid buying clothes that must be cleaned!

4. It's a little rip . . . sew it now. Hoard extra buttons when you find ones you like.

5. Weed out the inevitable flaw: snagged stockings, pulled threads, a spot of Orange Julius on your capeskin glove, a rip in the lining of

your handsome ostrich handbag. Repair it before you wear it again . . . or give it away.

6. Prune the closet mercilessly. Don't drag rejects with you the rest of your life . . . if you haven't worn an item in two years (a decade?), discard it. Not in the trash can. Clean it, and donate it to a charity thrift shop. Ask for a receipt of approximate value. That makes it deductible.

How Do You Know What's Right for You?

1. Study yourself in a leotard before a well-lit, full-length mirror. If this experience drives you to drink . . . vow to re-form your form.

2. Who are you? What are you trying to say about yourself? What is your image? Are you playing a romantic Ali MacGraw? Or a carefree groupie? Are you a girl with her eye on Mary Wells's advertising throne? Are you a lean drink of spring water or a bubbly kewpie doll or a sinuous sensualist? Decide! Then you will develop antennae that tell you when gingham is right and where monkey-fur fringe is definitely excessive.

3. Decide whose style you admire or consider close to your ideal. Analyze what this paradigm has done and be inspired . . . don't imitate blindly.

4. If you see someone wearing an item you *absolutely* must have—even a total stranger on a bus—say so and ask where she bought it. *Don't* ask the price.

5. Read the fashion magazines. Out of the wild and exaggerated fancy there is a message: brown is great for summer . . . or . . . length doesn't really matter anymore . . . or . . . superstructured underpinnings are dead. Especially note the accessories: bags, belts, gloves, jewels, hats.

6. If you find a store that pleases you, make it your hangout. Loyalty is rewarded. When you stumble across a salesgirl with taste and energy, pursue her. Call to see if she's on hand before you venture across town on a shopping spree. Ask her to telephone you when she has something just your style . . . or when that Cardin cape you've been sighing over is reduced 20 percent.

7. If you are one of those indecisive creatures who cannot tell whether a dress with pleats and flounces in shrimp crepe is as good as it sounds till it's hung on the closet door at home for a week, then never *never* buy clothes marked "final sale," or "not returnable."

8. Learn about fabrics, seams, and construction. Go to fashion shows and try on a dress by Norell or Galanos so you'll get a feeling for what makes a $900 shirtwaist different from a $90 one.

9. If you find a bra or panty or shoe that's ideal for you . . . pantyhose that are like a second skin . . . a ribbed turtle sweater that makes you

feel like Jeanne Moreau, buy in quantity. That's what Jacqueline Onassis does. Even on *your* budget, it makes sense. If you wait until you *need* replacements, the style or color may no longer exist.

A Sampler of Specifics

Q. Is it better to put all my money into one status Gucci handbag or buy half a dozen bags for different occasions?

A. A recognizably fine bag has great impact and lasts ages. But it really won't go *everywhere*. Invest in the quality leather as your mainstay. And then collect for pennies—a larger canvas carryall, an old doctor's satchel ($2 in a junk shop), a small wicker basket or champagne wicker tied tight with a bandanna hanky, an Oriental brass box from an imports bazaar, a denim over-the-shoulder newsboy bag you make yourself.

Q. Are there any rigid fashion rules that still count these days?

A. Yes. White for tennis (unless you're playing on your own court at home) and sneakers. Warmth for skiing, hunting, cold-weather sailing—if you neglect warmth for chic you'll ruin your day and everyone else's as well. Rubber-soled shoes for yachting, preferably those with a special-grip rubber bottom. Rules for formal riding and the hunt are specific: visit a shop that specializes in riding clothes and do what they tell you.

Q. Must I wear a hat to church?

A. Women should wear hats in Roman Catholic churches and Orthodox synagogues. And many women do wear a hat to church even where it is not a must. But today a lace mantilla (like Jackie wears) or a bit of veiling is considered "hat enough." No woman should ever let lack of hair covering keep her from entering a church on impulse for a few moments of meditation. Attitude is more important than a hat. And anyway, hats are back. I couldn't live without my giant wolf beret that covers my ears in winter or half a dozen felt and straw cowboy hats in spring and summer. You need to learn clever scarf tricks for your head, a flattering all-over hat for days when your hair just doesn't cooperate.

Q. Is it right for a divorcée to wear her wedding and engagement rings? Mine are so beautiful.

A. Do you really want a constant reminder of the past? Why not have the stones reset into a marvelous ring you can wear on your index finger or, if you're not the type, something smashing for your pinky.

Q. Where can I go to find out what to wear at a Bar Mitzvah?

A. A standard etiquette book, such as Amy Vanderbilt's or Emily Post's will tell you what dress is expected at weddings, funerals, and other ceremonies of life. Or you might call the women's news department of the local paper and ask advice.

Undress

Undressing for an audience is a sadly neglected art. Too many women just peel everything off with no thought to the effect . . . rudely tossing crumpled garments here and there . . . and then slopping around in an abused and mutilated housecoat.

COSMOPOLITAN once ran a wise little article about "How to Strip for Your Husband." Tassels and twelve-button gloves are not necessary. But attractive undressing, sensuous underpinnings, and flattering, fresh at-home wear is kind to your audience—that one *special* person.

THINGS THAT ARE TACKY

Your sweet little lace blouse worn one day too many.
Tattle-tale-gray nylon underwear (tint it purple or red or
     espresso brown).
Structural safety pins.
Wrinkles, spots, baggy anything, runs, rundown heels.
Shoes clearly beyond their prime.
A handbag that had it two years ago, still "making do."
Rhinestones and satin pumps in the office.
Ruffles when you are much more the slinky jersey type.
Too-big coats and shoddy tailoring.
Super clunk shoes.
Ice-cream-cone bosoms.
Bulges . . . panties that bind and show-through.
Drooping hems . . . make a fast temporary repair with sticky tape,
     then sew that very evening.
Baby-doll costumes on women over thirty-five unless you
     have the figure and complexion of a twenty-year-old.
See-through blouse with a utilitarian bra in full view.
Anything that looks like it's wearing you.
Itsy-bitsy fragile little jewelry. If you can't afford knock-out
     jewelry in 18-karat gold, buy some smashing fakery.
Last year's rejects or rotting nightgowns as at-home clothes . . .
     give the home folks a break.
Toting an adorable Lilliputian evening bag and loading your man's
     pockets with survival paraphernalia . . . learn to survive on less.

4. FASHION CUES

Six fashion experts gave Cosmo their advice for career girls who want to dress well.

BILL BLASS has been designing for more than twenty-five years. Jackie Onassis, Happy Rockefeller, Mrs. Henry Ford II, have been among his customers.

"Let's start with the woman inside the clothes. Whatever she does about fashion will be pointless unless she is thin, healthy, and clean. Without these basics nothing else matters.

"America has never had a fashion 'look' the way the French have. You can tell a Parisian anywhere. About the only thing American women seem determined to do with a vengeance is match their accessories! This may be the single worst crime in fashion. A best-dressed woman like Mrs. William Paley spends a lot of time and money on buying the right *mismatched* accessories. Why not try it? How about a small red alligator bag with navy calf shoes! Also, you must be a little practical about the realities of your life. Do you go to formal parties often? If not, don't let yourself get hung up on an evening dress for one occasion, no matter how beautiful it is or how important the man who's taking you to the ball.

"The next rule may surprise you: Don't shop with your girl friends. They may adore you but, psychologically, women do not particularly want to see *other* women look great. You just can't trust their advice. Put your faith in a reliable saleswoman. Try to have the same person help you each time. If she likes you, she'll give *good* advice and help build your fashion sense and self-confidence. Of course, *you* make the final selection.

"Do you have an open mind about fashion, or do you say, 'Oh, I never wear splashy prints,' or 'I hate pink'? How do you know until you try them? Maybe you haven't experimented recently enough. Let the saleswoman show them anyway. Just think of all the people who told you they would *never* wear patterned stockings, or a mini-dress, or

21

go without a bra. Maybe *you* ought to try some new—becoming—things you said *you* would never wear."

DONALD BROOKS: the Parsons School of Design honored him with a rare award presented to only three other designers—Norman Norell, Christian Dior, and Hollywood's Adrian.

"One problem that women have is their inability to be truly honest about their looks. The average woman can't or won't see her own shortcomings. She *must!* She should also recognize her assets and capitalize on *them.* Analyze yourself, play down the faults, play up the assets! Yes, it can all be done with the right clothes. Create your image around your best features . . . small waist, slim hips, or whatever.

"Women sometimes make the mistake of buying clothes that are very fashionable but not particularly becoming. They often choose the wrong shape or an unflattering color simply because it's In!

"I love the pulled-together look. This means thinking about your wardrobe in terms of color and texture—what works together. You can study people you know are well dressed and see what elements make them look marvelous.

"Naturally, the career girl should select her wardrobe and accessories with an eye toward multiple use. I always say fewer things of greater quality will make you look better and feel better."

RUDI GERNREICH is the most daring and youthful of U.S. fashion trendsetters (remember the topless bathing suit?). Barbara Feldon, Carol Channing, Betty Furness are a few who adore Rudi's dashing clothes, and he is a favorite with fashion models too. Winner of many fashion awards, Rudi now is accepted as a visionary even by the fashion establishment that once opposed him.

"A new fashion must be overstated to make its point. You don't think I seriously thought women would buy and then *wear* a topless bathing suit? But the impact, startling as it was, made my point—that nudity was the thing of the future. And now it is. But modified!

"So the first 'don't' I would tell a woman is: Don't accept verbatim what has been done and imitate it. Do extract from that look and adapt it to your own personality.

"I like clothes to be expendable. One of my biggest don'ts is: don't invest a fortune in clothes and then be stuck with last-season's look, when your heart is breaking for *this* year's new things.

"A career girl must have clothes that are basically practical. The most practical dress a girl can include in her wardrobe is the basic shirtdress. But—and here's the challenge—how does one adapt this classic to today's times? The timid girl sticks to her 'safe' look of years past. Her skirt is too short, her heels are too low, her bag is too big, and her makeup is too safe. Yet, the same shirtdress can be bought in an up-to-date midi at the right length and worn with colored tights, boots, a modified Sassoon haircut, and her own imaginative makeup. She may not know it, but what she has done is adapt fashion to suit herself.

"Don't imitate. Do adapt. But most of all, *have fun* with fashion."

TOM NASSARRE is the designer at Schrader Sport Division. Self-taught, he broke into the market on the basis of a portfolio of great fashion sketches. Many top models in New York are his customers.

"The career girl has a new problem today; her usual worries over how to dress have been compounded by the revolution in men's wear. So, don't be afraid to ask your date what he is wearing for the evening. You don't want to clash with him. There was a time when you could count on a nice dark suit—no more. You don't want to look like two people who ran into each other accidentally.

"Accessories are important: good-quality bags, shoes, scarves—in fact, scarves are the 'jewelry' of today. But the accessories most girls overlook are the ones they have with them at all times. For example, glasses. Nothing is more damaging to a woman's good looks than that 'sudden squint' as the menu goes out of focus. Wear your glasses, but let them be chic, simple, contemporary.

"One thing I firmly believe is that young women must be contemporary. If you go against the current look, you call undue attention to yourself.

"Career girls certainly shouldn't try to be sexpots. A girl must be natural, not overdone. Too many women dress according to some previous heyday . . . maybe high school or something.

"It's a good idea to find yourself a color story. Decide your best color and *use* it—perhaps for the entire season. This solves a lot of fashion *and* budget problems.

"Skip the extra dress and spend the money on good alterations. If the clothes you have are any good at all, you should pay to save them.

"And be as attractive when undressed as you are fully dressed. Mother's old cry as you pinned your bra strap—'What if a bus hits you?'—was pretty smart. What if a bus did hit you and the handsome intern zipped off your dress and there was a hideous safety pin? How *could* you?"

GEOFFREY BEENE started his career as a med student, making fashion sketches all over his chemistry and biology papers. When he turned to designing, more than fifteen years ago, his knowledge of anatomy was helpful, making him a master in the art of cutting cloth to serve the body. Geoffrey has won many fashion awards. Some of his newsy clients are Lynda Johnson Robb, Faye Dunaway, Vanessa Redgrave, and Joanna Barnes.

"I can tell you in one second all my 'dos and don'ts.' The wrong accessory piques me more than any other mistake a woman can make. You have to remember that everything you put on is part of the total look. Shoes have never been so important as today . . . they're no longer a simple matter. Once a girl just had to buy pumps in a few colors.

The heel height was constant and she could wear the same shoe morning, noon, and night. It isn't so any more. Proportion is the key to the right shoe.

"Hosiery has become *the* key accessory. Stockings can enhance or ruin the effect of your outfit. No longer can a girl just go and buy a dozen pairs of stockings in a neutral shade and forget about them. She has to choose daytime, evening, sport, dress pantyhose in different colors and patterns.

"Gloves are important, too. There is the right length and style for each ensemble.

"A woman's hair is *always* an accessory. With falls, a girl has a complete wardrobe of hair to choose from.

"I believe the total look is all that matters. Back away from that mirror—what do you see? Are you in balance? Top-heavy? Pear-shaped? Too long and thin or broken up into clumps? If you are not satisfied, then try changing your shoes, your jacket length, your glove length; imagine how you would look with shorter hair, or longer. Consider *everything*.

"Do it all with a sense of humor. After all, you're alone and you can't hurt anything by *experimenting*.

"I prefer black, always. Start with a basic black something-or-other—say, a coat, beautifully cut. A good suit. There is nothing so thrilling as a beautifully cut suit. It's so crisp, clean, and American.

"Do learn how to use separates; though I don't design them, I appreciate them so much. They can stretch a budget farther than any other part of a wardrobe. And there is something about separates that is just so right for the American woman."

ANNE KLEIN has been described as a 'jetstream of ideas,' and twenty-odd years of fashion creativity have not curbed the enthusiasm. She, too, has a vast array of fashion awards. Clients include Lauren Bacall, Nancy Sinatra, and Mrs. Henry Ford II. "Shock treatment belongs to psychiatry, not fashion," she says. All Anne Klein's customers agree with her philosophy.

"I'm troubled when I see the right girl in a wonderful place in the wrong outfit. Our wardrobes have to be geared to the life we lead . . . and to our psyche.

"Far-out fashions can be fun, but I can't bear to see a girl who isn't relaxed and easy with these clothes. Watching someone yank at a hemline or endlessly fuss with her fall drives me crazy. With all this new fashion freedom a woman should surely be able to find a look that's right and comfortable for her.

"It's a time when you ought to be able to look better than ever, because you really *can* 'do your own thing.' You can choose from hemlines, hair lengths, cosmetics. You can be soft and curly with laces and eyelets, or sleek and tailored; you can be thirties, twenties, even forties;

Russian, Oriental, American gangster, romantic classic, Roman, Greek. Every fashion statement ever made in history is available again to the fortunate woman of 1971. It's fabulous!

"As to practicality, when you find something you like, buy it in quantity . . . shoes, bras, girdles, stockings, shirts, sweaters, slacks; you may never find it again! There is nothing more infuriating than discovering a bra that really does it for you, and finding, when you try to reorder, that it no longer exists. Naturally, you can't apply this rule to items of fad fashion or you'll end up with a lot of out-of-date clothes. But buying in batches is an old trick for many well-dressed women.

"Another rule is: Never pass up anything you want desperately when you first see it. Buy it! You may never come down that street again, or, when you do, the item will be gone. I presume I'm talking to a girl who knows her style by now and has great taste.

"Do be a bit daring at the same time that you are comfortable and right in your role. (I don't think a career girl needs to carry her office image home with her; I just assume she plays an entirely different part at home with the man in her life.) Staying daring will keep you individual, staying comfortable will make you more efficient and help you never to be ludicrous, staying practical will make fashion *simpler*.

"And remember: Never try to be something you aren't—in fashion or in life."

EDITORS NOTE: Your best friend is a full-length mirror. Buy one. Be merciless when you look in it.

5. WHY I WEAR MY FALSE EYELASHES TO BED

How do you look without your makeup? If you're one of those sunny creatures who only needs to pinch her cheeks to look pretty, I hate you and I don't want you to read this.

I want only kindred spirits to know my secrets, for I'm telling it like it is. I do not wear makeup "because I look about twelve years old without it." I wear makeup because my eyes are too small, my nose is too big, and my complexion is too complex. I am not repulsive in my natural state. I am just plain—*terribly* plain.

This is the reason that no one, not even my husband, has seen my face *au naturel* for three years. Traumatic things used to happen to me when I ventured out in my naked face. Construction workers would pay scant attention to me—let alone summon up enough saliva to whistle. Storekeepers addressed me as "ma'am" instead of "miss." Other girls, girls with makeup, were nice to me, wanted to be seen with me. The boss asked if I were feeling sick. The neighbors mistook me for my mother.

If you have suffered similar disasters, take comfort in the knowledge that you are not alone. There are thousands of girls with "schizophrenic" faces, who look ravishing with makeup, ravished without it. We are the products of a cosmetic revolution. Ever since 1965, The Year of the Eyelash, certain cosmetics, once available only to show girls, have been transforming plain girls into beauties.

This has been a boon and a burden. Each of us risks exposure every time we have an intimate dalliance, go to the beach, or get caught in a monsoon. To prevent a catastrophe from happening, I have formulated a guide for the "plain but beautiful" girl.

These are my *essentials*. You probably need fewer cosmetics than I do. I admit I am a drastic case. Because of the seriousness of my condition, however, I have become extremely adept at camouflage. No matter

26

how rigorous the activity or how damaging the conditions, I have found ways to hang onto my protective coloring.

Here is my list of the most dangerous situations to be in, and how you and your make-up can stay completely intact through them.

THE HOSPITAL: Hospitals insist on no makeup during childbirth and surgery. To me, this is needless cruelty and is not only demoralizing to the patient and depressing to her visitors, it may actually prove to be detrimental to her physical condition.

How, then, can we fight off the antiseptic-soaked washcloth? Scream, I say—shout the nurse down!

If you are too timid to resist, my advice is to delay admittance until the last possible moment, even if you have to go in as an emergency case. Remember, if your condition is drastic enough, they'll operate on you, anyway!

"What if you are unconscious when you are brought in?" you ask. This is a favorite nightmare of mine. In such cases, you should, upon reviving, immediately demand your possessions and put on the *essentials*. If this is impossible (they burned up with your car), or you are too weak to squeeze the tube of eyelash adhesive, you must shut your eyes, and turn your face toward the wall or into the pillow. If you are in traction and can't move your head, I have one comforting thought to offer—there's always the chance that the men who visit you will think you look so awful because you're sick!

THE BASIC RULE: Decide which are your "survival" cosmetics—the ones that make the shocking difference. These are to become your *essentials*. You must wear these 24 hours a day, 365 days a year, until you are too old to care.

I have not been seen without my *essentials* for three years, and yet I lead an active, almost normal life. My *essentials* are:

1. Foundation—to cover gray skin and mini-acne.

2. False eyelashes—to bolster my real lashes, which are so sparse I cannot bat them.

3. The "primary line"—a line that I carve out with shadow in the hollow above my eyelids, and without which my eyes sink into my face like raisins in a rice pudding.

4. Dark pinkish-brown lip slicker—without this, my lips are a shade darker gray than my skin.

5. Brown contour makeup—to give me cheekbones. Before contouring, I appear to be storing nuts for the winter. I also dab a bit of the contour on the tip of my nose to prevent people from using my childhood nickname, "hose nose."

6. Hairpiece—my bureau is stuffed with the hair of a thousand Orientals. I feel occasional pangs of remorse when I picture all those peas-

ants going around half-bald in the hot sun. But it was either them or me.

SPORTS: You don't want to be one of those perfect-looking little girls who stands stiffly off to one side, unable to join in the fun because she's afraid to muss her makeup. During my three years of constant cosmetic wearing, I have found methods to take part in sports without falling apart.

Water sports are the most hazardous. Water is the natural enemy of makeup. But water skiing, swimming, snorkeling, scuba diving, and surfing can all be accomplished in full makeup—with only a few simple precautions.

Water skiing is the trickiest, but I've managed it while wearing a twenty-four-inch fall, false eyelashes, and eye-liner. The lashes and liner were easy. Certain brands are waterproof. But the fall—that took strategy! First, I practiced water skiing in a fluffy, flattering bathing cap until I could avoid rough spills. Although the bathing cap was fluffy, my head still looked too small for my body (the truth is, my body looked too big), so I was determined to wear a long, black fall that made me look thinner and kind of sea-nymphy as I glided along in my orange bikini.

The risks were high—a $70 fall might drown and be lost forever, and I might emerge from the water looking like a bald seal. I cut these risks by buying a $15 Dynel fall that *loves* the water.

I fastened it to my head with extra combs sewn into the matting. Then I glided gracefully along, relaxed my hold on the rope in peaceful waters, and gently slid into the depths at exactly a 45-degree angle. Once underwater, I clasped my hands over the fall and then surfaced. There I was, long tresses swirling romantically, when my date came zooming back.

Scuba diving and snorkeling are easy—the face mask protects all eye makeup. If by chance you feel one lash dangling, keep your mask on after you surface and wear it until you can make repairs. Snorkeling is preferable to scuba diving because the face rests on the water and a hairpiece can float along with you in no real danger.

The rule to remember when you swim is: Keep your head above water. This eliminates correct swimming technique. Dog-paddle!

Pool swimming is safer than ocean bathing. I met my nemesis in the Pacific when a monster wave swept away my eyelashes and two auxiliary hairpieces. I saw one swatch going down for the third time, so I swam after the other hairpiece (it was trying to get back to Hong Kong).

I emerged gripping that sodden clump of hair to my head, to the amusement of 3000 people. Since then, I do not venture into the sea unless I see birds' nests floating tranquilly on the surface.

THE SHOWER: Indoor water sports are as dangerous as any outdoors. Particularly if you are showering with a man. A man lathers himself and his stallmate with lots of deodorant soap. Then he blasts the water, full force, for a "needle-sharp" rinse. If you don't want your makeup to go down the drain, follow this advice.

Toy with the shower dial so that it is fixed at its weakest pressure and only a pathetic drizzle results. When it's turned on, tilt your head so that the spray catches you only from the neck down. If all else fails and your shower companion is scrubbing you with his pumice stone, hurl soapsuds in his eyes. This way, if your makeup has worn off, he won't be able to see how you look!

Avoid shower caps at all cost. I look like a growth in one, and I've never seen a girl who didn't. A nice Turkish towel in bright colors, wrapped turban-style, will look glamorous and protect your hair, too.

THE BED: Virginity is not all that is lost in bed. More makeup disappears here than anywhere else. And the bed is where you need it most! Every girl having an affair should have a magnifying mirror and her *essentials* makeup kit hidden under the bed. While her lover sleeps, she can make repairs. Note: Always wake up before he does. You will have to survey the damage.

Can a hairpiece survive a romantic tussle? My answer is an affirmative Yes, accompanied by an Excedrin headache. Those extra combs really dig into your scalp. On special occasions, however, I think it's worth it. The only risk is that your hair will look so lush, he will want to run his destructive fingers through it. The strategy here is to tell him to touch you somewhere else.

How do you sneak away from a bed partner? The side of the bed on which you sleep is the crucial factor in this maneuver. Do not hem yourself in between him and the wall!

If, by chance, you awaken him in bed and do not wish to be seen, playfully (and quickly!) wrap the blanket or sheet around you in Hindu style—covering your hair and most of your face—and make your escape.

THE MAN: The man is a walking, talking, love-making makeup destroyer. Most men, if asked, will say they hate makeup and adore "the fresh-scrubbed look." My husband has steadfastly clung to this bumpkinish sentiment throughout the three years I've known him. And yet, during all this time, I have never seen his blue eyes follow any girl but the kind who is wearing enough makeup to stock a counter at Marshall Field. The ones who are truly "fresh-scrubbed" go completely unnoticed. More amazing still, he constantly insists that the girls who are wearing makeup are naturally beautiful.

In all fairness to men, however, I must say they are getting less naive every day. I was alarmed one night at a party to hear my own innocent darling ask a woman if she was wearing a fall. If he was wise to her tricks, I thought, can my unmasking be long delayed?

I hurriedly devised several sure-fire techniques to keep the male swaddled in ignorance.

1. Faster Than Highlighting:
My old makeup time was a dragging fifty-five minutes. When you spend *that* much time in the bathroom, a man might realize you are doing more than powdering your nose. If he is sophisticated, he may even guess that you are not only powdering it—you are narrowing it, shortening it, and highlighting it. The trick is to break the makeup barrier. Whip through in fifteen minutes. Practice over and over until your time is in this safe category. When you dash out in twelve minutes flat, even the most cynical man will not suspect you have done a major overhaul.

2. Moment of Truth:
If your man has already expressed suspicions, this trick will squelch them. You stage a "moment of truth"—he sees you without makeup! That is, he *thinks* he sees you without makeup.

In absolute seclusion, you spend hours applying subtle makeup. Instead of wearing strips of fake lashes, for instance, you apply individual hairs, lash by lash. You omit the most obvious makeup—dark eyeliner, bright lipstick, and eyebrow pencil. Instead you painstakingly put on a sheer-looking foundation, delicate contouring, and liquid rouge. If you do all this right, you should look as if you have no makeup on at all.

When the natural look is complete, have your man come over. Act flustered when he arrives. Hold your hands before your face and cry:

"Oh, here you are, and I haven't had time to put on any makeup!"

He will scrutinize your features. You will appear almost as attractive as usual. His fears will evaporate. Men are only afraid of the unknown.

3. Moment of Half-Truth:
Another successful technique is to say that you do not "have to" wear makeup. Other "reasons" for wearing makeup are:
A. The standard, "I look like a twelve-year-old without it." Back this up with tales of being let into the movies at children's prices, and so on.
B. "I wear makeup because I'm constantly being photographed." Tell him you do a little free-lance modeling. Models are expected to wear gobs of makeup, and are never suspected of being ugly without it.

4. The Power of Understatement:
Another easily accepted white lie is: "I don't wear very much makeup." Here are some useful variations and supporting gray lies for this one:
A. "I just use a dab of lipstick and powder." Constantly reiterate this by saying, when he arrives, "Oh, my God, I haven't put on my lipstick and powder!" Always let him see you putting on your lipstick and powder. Call this perfunctory gesture "Putting On My Makeup."
B. "Look at that girl! Look at all the makeup she's wearing!" When you see a girl wearing blatant-looking makeup, exclaim this in a tone that

registers sweet astonishment, not snide bitchery. Little ole natural you is just shocked that such painted creatures exist. Somehow, when you say other girls wear too much makeup, this lets you off the hook. *"J'accuse!"*

C. Show him your yearly budget. Under makeup, write the figure $3.50 and add hopefully in the margin—"If the price of blush-pink lipstick doesn't go up!"

D. Build a secret compartment in your purse. In the open part, display a neat little comb and compact and a new tube of Chapstick. In the hidden section, deposit all messy creams, powders, daubers, and any surgical-looking equipment such as eyelash curlers. Carry your pocketbook as though it weighs only a few ounces. A sagging shoulder is a telltale sign!

5. *The False Assumption:*

If you can plant a false assumption in a man's brain, all other deceits will flourish there until, in the end, he is a garden of misconceptions. Here are several false assumptions that can fertilize your relationship with any man:

A. He asks the question: "Have I ever seen you without makeup?" You reply with a potent lie: *"Of course* you've seen me without makeup! Don't you remember? I wasn't wearing any the day I met you!" Most men have weak memories for detail, and will actually assume you are telling the truth.

B. "Remember what fun we had on the beach last summer when I ran around without makeup the whole time?" NOTE: Be sure the instance you cite occurred at least six months previously, and that no close-up snapshots of your face were taken on that occasion.

C. The most powerful false assumption is the one that lets the man assume he sees you without makeup constantly. Lines like this one will build the required synapses in his brain: "Tell me, truthfully, do I look that terrible without my makeup?" Since he has never seen you without it, he is sure to say, "I never noticed you looking any different. You always look great."

D. Denial is your last and most powerful ally. A strong denial is better than a weak admission, no matter how incriminating the circumstances may be.

Open your shadowed eyes wide, suck your cheeks in, and cry out in righteous indignation—*"What?* Me, wear makeup?"

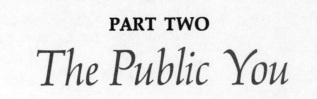

PART TWO

The Public You

1. HOW TO HAVE A LITTLE BIT OF CLASS

"Hot dogs don't make it," intoned the voice-over on a recent TV commercial. "But hot dogs and *champagne* make it."

How many of the things that *you* do just don't "make it" because they're all hot dogs and no champagne . . . because they lack that elusive quality (though we'll do our best to capture it as we move along here) that might be called "class"?

Class has nothing to do with the trappings of the rich—Vuitton luggage, your name in Suzy's column, a private Beechcraft, Daddy's being in oil. It goes far beyond finances, all the way to matters of style and character. If you have class, you may not even know it; if you don't have class, you may not know it either—but your *friends* have probably noticed. You reveal the lack every time you do something cheap or small or discomforting to others—from lunch to snarling at the mailboy because you haven't had your morning coffee (and you're more important than he, you figure, so he's "safe" to snarl at).

There are no absolute rules for what's classy and what isn't (I'm not certain the word "classy" isn't somewhat *déclassé* itself, but it's useful at the moment). Some examples, though, can give you a *feel* for the kind of behavior that is definitely classless—we'll get into some generalizations later on.

One of the areas where a girl (especially a not-too-affluent career girl) can unthinkingly tumble into the classless category is

MONEY: Why is it that some girls, *presumably* because they lack money, seem merely cheap, while others (not necessarily from rich or prominent families) have a flair for doing something splendid? Maybe because that first group is *thinking* cheap, *thinking* small.

The classless girl lets her rich friends pay and pay and pay, pick up every single tab—treat her to dinner, take her with them on vacation, give her lavish Christmas and birthday presents. "They can afford it," she says, and never bothers to reciprocate. A classy girl *finds* a way to reciprocate, and not just with an obligatory annual box of peanut brittle, either. If she has no money to spend, she'll spend time and thoughtfulness—poking around in fascinating old shops to track down an out-of-print book somebody's always wanted, or taking the children of her wealthy friends on a Saturday ice-cream-and-zoo romp.

A classless girl *always* gets more than she gives at Christmas, and the many presents she receives are almost invariably a shade better than the few she gives. She's constantly wrapping up old beaded cardigans or Formica ashtrays she got from somebody and palming them off on someone who doesn't want them *either*. The classy girl, again, spends *time* if she has no money. (One of the nicest presents I received last year was a jar of homemade wild-blueberry jam from a penurious couple in Maine.)

The classless girl (rich *or* poor) is ruthlessly petty. She tries to get everything wholesale . . . then, when her order doesn't turn out the way she thought it would, she immediately tries to return it to the company—against wholesale courtesy. This is the same girl who imposes on remote acquaintances to borrow their interior-decorators' cards or to drive a carton of wholesale liquor in for her from New Jersey. She's always asking the grocer to give her a free onion—it's just one little onion, worth only about half a *cent*—or looking for minuscule flaws in sweaters so she can demand a markdown. (I've seen some stunningly furred and bejeweled women enmeshed in this unattractive activity.) The classy girl *knows* when a bargain is a bargain and when it's a waste of time or an exercise in self-humiliation or rudeness. If *she* buys a few things wholesale, for instance, she'll abide by the unwritten rules and keep what she ordered, no matter what.

The classless girl (aren't you developing a warm affection for her by now?) gives a party and orders the minimum amount of liquor (even if it *is* wholesale!), convinced that when the bar dries up, the guests will know it's time to leave or the men will order more liquor *for* her. The classy girl gives a party *right* or doesn't give it at all. If she can't afford a lavish variety of liquor, she'll plan a noontime open house with Bloody Marys in a giant punchbowl. *And* she'll have the foresight to lay in something for Bloody Mary spurners.

The classless girl surreptitiously steals and steals from her company's supply room. What does it matter if she doesn't really *need* sixty grease pencils; they're free, aren't they? The classy girl may occasionally take home a package of paper on which she'll do office work and perhaps write a few letters of her own, but she isn't compulsive about looting the stockroom—and if someone saw her taking the paper, she wouldn't feel pressed to make excuses.

Finally, the classless girl tries to stretch her money by fakery. Thinking cheap, she'll decorate her new apartment with a full set of inexpensive, mix-'n'-match Danish modern, color-keyed right down to the Kleenex box in the bathroom. What she ends up with, of course, is *fake*—fake walnut veneer, fake satin pillows, fake mother-of-pearl waste baskets. She probably serves let's-pretend beef Stroganoff, too, made with canned tomato soup and hamburger meat, or bogus chicken Kiev swimming in margarine. The classy girl is honest with whatever money she's got. Her apartment may look slightly Early Miscellaneous, but what's in it is probably *real*, whether it's a sheepskin rug on the lone brass bed, a Lucite table, or wicker chairs. The point is, the Lucite is frank plastic, and the wicker is frank wicker. And when a friend comes over for dinner and all she has in the house is ground chuck, she won't flambé it in cognac; she'll make "honest" spaghetti and meatballs, or hamburgers on buns cooked over a grill on the Franklin stove.

Another area where you don't want to be the classless girl is in your relationships with

MEN: The classless girl's smallmindedness filters into her emotional life, too. She is forever picking and badgering, whining and sulking, because all she can think about is *herself*—and a paltry image it is at that. This girl holds herself so cheap that her entire value as a person, she thinks, hangs on her attachment to her current man—she deliberately seeks her identity through him. The classy girl's more generous life encompasses *more* than a man, and so she has more to offer him. She also treats him better. Because she's not so wrapped up exclusively in her *own* problems, she's able to consider *his* feelings . . . to tell if he's worried about his taxes or how to fire his secretary.

The classless girl is always telling men how bad she looks, or apologizing for *something*. If it's raining, she points out that her hair is frizzy or limp. If there is a run in her stocking, she calls it to his attention. When she smiles, she covers her teeth so he won't notice they protrude ever so slightly. She uses up so much emotional energy defending herself she hasn't much left to use for more appealing purposes. The classy girl cares about her faults and tries to correct them, but she won't harp on the unfixable.

The classless girl is always ingratiating herself with a man's friends, using them as insurance against the day he might decide to drop her. In this one respect, she stumbles *too* far down the road to thoughtfulness—remembering all his friends' birthdays (*and* their wives') and sending cards and presents, linking her life to theirs in a network of entanglements designed to hold *him*. The classy girl treats his friends like anyone else (although she may have to force herself to be civil to the ones she doesn't care for, a pretense she goes along with only out of *consideration* for him), but she won't ever try to *use* them.

The classless girl thinks men owe her *everything*—constant attention, dinners at chic restaurants, expensive gifts. She may seem like a gold digger, but she's really not; she's just so ego-centered that she sees men as self-esteem-bolstering objects rather than as human beings. Or sometimes she's simply plain *scared*. Not knowing quite how to do or say the right thing, she thinks the "easiest" date (where she won't have to make too many decisions or get into "deep" conversation) is a formal little evening of cocktails, dinner, and dancing—even if the man can't afford the tariff. The classy girl knows how to handle *any* situation, and isn't afraid of drinks or dinner at *her* place, or coffee and gallery-hopping, or merely talking somewhere. (Maybe you're beginning to almost *hate* the classy girl a little bit and feel almost sorry for her opposite. Read on.)

You'd think the classless girl would relax sometimes and stop *trying* so hard, but she is even classless with her

FRIENDS: Afraid to contribute her own thoughts, the girl *sans* class repeats everything she hears as soon as she can find somebody to tell it to: office anecdotes, unsubstantiated gossip, David Brinkley's latest quip, even classified information her boyfriend may tell her about his company. And when her storehouse of secondhand conversation runs dry, the classless girl tries to shore up her sagging ego by talking non-stop about *herself*. She'll call a friend, ask, "How are you?" and after an acceptable time (say three seconds) launch into the details of her love affair or how she was pinched in the subway. Subtype A here is the name-dropper—the girl whose ego is *so* bedraggled it can only be salvaged by letting people know that *she* knows, or, even better, has made love with, real or ersatz celebrities. "I met Philip at this party . . . oh? Philip *Roth*, naturally." Or, "I'm seeing this man who's a *very close friend* of Eugene McCarthy's." The classy girl may be thrilled to meet someone she admires, but her success in life isn't tallied by the number of famous acquaintances she can tot up.

The classless girl just has a *gift* for making friends uncomfortable. She talks about other people in the third person—when they're right in the *room*: "George thinks the movie was awful, don't you, George? I told him it was the most inventive film of the decade, but what does *he* know?" And if she has to dispose of an extra theatre ticket, she manages to do it in the most awkward way, promising it to one person and giving it to another, creating an embarrassing situation she worries about all evening. The classy girl looks out for the interests of others—drawing a quiet guest into the conversation without making a big thing of it, making life a little easier for others . . . a little more graceful.

One of the most revealing indications of classlessness is how a girl treats

PUBLIC PROPERTY: The classless girl thinks nothing of abusing property that's not her own; actually, she practically *insists* on it. She grinds hot ashes into the hotel-room rug, or leaves cold-cream handprints on the wallpaper. It's *only* a hotel, after all, and, besides, they soak you plenty! The classless girl filches that cute little pepper mill from the restaurant table ("They have so many of these things, and they'll never miss just one"). She also doesn't hesitate to litter the street with empty cigarette packs or candy-bar wrappers. "It's only one little piece of paper," she says, "what's the difference?" The girl with a little class *knows* the difference. She has enough concern for others not to put them to any extra work—or expense.

Finally, the real tattletale mark of a classless girl is how she keeps

HER OWN BELONGINGS: The classless creature is a slob-in-hiding. The inside of her purse, a disgusting jumble of tobacco flakes, dust, lint, used tissues, combs minus teeth, and other paraphernalia, looks like a disaster area. And her bureau drawers are even messier. If you ever opened her linen closet, you'd be lucky to escape with only a mild concussion because she has so much junk cascading off the shelves. The classless girl says, "It's the *inside* of my purse, and I need all that stuff. . . . It's *my* bureau/closet, who sees or who cares?" The classy girl *cares*, even if nobody *sees*. She may not be a fanatic, like your mother, who told you never to go out with a pin in your bra strap because what if you were hit by a car; but she has enough self-respect to be fairly neat in private, and enough pride in ownership to take care of her possessions.

The kind of misbehavior we've been talking about is spurred on by one motivation: *fear*. Fear of doing the wrong thing, not looking attractive, being rejected. And such fear leads to an all-absorbing self-consciousness, which in turn makes a girl indeed do something . . . classless! She's so wrapped up in herself, she's just not *noticing*.

Self-consciousness is, historically, an invention of the middle class. The bourgeoisie of the late Middle Ages and the Renaissance were the social climbers of their era, eager to disassociate themselves from the poor and ingratiate themselves with the rich. We have these insecure strivers to thank for the onset of portrait painting, which allowed *nouveau* rich merchants to commission oils of themselves dressed up in all their finery. But by Victorian times the climbers were foisting worse things than portraits on us—all those tacky values we think of as "middle class": hypocrisy, bootlicking, euphemisms for bodily functions, cutthroat bargaining, unquestioning obedience to rigid social codes.

Meanwhile, the upper class had originated what we call "classy" behavior. The very rich, or powerful, or elite of one sort or other tended to be isolated by their position (the poor-friendless-little-rich-girl motif got its start here). Outsiders felt uncomfortable around the great, so the great found ways to put such people at ease in their presence. *Real* class, then, is oriented toward others.

The lowest class, interestingly enough, resembled the top class in its social patterns. Locked into their poverty, the poor had no place to climb to, hence no reason to adopt middle-class values. Like the rich, they used the straight-talking expression, not the euphemism. They may have had to pinch pennies, but they could also afford to be generous—having little to lose and a natural empathy with somebody in a jam.

The point in bringing up this little seminar in social history is to show the futility of trying to identify with any particular class. What you should do instead is avoid acting like the middle class *stereotype*. Say a guest brings you a bottle of champagne, and all you have to serve it in are jelly glasses. You might say, "How I wish I had some champagne glasses for this lovely stuff," but then you pour it—*with no excuses*—into the jelly glasses. At worst, you'll be considered eccentric or impoverished, but you won't be thought classless. The classless girl would apologize and blush all evening, making her guest feel stupid for having brought champagne in the first place.

Some general guidelines, then:

First, stop being so *scared*. Class is a state of mind. If you *think* classless, you'll never be daring enough to take risks—you'll be too afraid of failure, and you could find yourself in the position of turning down a demanding job promotion without giving yourself the chance to try. One girl I know even refused several invitations from a remarkably sought-after man—she thought he was too *good* for her and was afraid to aspire to his league. The classy girl doesn't fear the Big Time.

You don't have to be afraid of being yourself, either. The United States is full of girls who have pasted a clenched-jaw English accent (which they've apparently learned from old *Punch* cartoons about Balliol men in the Crimean War—you know the sort of thing: "Haw, haw, I've lost my valise") on top of their regional twangs—and they sound ridiculous as *well* as classless. If your voice or some other quality is offensive, please fix it; but affectation is decidedly *déclassé*.

Nor do you have to be scared of being out without a friend. A classy girl won't be uncomfortable going to the museum alone, or waiting in a restaurant for her date to arrive, or even lunching by herself instead of with a group of girls. Nobody is going to snicker and point.

Another guideline to keep in mind: stop thinking about *yourself*. Most classlessness is simple *care*lessness about the feelings of others. Girls who dwell on *their* looks, *their* clothes, *their* men, and *their* jobs are the most classless of all. The classy girl listens when others talk, and asks them questions instead of opening a monologue. Also, she may devote some of her free time to politics or some other socially conscious cause (and not *only* to meet men). But even if she doesn't take an active part in community affairs, she at least *cares* about what's going on outside her tiny world.

Some girls are so self-absorbed that they're totally at sea when they meet the unexpected. Real class, on the other hand, shows best in times of adversity. The most stunning example of class-under-stress that I've ever heard of is the true story of a girl who was coloring her hair (a two-hour procedure) when the doorbell rang. She had just moved into a new apartment and didn't have a phone, so two friends had stopped by unexpectedly, and brought with them an attractive man she had recently met and wanted to know better. Instead of sending them away or letting them in and disappearing into the bathroom for an hour, she wrapped her head in a flattering pink towel, mentioned briefly that she was doing her hair (but didn't apologize or fidget), and went on to enjoy her guests with great ease. She had to make a ten-minute disappearance while she washed out the dye, then came back with straight, wet, clean hair. The attractive man mentioned (somewhat later in their relationship) that he had been charmed by her lack of self-consciousness when most girls would have gone into cardiac arrest. This impressive display of class cost her nothing (unless you count a couple of dollars for the dye-stained towel) and probably helped her attract the man she wanted.

A little bit of class won't cost *you* anything, either—so can you afford *not* to have it?

2. THE NEW LANGUAGE

It seems like a thousand years ago that Norman Mailer stormed the literary world with *The Naked and the Dead,* an epic studded with the coy euphemism "fug." Upon meeting Mailer, Tallulah Bankhead greeted him: "Oh, yes . . . You're the young man who doesn't know how to spell - - - -!"

Times have changed . . . some. We still can't spell out—and don't want to—four-letter words most places. But unless you have been wearing blinders and earmuffs for the past ten years, there is not likely a four-letter expletive a nice girl has never heard or even used!

So you know a few four-letter, ten and twelve-letter expressives. Is it *ever* good manners to use them? Does a lady say - - - -? Or does she just save her rare "lingua franca" for spicing her novel?

Surely you know women who can say nearly anything with elegance and propriety, while others sound like stevedores or 100 percent brass. The new uninhibited frankness has its place. Indeed, there is something vulgar and unpleasant about coy simpering circumlocution to avoid plain Anglo-Saxon English or straight anatomical nouns! Here are some general rules:

1. What is acceptable usage in your crowd might be considered outrageous in other circles. Don't bowl over new acquaintances with your linguistic frankness.

2. Something is seriously wrong if you can't express yourself *without* your scatological specifics. Are you language poor?

3. Language you might never use in a social situation may have its place in the bedroom. As one eminent Hollywood internist told COSMO-POLITAN: "Talking about each other's sex organs while making love can have an exciting effect. And the shock value of using dirty words, particularly with people who don't use them very often, could cause an excited response." Try it.

42

4. When you are offended by the language around you, don't assume a superior attitude. A teasing complaint ought to help . . . "Hey, America's Sweetheart isn't *quite* ready for this."

5. If you are a woman working with mostly men, you either take their vernacular and join in, or pretend you don't even hear whatever might offend you. You don't have to *imitate anybody*.

6. Sometimes you may want to complain. My mother was appalled at lunch recently by the conversation of two men at the next table. Numbed by a decade in the Manhattan jungle, I hadn't even noticed . . . but it seemed right to say to the two men: "My mother isn't used to hearing such language . . . could you speak a little lower!" They blushed and from that moment on, conversed quietly.

7. You needn't be the first to tell a dirty joke, but if everyone is telling one, tell yours. Learn one or two that don't offend you, and *are* funny. Many dirty jokes aren't. Avoid those!

8. There is real hostility underlying the rage for ethnic put-down jokes. But you blur the slur if the insults are distributed fairly. I felt myself growing uneasy recently when a friend spun off twelve Italian put-down puns in a row. I countered with one maligning Poles, one clearly anti-Jewish, and two poking fun at WASPS and Puerto Ricans. I felt much better . . . but all ethnic *put-down* jokes are bad taste.

3. HOW-TO-DO-IT GREETING GUIDE

In this complete capsule guide to gracious and sometimes-less-than-gracious greetings, we will begin by describing some elementary kisses and shakes, proceed to a variety of occasions where basic kisses *and* variations are applicable, and conclude with other off-the-lip tips.

MAKING CONTACT: MOUTHS

For purposes of greeting *for fractional kissing*, the mouth may be divided roughly into four sections: quarter lip, half lip, three-quarter, or full lip. The intensity of the contact desired is a deciding factor as to which section will be used. Intensity can range from a quick brush or peck on the designated area to lingering contact supplemented by the use of tongue, teeth, and fingers.

Our lips generally remain *stationary* for brushes and lighties, as we then employ the vague and partial puckers, the total pucker, the semi-open pucker, and a beguiling half-pucker twist for whimsicality.

Again, there are variants, such as both you and your opponent tightly tucking your lips inside and beneath your own teeth, then touching each other's mouths and holding "on the line" for the famous *Clam* encounter. Or you each form a stiff grimace until, with lips quite taut, you bop or bump one another's mouth and chin. This is classified officially as *The Fender* and is designed for offensive people. Since both of you rev up for *The Fender*, there is not much doubt where you stand with each other.

Moistening of lips is also significant. A slight wetting is often a plus for the receiver. The full *Wet Cow* kiss, however, is used exclusively for relatives, revenges, creeps, and cows. A refined limpid version is *The Limpy*.

44

Exaggerated kisses are becoming more and more commonplace. *The High Show Biz* between sexes is a series of full smacks augmented with slaps, hugs, shakes, grinds, rubbing, tussing, bear wrestling, punches, and sometimes actual sex or strangulation. All of this enthusiasm serves as the perfect alibi for murder—as you weep that you got carried away. A modification of *The Show Biz* is *The Panel*, where kicks are built up by its being witnessed by one and all on TV-game and panel shows.

CHEEKS

The cheek is the second most vital area involved in greeting contacts. It is a large, secure target with no specific value breakdown or division of areas. Except strategically, for a speedy cheek-to-quarter-lip brush, you should angle in below the cheekbone. *The Diplomat* is a kiss on the left cheek, then the right cheek, then either the lips or the left cheek again. *The Courier* starts on the upper-right cheek while you look suspiciously over the kissed one's shoulder; then you tiptoe around his back and finish off the left cheek with great intrigue.

The Double Cheek is merely brushing the kissed cheek with yours. Very cheeky!

(Other significant areas for kissing—though more casual and innocent—are the forehead, eyes, ears, nose, and throat. This last is recommended after midnight—and make sure your victim is snoozing. Also, be sure you have no latent vampire inclinations. *The Nanook*, a rubbing of noses, is divine. And surprisingly sexy.)

HANDS

You don't have to *kiss* everyone you meet or fancy. Sometimes a handclasp serves equally well, is more diplomatic, and far more revealing! A hearty grasp, *The Long-Time-No-See Pump*, *The Tender Clutch*, *The Squish*, all leave their mark.

And there are numerous exotic variations with the hands: *The Roman*, wherein you grasp each other's wrists; *The Reform-School Shake*, in which you throw your girl friend or boy friend over your shoulder; the meaningful entwining of arms of *The Comrade*, and the old-fashioned but eloquent *Give-Me-Some-Skin-Man*, where you lightly brush palms and keep moving.

Hand kissing is no longer limited to gentlemen. A woman should freely practice kissing men's hands. The back of the hand is acceptable. But if you're interested in the medium as a message, and an impressive one at *that*, it's preferable to take his hand and lightly lick the palm and/or the index finger.

(And, of course, there is foot and shoe kissing—only recommended if you really enjoy it or *he* does, and you're more than anxious to please.)

Now, with this basic primer of kisses and shakes spelled out, we know you're oscillating for action. So, let's put everything together and see what specific occasions go with which individual greeting.

When To Use What

● A chance meeting with a dear old friend, relative, or associate on the street, out of town, in a crowd, at a party: For a man, after the initial, "How desirable you look, darling," *The Double Cheek* is chic, followed by a quarter-lip brush. For a woman acquaintance, brush cheek and lip with lip. In both cases, a casual hug will add impetus and sincerity.

● A chance meeting with a casual but *important* acquaintance, male or female: A firm but casual cheek peck, warm shoulder grab—nothing overbearing or presumptuous. A strong handshake is also suitable.

● When introduced to someone potentially important, professionally or socially, for the *first time:* For man or woman, a good solid handshake; *however,* if the circumstances are frivolous and the person seems slightly tipsy, *The Diplomat* is quite effective and proper. Or a well-controlled half lip. If the notable greets you with a bit too much zeal or affection, keep calm but flutter lashes and politely go, "Tsk, tsk." And return the compliment.

● Meeting a celebrated ham or conceited oaf you're not interested in impressing calls for *The Narcissist:* You approach him with pucker, then kiss your own shoulder, pulling dress down to bare it, if possible.

● For a foe or creep to whom, because of circumstances, it's necessary to act friendly: Reinforce a three-quarter-lip brush with mean tooth nip, toe crunch, or ear pinch not discernible by others, but *he'll* know. Duck fast.

● When aggressively greeted by anyone hideous that you wish to eliminate for good from friendship list: Cough, or kiss the first person to your right, point to monster, and run.

● Accidentally meeting a friend while you are cheating, hiding out, or in forbidden, unlikely territory (it may be that the *friend* you meet is with a secret romance, also): Kiss your secret romance and *his* secret romance and ignore the friend. Recommended: three-quarter lip-to-lip.

● If the same strained situation occurs when you run into an *enemy:* Present an equal cheek brush and half-lip peck to both enemy and her secret romance.

● When introduced to any group of more than two people, use a standard over-all greeting: A congenial lip or cheek brush, but appropriately fortified for each individual with secret pats, nudges, and gropes. If an attractive man is in the group, greet him as you do the others, but whisper "Later" as you alert him with a pat on his chest or upper thigh.

● Whenever you're introduced to a possibility: Use polite but encouraging kisses. Never more than a three-quarter or four-fifths lip (but always leave something to be desired), reinforced by a playful tug of his hair or ear (*never* mess a man's hair or you're through). A half-lip kiss while touching the back of his neck—and lingering there after the kiss while you look at him—is solid!

46

- If you spot an attractive stranger, anywhere: Run up and give him a full gusher. Then apologize and claim mistaken identity.
- When quite *properly introduced* to a possibility: Smother-hugging and the full lip are risky, but risk away. Your passion will flatter him and finally either entice or (we never *said* kissing was *safe*) repel. If on-lookers appear jolted, claim he's your second cousin you thought was lost in the jungle.
- In a tight crowd where you can't appear too obvious: Slightly moisten your lips for him alone to see; aim for his cheek, but accidentally lay on a three-quarter lip. If he's with a girl, use a combination cheek brush and secret hand-tickle handshake.
- If you're *interested* in him but wary: Pucker and fake an approaching hot blast but serve no more than a polite quarter- or half-lip brush. He'll be intrigued but you won't be out of line.
- As a guest at a party: Any host or hostess, whether well known to you or not, is entitled to a *Party-Full-Lip* or a *Semihollywood*. If the party is a bore, all you're required to do is throw a *Limpy* on the way out.
- If you're the hostess: *You* are the best possible icebreaker. Kiss *everyone!*

Other Situations

- For an obligatory kiss: With man, woman, or beast, fake it in the ways described: by partial puckers, then missing or brushing.
- For uglies or smellies: A definite *Aerial Brush*. For mouth and/or cheek, this involves a lightning swipe. You get as close as possible, almost cheek-to-jowl, but your mouth glides right by. You never actually touch the recipient, but it appears and almost feels as if you did. Requires timing and practice, but worth cultivating. Or kiss your fingers and apply to the ugly's lapel or face from a distance.
- For homosexuals: A full kiss is compulsory. For the local boys: The *Diplomat* impresses any tacky mob. For children and men you aren't sure you like: A forehead or nose kiss is sweet and tender. For panel shows, if you're a guest: *The Panel* (mentioned previously).

And when meeting for the first time a man who sets off certain distinct chemical charges: No kiss or greeting so far described is quite profound enough. Just take his hand and lead him off into your own sunset.

4. YOU LOOK GREAT!
HOW DO YOU SOUND?

"I want a word with all you *ti*-gers!"

Remember those words from that famous television commercial? You probably *still* buy Top Brass for all your beaux because you *do* remember this particular TV commercial, the girl who spoke—and her sexy voice.

The voice in the commercial was Barbara Feldon's (costar of NBC-TV's *Get Smart* series). Barbara describes her velvety sound as "throaty, low-pitched, and sultry." She believes that you, too, can acquire such a voice if you're willing to work at it—and, most important, if you can learn to relax.

What does relaxing have to do with a pleasing voice? Plenty! Haven't you noticed that after sleeping or making love your voice is lower-pitched, warmer, and more resonant? (How relaxed can you *be*?) That's the way you should talk *all* the time!

Talking is one activity that proves practice *doesn't* necessarily make perfect. You've been vocal for some (twenty?, thirty?) years now; yet, instead of your voice improving with use, it's most likely gotten *worse*. Marian Rich—the New York instructor who has worked to bring out the best vocal qualities in such well-modulated women as Olivia De Havilland, Phyllis Kirk, Mrs. Joseph P. Kennedy, and Eileen Ford—tells us that almost every American adult speaks in an *unnatural* voice. Our natural voice is the one we were born with, but somewhere during the growing-up process, we lost it.

"As an infant," Miss Rich explains, "there was a one-to-one correspondence between the *sounds* you made and the way you *felt*. It was easy for your loving family to distinguish between your sounds of fear, hunger, anger, joy, or contentment." This is because a baby's posture is free and relaxed, his breathing deep, his throat open—forming a perfect channel through which sounds can escape.

But, as we grow older, we grow more cautious about expressing our emotions. Our throats become tight and constricted, our breathing grows shallow, our posture tense. As we become more "civilized," we literally choke back our feelings and our words. We've learned to keep our emotions to ourselves.

Fortunately, *any* time is a good time to start cultivating a voice that has life and color, variety and melody—a *sexy* voice! The following test will help you recognize your particular voice faults:

1. Do people constantly interrupt you to ask, "What? What did you say?" (MILLIE THE MUMBLER)
2. Are you a grown-up girl, but do salesmen calling on the phone ask, "Is your mother at home?" (THERESA THE TODDLER)
3. Have you ever answered a job advertisement only to be told over the phone, "I'm sorry, *sir*, this job is for a *woman*." (LOLA LOW-PITCH)
4. When you're talking, do you ever notice a look of pain creeping over your listener's face; does his hand wander protectively up to his ear? (HEIDI HIGH-PITCH)
5. Has a man ever fallen *asleep* while you were talking to him? (MARY MONOTONE)
6. Do you get tired of people asking if you have a cold? (NELLIE NASAL)
7. When you call out greetings to friends, do nearby windows shatter? (STELLA STRIDENT)

If you answered yes to any of these questions, the pointers and exercises we're going to give you will help you get *back* that natural, expensive, fully-rounded voice you were born with. If you didn't recognize yourself in our little test, try these tips, anyway. (Your friends may be too *kind* to let on that anything is wrong with your voice.)

LISTEN TO YOURSELF. You can't start to improve your voice until you've heard it . . . and that means to *really* hear it. One way to listen is to *talk into the corner of a room,* so that the sound is thrown back to you the way others hear it. The ideal way, of course, is to make a tape of yourself talking or reading aloud. This may be a destroying experience. Your first reaction will be: "*That* doesn't sound like me!" But keep at it every day and you'll soon be pleased with the results.

One tape recorder I found that is ideal for this kind of practice is a sound-with-sound, four-track model. It allows you to play back, simultaneously, recordings made on two separate tracks at two different times. (I saw this demonstrated on the Panasonic RQ-194, an attaché-case-enclosed tape recorder that the manufacturer refers to as a "portable language lab.")

Each day there should be a marked improvement on the second track, which can then be erased and repeated over and over again—leaving the first track (your original tape) intact for daily comparisons.

IMPROVE YOUR POSTURE. Unless you were raised at a military academy, your posture probably needs improving. A free-and-easy posture, with your body always in a "long and thin" position, is essential for good vocal projection. If you already know and use a posture exercise, that's fine. If not, try this one from the Royal Canadian Air Force Exercise Plan:

Sit on floor, knees pulled up, feet on floor. Clasp hands around knees and bend head forward until forehead rests on knees. Relax body. Then, straighten body and lift head so that you are looking ahead. Pull in tummy muscles. Relax to starting position. Repeat.

BREATHE! Did you know there is a right way and a wrong way to breathe? The right way will make your voice warm, intimate, and inviting. The wrong kind of breathing can produce seductive sounds similar to the mating call of a moose.

If you breathe from the depths of your lungs—which is correct—your stomach puffs out when you inhale and deflates when you exhale. Most of us do just the opposite when we consciously inhale. Some of us never breathe with our stomachs at all but take short, gasping breaths from high in the chest. To get into the habit of breathing correctly, blow up balloons! You'll be forced to breathe deeply. When your backlog of balloons threatens to take over your home, don't waste them. Have a party! Try out your new velvety voice!

RELAX. A tense person has a tense voice. Relaxing will help open your throat—a necessity in achieving resonance. There are two simple ways to relax your throat. One is to *yawn*. With your lips closed, yawn a big yawn until it forces you to open your mouth. Once you get started, you won't be able to stop. That's good. The other relaxing technique is one that Miss Rich suggests to her voice students. It couldn't be simpler, and it's fun. Imagine yourself an idiot. That's right! Let your mouth fall open and your jaw fall slack. You'll relax in spite of yourself.

LIMBER UP TONGUE AND LIPS. A pleasing voice requires a glib tongue—literally. Tongue twisters are wonderful in this phase of speech improvement. And by energetically *whispering* the twisters, you'll benefit doubly because you'll also be practicing good voice production. Try the following twisters, consciously exaggerating the movement of your tongue and lips and whispering as fiercely as you can:

She says she sells seashells by the seashore; and the shells she sells are seashells, I'm sure. The seething sea ceaseth and it sufficeth me. Peter Piper picked a peck of pickled peppers.

SPEAK A SONG. We want our voices to sound as pretty as a song—lilting, dipping, and soaring up and down the scale. Monotonous speech tones are boring and tiresome to listen to. To overcome the one-note blues, try *speaking a song*. Don't sing it, but speak it, going up and down the scale as the music does. Try it with "Do, Re, Me," from *The Sound of Music*.

As you begin to develop your velvety voice, there's one important thing to remember. Marian Rich says, "Something wonderful—and a bit frightening—is going to happen to you. As you practice, your voice will improve; there's no question about it. As your voice improves, you'll attract more attention . . . people will *like* listening to you. So you'll have to live up to your new image and make *what* you say and who you are as exciting as how you *sound!*"

Conquer The Eliza Doolittle Syndrome

The girl at the table next to you is wearing all the right things. Her blue-lensed sunglasses (huge) are pushed back just far enough on a head of long shiny hair. She has the right number of signature scarves (one), chain belts (two), and rings (three). The man she's with, not bad, not bad at all, risks the bottom of his tie leaning over his onion soup and asks her a question. You're not about to miss this so you, too, ever so imperceptibly, lean toward the shiny-haired girl. *And then she opens her mouth.*

"Oh, I can't tonight, Robert. I'm going over to my girl friend's."

If this girl were Cinderella, the clock would immediately strike midnight, changing her skinny-ribbed bodystocking into a tight pink angora cardigan. Her thigh-slit, suede midiskirt would instantly become a skintight black satin cocktail dress. Her lace-up granny boots would turn into spike heels; long straight hair would rise in a lacquered and teased bouffant. In other words, she would *look* the way she talks.

Upper-class clothes will never make up for lower-class language. If a girl is going to dress as if she belongs in a slick magazine, she'd better learn to *speak* as if she does. It is more a matter of vocabulary than accent. There are certain words and phrases that must go.

Back to the girl in the restaurant. You would never hear a little rich girl say she's "going over to my girl friend's." What she would say is something like "I'm seeing a friend of mine." The ambiguity about the "kind" of friend is completely intentional.

Fifteen years ago, when ideas of class and status were first really being examined from a sociological point of view, Nancy Mitford wrote an article called "The English Aristocracy" for an English magazine. In that article she made the now famous point (admittedly borrowed from an earlier article written by a Scandinavian professor of English) that the only way you can tell the upper classes from the lower classes is by their use of language, "since the upper classes are no longer cleaner, richer, or better educated than anyone else." The professor's idea, which Nancy Mitford made public, was to study the language of class, and to categorize upper-class speech as U and lower-class speech as Non-U. Some of the examples Miss Mitford gives of U and non-U language are:

The word *rich* is U; *wealthy* is Non-U.

Sick is U; *ill* is Non-U.

House is U; *home*, as in "They live in a lovely——" is Non-U.

Most of her other examples are too British to be translatable; but the formula she proposes is a very useful one. The U speech of the upper classes is direct and without pretension; Non-U speech is full of incredible affectations.

Vance Packard's *The Status Seekers*, another well-known study of class behavior, this time American, quotes *his* English professor as a source to illustrate "language that gives us away": The upper classes *live* in a *house* . . . use the *toilet*, the *porch*, *library*, or *playroom*. The middle classes, more pretentiously, *reside* in a *home* . . . use the *lavatory*, the *veranda*, *den*, or *rumpus room*.

What the whole U and Non-U theory is telling you is that to speak as if you were affluent, successful, and secure, you must simply talk unpretentiously. Talk that *pretends* you have the goods is an immediate giveaway that you don't. Eliza Doolittle's practiced party speech, "How kind of you to let me come," is pure and transparent Non-U.

In real life, the have-nots (and of course you want to sound "having"!) give themselves away every day by unconsciously using the wrong words. For example, the Even If It Is One school:

You should say *car* (U), and not *limousine* (Non-U), Even If It Is a limousine.

House, never *estate* or *mansion* (as in "I'm going to his——").

Boat, not *yacht*.

And you say my *coat*, not my *mink* or my *sable*, Even If It Is One.

A *dance* is never a *ball*, a *party* never an *affair*, a *dress* is never a *gown*, and *servants* are never *help*. Understatement and directness are the keys. In every case the more pretentious word indicates either that you are impressed or that you're trying to impress someone else, neither of which a nice little rich girl would do.

There is probably no one thing as obscured by euphemism as the bathroom. If, for example, you're in a restaurant and you want to announce your intention of leaving the table in search of a toilet, what do you say? *I'm going to the toilet?* No. Too crass. *Lavatory* and *powder room* are baldly Non-U. *Little girl's room* is far too precious, and *I'm going to powder my nose* (who does *that* anymore?) or *I'm going to wash my hands* are both too obvious cover-ups. The only alternatives are *I'm going to the john*, which, although it types you as College Dorm of the Forties variety, is far better than *loo*, which is a British affectation. The best procedure is just to get up, say *Excuse me*, and figure everyone else is as tuned in as you.

While it is generally true that pretentious words will give you away as Non-U, so will common words (*my girl friend*):

You never *have company*, you *have people in*.

You don't *eat*, you *have dinner*.

The word *cocktail* is out altogether. You don't *have cocktails*, you *have drinks*. Consequently you don't *have a cocktail party*, you *have people in for drinks*, and what you wear is not a *cocktail dress* but simply a *dress*.

You do your *laundry*, not your *wash*, but you *wash* clothes, not *launder* them. If you have your hair *done* (*fixed* is Midwestern), you go to a *hairdresser*, not a *beauty parlor*. You are not *single* (single is a mass put-down), you are *unmarried* or *not married*. You can go to a *play* or to the *theatre* but never to a *show*. And you *see* it, you don't *catch* it. Movies are *movies*, not the *pictures* or the *cinema* or the *films*. People in them are *actors* or *actresses*, not *stars*.

Certain common turns of phrase are instant lower-class betrayals. One of the most flagrant is using *he goes* for *he says*. For example: "I said 'Really?' and so *he goes* 'Why not?' " The other is describing someone's work as "He is *in* cosmetics." But this is subtle, because if the work itself has a lot of status, then you can use the *in* as "He's *in* the book business" or "*in* the market" or "*in* government."

There is a group of Old Home words too middle-class to be left in the vocabulary of the seventies. The point here is not to adopt a fake upper-class Piping Rock lockjaw way of talking, like Daisy in Fitzgerald's *The Great Gatsby*, whose voice was "full of money." The intention is merely to rout out of your vocabulary words that are as old as the clothes you threw out years ago—cinch belts, baby-doll blouses, crinolines.

Old Home words that should go are, for instance:

Couch or *divan* for *sofa*.

Icebox for *refrigerator*.

Hi-fi or *stereo* for *record player*.

Drapes for *curtains* or *draperies*.

Bedroom set.

Romance words associated with an Old Home kind of titillation have to go, too. Like *mistress*. "She's his *mistress*." And *thing*, as in *having a thing* with somebody. To *propose* is as old as the getting-down-on-knees picture of it. Love is *love* and sex is *sex*.

Abbreviation is tricky. It can sometimes indicate familiarity and therefore be good (*Saks* for *Saks Fifth Avenue*). But it can also sound common and therefore bad (*L.A.* for *Los Angeles*; *Vegas* for *Las Vegas*; *Frisco* for *San Francisco*; *Jersey* for *New Jersey*).

In the Abbreviation Is Class category are most, but not all, department stores: *Bonwit's*, *Bergdorf's*, and *Bendel's*, but never *Neiman's*. The *B. School* for *Harvard Business School* is O.K. Abbreviation is necessary in such declarations as "I'm going to *the Shore, the Hamptons, the Islands.''* A U person would tell a friend he's going to the Plaza and a taxi driver *Fifty-ninth Street and Fifth Avenue.*

Abbreviation Is Crass with such things as *burger* for *hamburger, martins* for *martinis,* and expressions like *frat brother* (which is really not much of a problem since fraternities are on their way out). All too common, and therefore Non-U, are *the Coast, the store, the track, the States.*

When you're talking about clothing, the best thing is to be completely straight. Probably the best example ever written of pretension in clothing is in Sue Kaufman's *Diary of a Mad Housewife,* recently made into a successful movie. She has a superstatus-conscious, social-climbing young lawyer-husband call his wife with a list of things he wants her to pack:

"First of all, I want to take my tan cowhide two-suiter. Not the one from Mark Cross, the new one from T. Anthony. Then I'll need two suits, the gray Glen-plaid Dacron and the Oxford-gray basket-weave polyester worsted from Press.

"I'll need six pairs of gray lisle socks, the ones with clocks. And six shirts. Give me three white oxford voiles and three Sea Island cotton stripes, two gray, one tan."

Non-Uness in talking about clothes comes from name-dropping and from using a modifier to replace the thing itself, as in *my Pucci* or *my Guccis.* Or, calling a sweater a *V-neck,* a skirt an *A-line,* a dress a *drip-dry,* instead of just plain *sweater, skirt, dress.*

Some more clothing giveaways:

Evening clothes, dinner jacket, black tie are right; not *tux* or *tuxedo.*

Underwear, not *lingerie.*

Stockings, not *hose* or *nylons.*

If you must say it, *bra,* not *brassiere.* All other hybrid forms of underwear, like *bra-slip, bodystocking, pantyhose,* have to be called by those names because they haven't been around long enough for anyone to think up better ones.

Nightgown, not *negligee* or *peignoir,* which were made obsolete when women stopped needing to slip into something more comfortable.

Shirt, not *blouse.*

Pants or *slacks,* not *trousers.*

Pumps can only be a man's black patent dancing slippers. There is no such thing as the needle-heeled black-kid variety.

In the *bag, purse, pocketbook, handbag* area, the first two are preferable, but this is one word with great regional differences.

Coat, not *furs* or *wrap.*

Working-girl phrases are quite obviously alien to a little-rich-girl way of talking. In this case a bit of deviousness is necessary. For example, if you say *I'm going on my vacation,* that implies no volition of your own. Where's the magic in a two-week salary check in advance? But *I'm going away* or *out of town* is just vague enough to erase the nine-to-five image. In the same way, *a girl in my office* should become *someone I work with*, and phrases like *my boss* and *on my lunch hour* should be done away with completely.

Also to avoid—words you can't pronounce. Chic little French phrases like *"le dernier cri," "pièce de résistance,"* or *"à bientôt, mon ami"* misparlayed into conversation can do you in. And things you don't know the difference between (*writer* and *author*) shouldn't be used interchangeably. *Writer* is the occupation; *author* usually means he's written a book.

About playing with words. It is true that anything said with the right tone of irony or playfulness or mockery is O.K. Creativity of language, or "It's not what you say, it's how you say it," is just fine if you can pull it off. If you can't, then learn how not to give yourself away.

TIRED NON-U WORDS AND PHRASES TO AVOID

Sock it to me
Steady ("He's my steady.")
Like ("Like he has this Mustang and like it's dark blue.")
Groovy
Double (as in a double date for the movies)
Ritzy or swanky
Gal or chick
Business ("I go to business.")
Swoon ("Couldn't you just swoon?")
Boyfriend
Garcon (U people say waiter or sir)
Hubby
Fink
Crush ("He's got a crush on Thelma.")
Beatnik
Cool ("He's real cool.")
Flower power
Neat ("The movie was neat.")
Intended ("I want you to meet my intended.")
Lover, sweetheart (unchic words of endearment)
Call up ("She called," not "She called up.")
Coming over (The rich never come over; they drop over or stop by. They also drop by and stop in!)
Cup of coffee (I'll have coffee is sufficient.)

Luncheon (lunch is better)
Fun time (or a fun anything)
No-no (as in "That's a no-no.")
Stacked or built (to describe a well-proportioned female)
V.I.P., B.O., T.L.C. (initials are déclassé)
Hunk (for great-looking guy)
On the ball
Jazzy
Swear word or curse word
Bag (as in "That's not my bag.")

5. STARTING A CONVERSATION

Once upon a time there was a little girl who spent her days sitting on a lily pad watching a frog. Now the little girl knew that the frog was probably a prince. And the frog, who was indeed a prince, knew that the little girl could kiss his nose and break the magic spell that had been cast at his birth by the wicked Witch Grushenka. But the little girl on the lily pad couldn't think how to begin a conversation with a frog, and the frog could hardly bring himself to tell her how badly he wanted her to kiss his nose. So the little girl went on sitting on the lily pad watching the frog, and that is the end of the story.

And the worst part of the story is that it happens every day. Every day and every night, thousands of girls sit in offices, go to parties, wait for elevators to come and lights to change, buckle their airplane seat belts and straphang on subways, and look wistfully at princes, near princes, and knaves they cannot quite start conversations with.

How can you begin a conversation—and begin it so well someone else will want to go on with it?

First off, why are you having trouble with it?

Ask any girl who does have trouble, and she'll probably claim she's just shy. Or reserved. Or afraid of being mistaken for an aggressive female. Or afraid of being raped.

Well, let's take these explanations one by one.

Shyness, if you really think about it, is usually the result of thinking that what you have to say cannot possibly be as interesting as what everyone else in the world is saying. If this is your problem, next time you're at a party, try listening to what others are saying and match it against your own conversation. What you'll find is that what that charming-looking girl is saying to that pipe-smoking man who is doubled up with laughter is about as scintillating as the copy on the back of a breakfast-cereal box.

Some people occasionally mistake *reserve* for shyness, but the two problems—though outwardly alike—couldn't be more dissimilar. A reserved person, far from feeling inadequate to conversation, feels that she is so much more entertaining than anyone else that she isn't even going to dignify the conversation by entering into it. In many ways, reserve is a kind of *selfishness*. And if it sounds like your problem, you may want to think about whether you actually *want* to start a conversation with anyone at all. In fact, you may want to think about it with a good psychiatrist.

As for being taken for an aggressive female when you open up—if you are an aggressive female, you probably don't have much difficulty starting a conversation. And if you aren't an aggressive female, no one—except possibly a misogynist—will mistake you for one. And remember this: Men have as much difficulty starting conversations as women do, and most of them are extremely flattered and relieved by a direct approach. (Incidentally, there is a corollary to the aggressive-female phobia. My friend Vanessa believes that it is written somewhere that Men Start Conversations and Women Don't. This rule is probably written in the same book that says Women Never Let Men Lose Athletic Contests. In any case, my friend Vanessa believes it, and as it happens, she hasn't met a man in seven months.)

No one gets raped when she starts a conversation. No one gets mugged, either. The notion that any girl who asks a nice-looking man how to get to Rockefeller Center is immediately bundled up in a burlap bag and sold into a Middle Eastern harem is approximately as valid as the myth that frogs give you warts.

No, when you get right down to it, the real reason most people have difficulty starting a conversation is none of these. It's simply that no one wants to be rejected. No girl wants to walk up to a strange man, lob off a twinkling remark, and be met by a cold stare and a furtive escape to the bar. Rejections are awful. But if you spend your life avoiding rejections, you will never meet anyone. And if it helps—any man who rejects you when you open a friendly conversation is probably too fearful and too inhibited or stuffy a person to be any fun, anyway. Mainly, try not to take the rejection personally. He'd probably be the same way if Raquel Welch undulated up to him.

Now, your fears of rejection aside—or shelved temporarily—how can you begin a conversation so that someone else will want to go on with it?

The answer, of course, depends on where you are, what time of day it is, and whom you are approaching; but, generally speaking, there are two rules for conversation openers:

1. What you say to begin a conversation doesn't have to be extremely clever or witty or remarkable. It just has to say, "I'd like to know you." (Haven't *you* responded, favorably, when a man has made some banal remark like "Gee, that's a pretty scraf" or even, unbelievably, "Do you

know what time it is?") All that's needed is to get the two of you *started* talking. The emeralds, diamonds, and sapphires of conversation can be mined later.

2. It's better if what you say is *prolongable.*

EXAMPLE OF POTENTIALLY UNSATISFACTORY OPENING GAMBIT:

SHE: Do you have a match?
HE: Yes.

EXAMPLE OF EVEN MORE UNSATISFACTORY OPENING GAMBIT:

SHE: Do you have a match?
HE: No.

EXAMPLE OF NEW IMPROVED OPENING GAMBIT:

SHE: I'd give you my martini olive if you could find me a match.

Where The Action is

There are three kinds of situations in which you will be called upon to open a conversation: in familiar surroundings (party or your office); in semi-impersonal situations (airplanes and doctors' waiting rooms); and in totally impersonal situations (on the street or on a bus). The more personal the situation, the more personal your opening remark must be.

In situations where you've been invited or where you belong, there is a certain element of safety involved in making a direct approach. For one thing, it is relatively easy to find out before you talk to him whether the man you would like to meet is married, rich, divorced, available, or whatever you want to know. For another, you have a certain amount of time to strike.

In these situations, whenever possible, start your conversation with a remark directed squarely at the man you are approaching. In the movie classic, *A Place in the Sun,* Elizabeth Taylor found Montgomery Clift, isolated, during a party, practicing shots in the billiard room. They had never met but she said. "I see you had a misspent youth." It was a perfect opener . . . personal . . . soliciting information without asking for it . . . an astute observation directed squarely at the man she was approaching.

The remark you open with can be nearly anything—a compliment on the man's tie, on the way he tamps tobacco into his pipe, or his mahogany tan; it can be a question asking when he thinks the taxi strike will end; it can be as blunt as "We haven't been introduced," or as oblique as "Do you have any idea who these people here are?" But it should deliberately make the man talk about *himself* and what *he* thinks. (If you simply cannot walk up to a man and open a conversation, ask the hostess to introduce you or let you help pass the hors d'oeuvres.)

SUGGESTED OPENERS FOR PERSONAL SITUATIONS:

"Can you suggest a good French restaurant for lunch?"

"If you were a vegetable, what kind would you be?"

"Which do you think is more loathesome . . . a landlord or a cab-driver?"

"Have you ever had your handwriting analyzed?"

"I'm doing an article on how to begin a conversation. Do you have any suggestions?"

OPENERS NOT TO BE USED UNDER ANY CIRCUMSTANCES:
"I hate cocktail parties—don't you?"

"Do you happen to have an aspirin? I have a splitting headache."

"Don't you think that girl in the corner is marvelous-looking?"

OPENERS IN IMPERSONAL SITUATIONS:
In a *somewhat* familiar place where you have been plonked down with a stranger (waiting room, train, lunch counter, drivers'-license lane), your opening remark should be directed not at the man but at the common situation you share.

DOCTOR'S WAITING ROOM:
"There was only one man who could save me, but he's in Vienna, so here I am."

LUNCH COUNTER:
"Will you please pass the salt—and would you set it down because I'm superstitious about handing salt."

AIRPLANE:
"I don't care what the statistics say—I'm absolutely terrified of flying."

In a totally *impersonal* situation (street corner, department store, subway) your remark should be even more impersonal, but as clever as it can possibly be (after all, you have only a few minutes to make contact); the remark *should* pass for a friendly gesture. If a salesperson cannot tell the man you've been eyeing where he can find a South African elephant tusk and *you* know, say: "Excuse me, I hope you don't mind my butting in, but I think what you're looking for is at Abercrombie and Fitch." You're attracted to a man on the street wearing a wonderful trench coat; stop him, apologize for taking his time, and tell him you've been looking for one just like it—for your brother. Bold but not *that* bold: Ask a man directions on how to get where you're going—when where you're going is in the direction he's walking. Crammed next to a desirable on a bus or subway, say, "I suppose there'll be the same pushing and shoving on the Monorail." Do pick your target carefully—by the look of his attaché case and the cut of his coat—or you may end up having a drink with a machine-gun salesman from Connecticut.

Starting a conversation so that someone else will want to continue it isn't really difficult. What you say is almost unimportant—what matters is that you get up the nerve to talk to this man in the first place. The worst thing that can happen to you is a cool rejection. The best thing—well, who knows?

6. HOW TO REMEMBER NAMES

Isn't it delightful to run into someone you met at a party and be greeted with your correct name? And isn't it awful to mumble and hesitate and search frantically through *your* numbed brain for some connection, *any* recollection, of *his* name? Of course he's disappointed; and you feel ashamed and guilty! What an easy situation to avoid!

The reason you can't remember names is that you never *learned* them thoroughly in the first place. Were you distracted by nervousness, or hostility, or the man's attractiveness at the first meeting? Well, for *some* reason you weren't listening attentively. The next time someone is introduced to you, try the following:

1. Be sure you've heard the name correctly.

If at all unsure, say the name aloud as you think you heard it, so any mistake can be corrected immediately. If you don't catch the name at all, ask that it be repeated. Still don't get it? Ask how it's spelled—tell him you're reading a book about European nobility and thought you'd come across his very name, so he won't feel odd at such insistence.

2. Hammer the name in by repetition.

While talking to the new acquaintance, repeat his name to yourself several times. Call him by name during the conversation and again when saying good-bye—your caring about and remembering who he is, after all, is flattering.

3. Anchor the name by association.

A sure method for remembering names is to make a connection immediately which will come to mind when you meet again.

a. Think of a friend, celebrity or product with the same name.

b. Make up a silly but appropriate rhyme—Joe Stein's fine; Robert Hull's dull.

c. Divide the name into syllables with some meaning, however nonsensical (Mrs. Divinsky—dive-in-sky, sky diver).

d. Interesting facts your new friend tells about himself may help you make the connection—ask a mutual friend to tell more!

As you continue to meet people, many names learned earlier (but haven't used) will fade. This won't happen if you reinforce original connections occasionally for practice. Before going to bed, write down the names of people met recently, along with the date and the event.

4. Imprint the face on your memory.

Focus sharply on the person. Notice posture, features, coloring. Listen to the timbre of the voice as well as the words. Guess an age. Try to imagine the speaker in other surroundings. If a person makes you angry, or you take a quick dislike, form negative associations. Writers like Truman Capote are continually interested in everything and everyone around them. Friends claim he never runs out of questions to ask—his curiosity is *boundless.* Everyone has more to his life—even the crashing bore—than the part of it you see at first meeting. Try to *discover* more.

Practice *sharpening* perceptions—watch people on the street, at the office, on buses and subways. Each is an individual . . . unique. Try to imagine his life story. When at the theater or the movies, learn names of minor actors whose faces are unfamiliar. See if you can remember them for a week, a month, or even a year.

All this organized effort may sound a bit cold and calculating—but it's only suggested as a training program. When you learn to concentrate sharply on others, their idiosyncrasies stand out—and then you're almost *unable* to forget their names. And while paying closer attention to those you've been introduced to, and discovering how interesting and surprising each one is, they, in turn, are being encouraged to discover how different and surprising *you* are!

7. NEVER AMISS AGAIN

Etiquette evolves. Styles of life change. And here is one style caught mid-evolution . . . definitely worth encouraging. The new way to address women: Ms. replacing Mrs. and Miss. Under the old rules, a married woman was addressed: Julie Eisenhower or Mrs. David Eisenhower. Under the new convention she is Ms. Julie Eisenhower. And Tricia gets similar billing, Ms. Tricia Nixon. Although the rule is still not widely used, it is logical and proper, and you might want to start using it in business letters immediately.

8. HOW TO WRITE
THAT LOVE LETTER

Four . . . three . . . two . . . one . . . blast-off! There goes his train (or plane or car or motorcycle) and it gets smaller and smaller in the distance—and so does he. And here you stand in your crimson (for bravery) mohair sweater you saved especially for today and wonder if you'll ever see him again. You also wonder why he didn't ask you to marry him or ask you to wait for him or ask you *something important*, but all you managed to get out of him was "I'll write—you, too."

So what do you do now—wait for him to write those tender, deeply-committed-to-you words he wouldn't say? Not on your gold charm bracelet you don't. You go home and begin a campaign by mail that will shatter his resistance. That sounds superoptimistic but it's been done by smart girls before, and there's no reason why you can't do it, too. Who were some of the smart girls?

Well, there was Elizabeth Barrett. Her romance would never have gotten off the ground if she hadn't responded to Robert Browning's letters praising her poems. The letters got more intimate as the correspondence proceeded—and this with a father who never let her out of his sight!

How about Adèle Foucher's secret romance with Victor Hugo—by mail? For three long years Adèle supported the postal department *and* her lover's ego with encouraging letters until he had enough money to defy his family and come to her. And don't bother to say, "But that was aeons and aeons ago." My friend Heidi went with a darling but very *bachelor* bachelor who kept her cliff-hanging for two years. Then off he went to the induction center one cold morning with no more comforting word for Heidi than that old promise to write. Well, with nothing *else* to work on—she wasn't anyplace *near* the boy anymore—she worked on her *letters*. Within two months he wrote that he wanted to marry her on his first long leave in June. (Although Heidi got to be a June bride, it's probably better not to hold out for that. Accept anything written on a Halloween or May Day card that even *hints* of a proposal.)

Heidi really did nothing so special with her letters. She wasn't an Elizabeth Barrett, but she *was* in love and finally convinced him that he was, too. She just kept pouring love—in a nongushy way—and care for him into her letters.

Results aren't guaranteed, but if you follow these simple rules, used by Heidi and other girls who have only the mail to keep them warm, they should help you cement a relationship. Edit a little for your special situation and you'll be surprised and delighted with what you create. You *are* creating, not bulldozing. Subtlety and charm will get you everywhere whereas pummeling, pounding and attacking too "frontally" will scare him. No, you mustn't propose by letter. He's still got to do that. Incidentally, some girls augment a person-to-person romance with a few little love notes. Nearly everybody loves to get "mail." Right now, though, we're talking about regular letter-type letters to send when a boy is away.

RULE ONE: *Arrange your thoughts* in a brief little outline before you start to write. That will make you sound like the logical and organized girl you really are. Prepare for this date by mail as painstakingly as you would if he were calling for you at the door. (He *will* be home at your door one of these days, you know, so don't cry.) You are going to accomplish in three or four paragraphs what you would in three hours if he were with you, so you must cull only the interesting information to pass along.

RULE TWO: *Keep it short and to the point.* Remember the crazy Russian who told his friend he was writing him a long letter "because I don't have time to write a short one"? Well, he wasn't crazy—or illogical—after all. It *is* easier to write a long rambling letter because you don't have to bother to be selective. Anybody can go through her dull little day, moment by moment, telling him what Myrna said about Selma's cousin's draperies and how the teal blue zipper you spent your whole lunch hour shopping for didn't match the teal blue dress you made last weekend after all, but who needs it? Rather than leave him definitely *not* palpitating with excitement over what you had for breakfast this morning, why not write three or four paragraphs that are of interest solely to *him*. He'll prefer that to sixteen pages of what he might consider junk. (That is, if he didn't *love* you so much!) Which brings us to . . .

RULE THREE: *Keep the letter person to person.* He doesn't want or need a letter from you that could just as well start out, "Hi, Gang!" This is to and *for* him. Think of the goodies *you* madly search out in his cherished little missives. Are they things he could quite appropriately have written to Aunt Gertie or his sister? Of course not. They are those gorgeous tidbits that are all for you and might as well be Morse code as far as anyone else can figure out. If he signs off, "Softly, softly now I leave you," anybody who had nerve enough to read your mail might think this was his way of tiptoeing out of the whole affair. But you know he's remembering the song Bobby Short played one wonderful night when you sipped on champagne and couldn't be close enough to each other.

You do have to be careful about one thing. It's frighteningly easy to get carried away with red, white and purple prose—especially when you're about to perish from loneliness. But use your head. What you *say* can only be remembered—what you write can never be erased and may come back to haunt you. Lana Turner wrote some impassioned lines to her friend Johnny Stompanato. She must have sincerely meant them at the time, but later, when they were on the front page of every tabloid in the world, they must have saddened her. Probably you won't be part of an international scandal—you and your friend are not famous—but if this *shouldn't* be the man you marry, how would the letters seem to you ten years from now if they were read aloud? It's wonderful to race his libido but you must be clever about it. If you only hint at passion, he'll get the message. Men have powerful imaginations in this area, you know. Besides, he'll respect your judgment and finesse if you're *subtle*. "I know how fond you are of chiffon, darling—you once said it was feminine and fatal—so, of course I shall wear it every night when you come home" is better than a graphic description of how you look in you new nightgown. Enough said!

RULE FOUR: *Use everyday language.* Just because you have a pen in your hand, don't go all flowery. Try to be yourself. He doesn't want a letter from a stranger. If he loved you before he left, no need to change now and frighten him. The main thing is to sound as though you were right there with him, hand-holding over a candlelit table. Come now, would you *really* say *procumbent* instead of *prone*?

Do try to avoid clichés. That means saying something the way it's been said thousands of times before: "She weighed one hundred pounds soaking wet," "everything but the kitchen sink," "a face only a mother could love."

No, they're not ungrammatical . . . just *tired*. By weeding out clichés in your letter you'll probably find a new way to say something and be more of a writer than you dreamed possible.

RULE FIVE: *Use short sentences varied in structure.* That means some of them will be questions, some will have three adjectives in a row, and some may be only two words long. Your sentences shouldn't ramble any more than your letter should.

RULE SIX: *Keep it light and amusing.* So he's off in Vietnam in the steaming jungle or his kid sister eloped with a bookie. You're not going to write a jokebook, but you're not going to depress him any more than he already is, are you? Acknowledge the misfortune he's written about but then be positive about something else—like his coming home to you. Don't bother to dwell on his taking care of himself or being careful. You're not his mother. What he needs is something to make him feel that it's all worthwhile and that there's a ray of sunshine somewhere—you. You may have just gotten over the most destroying case of flu on record, but do you really think it's going to help him if he has to plow through every morbid symptom? You'd like him to worry a little about you, too—that's only natural—but this is a campaign to please and delight a man. You can share your life and its unavoidable woes later. Right now he needs shoring up more than you do. . . . Men are like that. Instead of being a hollow-eyed martyr, you're a tranquil golden girl in a stormy time. He'll never forget you for it . . . and he'll never put off opening *your* letters because they're *dreary*. (Remember, Napoleon wrote to Josephine during his grueling Italian campaign begging her to send "Pages full of agreeable things which shall fill my heart with the pleasantest feelings.")

RULE SEVEN: *Be sincere and honest.* For almost a lifetime, George Bernard Shaw remained enraptured of Ellen Terry who wrote him of her mixed emotions, "You have become a habit with me, Sir," and, referring to his daily letters, "Each morning I take you like a dear pill." Times change, of course. Today it just isn't nice to call someone a pill, but the charm and wit of Ellen Terry's letters remain. For a more formal era, they're little jewels of sincerity and honesty.

Are you torn between saying what you think you should say and what you really mean? Try the latter. Tell him you miss him if you really do, but don't declare undying love unless you can mentally say, "Scout's honor," and are perfectly capable of leaving that adorable bachelor in the next apartment *alone*.

RULE EIGHT: *Gimmicks are worth a try.* Some people use these very well. A determined girl I know ate her way through seventeen bags of Chinese fortune cookies until she came up with five fortunes that fit "her and his" situations perfectly. She plans to lose the five pounds she gained before he comes home. Small price to pay; her letters with the fortunes enclosed convinced him that something "bigger than both of them" was giving him a message.

Another girl I know filled one letter with confetti from a New Year's Eve party (which wouldn't have been too smart if she hadn't hastened to assure him that she thought about and missed him every miserable second of the party).

There isn't much point in enclosing photographs of you unless they're smashing. Sneak one in a bikini every so often to show that you're still a girl—*his* girl—and that you're keeping yourself ravishing for him. Never, never send a picture of you and another man unless you enjoy self-destruction.

RULE NINE: *Build a bridge for his reply.* Polls show that men don't *like* to write letters. (They had to take a poll to find that out?) So unless you want to carry on a one-way correspondence, you'll have to learn to write the kind of letter he'll want to answer—or have to answer—because you've asked unignorable questions. The best way to get a reply is to ask specific, intelligent queries about things that interest him.

Ellen had tried to no avail to get at least one gurgle out of a junior executive of water-cooler acquaintance. (For the first time in her life she was drinking the recommended eight glasses of water a day—gulp, gulp, gulp.) She got a tremendous break when he was sent to Munich on business. Taking pen and courage in hand, Ellen wrote, "I know that Salzburg is only about two and a half hours from Munich on the Orient Express. Are you going to make it to the Mozart Festival next month? If you do, be sure and tell me about it—it's one thing I've always wanted to see." Now Ellen, bless her heart, couldn't sing a note and was tone deaf, but she'd overheard enough at the water cooler to know that he adored music. One little lunch hour at a travel agency revealed everything she ought to know about Salzburg. He was impressed enough to write back with impassioned descriptions of Alpine scenery, Bavarian costumes and, of course, the Mozart Festival. When he came home, they graduated from Dixie-cup companionship at the water cooler to dinner dates at little out-of-the-way German restaurants. She learned to love wiener schnitzel and constantly hums Mozart—off key.

RULE TEN: *Let your love show.* That means more than a "darling" here and a "darling" there. This is one rule that is most difficult to put on paper. All I can tell you is that your love has got to be *all over* that letter—in every word you write. This will come naturally if you are in love with him, but it's terribly hard to do if you're not *sure.* If your relationship hasn't reached the love stage yet, then the possibility of love—or at the very *least* tremendous liking—should come through. And it will, if it's there—and if you just follow these little rules for a letter to That Man. OK, Elizabeth Barrett—to your pen!

9. THE USE AND ABUSE OF FRIENDS

A friend is someone who likes you. Sexual *love* is cosmic, visceral, sensual . . . *love* for a friend is emotion fed by the intellect, it is *like* raised to the highest degree. Your need to *like* and *be liked* is as basic as your need to *be loved*. And friendship requires care and feeding and exercise. Friends are to be used. Use is not a dirty word. Abuse *is* a dirty word. Here is a chart of what one thoughtful friend can rightly expect from another . . . and some demands that strain the bonds.

DO, DO, DO

A friend is someone . . .

Who likes you and makes you know it.

You like and you make sure she knows it.

To do nutty things with . . . and not ever question what the hell are we doing?

You may borrow from . . . money (you always pay back promptly) and furs or costume jewelry unless you know she has a phobia about lending. Never take *anything* irreplaceable.

You can spill everything to—your secrets and wildest fantasies.

Who confides in you. Intimacy must go both ways.

DONT, DONT, DONT

A friend is someone . . .

You never gossip about behind her back except if it's flattering.

You never put on airs for . . . it's not necessary.

You never borrow a fragile dress from. Of course you would offer to clean it, but each dress has just so many trips to the cleaner's built into its life span.

You don't engage in hostile competition.

You are not trying to remake. Help, yes, but reform, no.

Whose confidence you will not betray for love or money or publicity . . . except to your husband. (But she knows *that*.)

70

Who understands . . . . even when she couldn't possibly agree or do the same thing.

With real empathy.

Who listens.

You can tease . . . but carefully; just a layer of love softens the hostility in a tease.

Warm.

Who always tries to reassure you.

Who laughs at your jokes and never shows that she's heard them before.

Who knows your faults but thinks your virtues far outweigh them.

Who acts as a buffer . . . shielding you from insults and slights.

Who loves you in good times as well as bad . . . your triumphs don't make her dissolve with envy.

Who makes being sick almost tolerable because of her kindness . . . Everyone comes to the hospital the first week . . . she's still coming six weeks later.

Who never crowds into your spotlight.

Who gets it for you wholesale.

Who remembers your birthday . . . but buys perfect little gifts every once in a while because "it just looked like you."

Who sends flowers because she knew you'd be blue today . . . or nervous . . . or she just heard the great news.

Brings cold poached salmon, a jar of homemade mayonnaise and some iced Moselblümchen because she knew you'd be too tired to cook first day back from

You would not make choose between her man and you.

You are not always breaking dates with because something better came along—a man. Sometimes but not always.

Whose boyfriend you do not feel compelled to seduce.

Whose husband's advances you tease off and do not report back to her.

Who *never* sends you copies of your bad notices or reviews or *ever* passes along the vicious gossip about you she overheard.

Who never passes along an ex-beau to you unless she really is willing to let him go . . . no games.

You never leave standing there when you should introduce her.

Whose family you never deride . . . she may, but you don't.

Whose borrowed possessions you never loan to anyone else.

Whose services you do not volunteer to a third party without checking first.

Who doesn't cry wolf . . . draining your emotions needlessly . . . well, not *too* often.

Who doesn't call you only when she needs a shoulder to cry on or lay analysis.

Who doesn't always wait for you to call first.

Who doesn't destroy you with frankness.

Who doesn't seek to dominate you or invent your life.

Who isn't more than normally paranoid . . . she is sensitive but not overly so.

getting a divorce in Nevada.

Who takes off the scarf you admired and gives it to you . . . but not always . . . that would dam up the compliments.

Who picks you up at the airport . . . even in a blizzard . . . or sends her brother when she can't.

Who doesn't mind returning a coat for you because you can't face *that* salesgirl . . . but not if it's a habit of yours.

Who shares her European addresses with you and gives you letters to friends overseas.

Who uses her pull for you. That's what pull is for.

Who doesn't mind your droopy phone call at 2:00 A.M.

Who understands why you have to hang up now . . . because *he* just walked in.

Who adopts you because you need a home.

Who takes you in . . . no questions asked.

Who rescues you at Christmas if you're alone.

Who takes you along as if you were welcome.

Who knows exactly what you want in a blind date . . . and often creates a whole little dinner party to make the meeting smoother for you.

Who is not a sponge or a parasite.

Who never has to put you down . . . She spares you her witty sarcasm.

Who doesn't stifle you with her possessiveness.

Who spares you the terrible truths about yourself.

Who doesn't put down your friends . . . She tries to see what you see in them.

Who isn't always bossing you around . . . for your good.

Who never says, "Why are you so blind?" or . . . "You're confused" . . . or "Don't tell me you're into *that* whole terrible scene again?"

Who never uses you as a kind of free-lance girl for her husband's business friends.

Who wouldn't dream of taking advantage of your weaknesses.

10. TWENTY TIPS ON MAKING FRIENDS IN THE BIG CITY

1. Be friendly; *smile.* On the bus, in line at the supermarket, be open to people—you may be pleasantly rewarded.

2. Call that cute couple you met at the party last night before they have a chance to forget you.

3. Take walks—along the main streets, through the park. Look so cheerful people will want to join you.

4. Choose a roommate who knows the city and has many friends—you'll meet *her* crowd.

5. Live in a small building so you bump into neighbors regularly.

6. Live in a building large enough to offer socializing facilities—a roof pool, a reading lounge.

7. Always go to the beach *totally* prepared—radio, food and drink, suntan lotion, cigarette lighter . . . so anyone can have a marvelous excuse for borrowing something from you.

8. Hail the same cab an attractive stranger is after. Then ask sweetly if you could possibly share it.

9. Visit museums. They attract interesting people, and the flexible atmosphere provides great opportunities for conversation-openers.

10. Put an ad in the paper: "Have antique lamp. Must sell immediately." Even if you don't have a lamp the response will prove intriguing!

11. Join a hiking association or bicycle club. You'll feel healthier and think of all the men you'll meet!

12. Take a college course. But choose subjects men are likely to take—*Woodworking* or *How to Repair Your Sailboat,* not *Needlepoint* or *How to Cook on a Budget.*

13. Gather a list of the most eligible bachelors in town—then call each and say you'd like to interview him for COSMOPOLITAN!

14. Put an extra long leash on your dog and let him make friends for you. All pets are useful this way.

15. Carry a camera—it's not only a good conversational gambit but you can offer to send *him* a picture of himself.

16. Don't underestimate the power of a consistent image. Dress and act like the people you want to attract; shop in places they frequent.

17. Get seasonal subscriptions to operas, concerts and ballets—you'll have the same person next to you all season!

18. Visit the piers on days when luxury liners leave for Europe—in the whirl of farewell parties, everyone will assume you're a beautiful stranger with a mutual friend.

19. Join a picket line; go on a peace march.

20. Look into a Women's Lib chapter—even radical girls know members of the opposite sex.

11. SCORN NOT THE STREET COMPLIMENT!

The happiest moment of my life (well, *close*, anyway) occurred on a sunny end-of-Saturday-afternoon when I was on my way to a post-shopping visit at my old friend Kenneth's for a glass of No-Cal and a look at his new co-op. As I waited for a light to change, a subteen A&P delivery boy careered toward me on a bicycle-wagon, lurched frighteningly in my path, grinned insanely into my face, and shouted blissfully, "Hey, mama, you lookin' fine!"

Actually, I had imagined I was looking only middling; no makeup except eyeliner, clean but limp-blown hair, an old navy sweater, and gray bell-bottoms—not exactly your pulled-together, minutely accessorized fashion-magazine plate. But if this cat said I was lookin' fine, then I was feelin' fine—and, as we all know, *that* gives you a 90 percent advantage in the battle for beauty.

I must have been glowing like an expectant mother when I reached Kenneth's apartment . . . and just this once didn't suspect that his inevitable "My dear, you look *divine!*" was the tiniest bit undiscriminating. For the truth is, there are some people in your life whose compliments become devalued. Like Kenneth's. Now Kenneth is the best tonic in the world to perk you up out of the lows, because when you're feeling frumpy, sleazy, grouchy, or plain ugly, you really can't get enough of his "You look divine"s and "How stunning"s. But after a while his compliments begin to pale—especially when your skin is a dried-out mess and your naked eyes look tiny, and still he says you're a ringer for Hayley Mills in *Tiger Bay* . . . or when you're madly overdressed at a party where everyone else is in surf-bleached jeans, and he tells you you're more chic than Vogue's Diana Vreeland.

Now *nobody* is perfect, and though we all love to be told we *are*, full-time delusion undermines the very fabric of human communication. As Tom Stoppard put it in his play *Rosencrantz and Guildenstern Are*

75

Dead, "Truth is simply what we agree to accept as true. Everything must be taken on trust. It's the ordinary currency of life." So what happens when all the inputs you get about yourself come from somebody like Kenneth, whose "truth" puts you in a crazy Rosencrantz-Guildenstern world where heads come up with every flip of the coin? What happens is that his compliments become devalued.

Not that the Kenneths in your life are alone in spooning out delusionary balm. Your lover tells you you're beautiful, and occasionally you wonder if he *really* thinks so or is just manipulating your sexual responses. Are your eyes *really* like emeralds (I mean, is he wearing a jeweler's loupe, or what)? How can you ever know for sure? Well, the answer is you can't. Shouldn't even try, because trying to know for sure leads to neurotic anxieties that can poison any relationship. When you love, you *must* trust—"It's the ordinary currency of life." If you're beautiful to him, you *are* beautiful, period. Yet . . . from that secret place deep inside you doesn't there always come the desire to know *How am I doing? How do I really measure up against all those other women out there? Am I pretty?*

When you marry, isn't the situation the same? After a while he may not even hand you the line about emeralds (count yourself lucky if he says your eyes are like Sara Lee brownies), but if he does, is it out of love? Honesty? A sense of obligation? Preparation for bad news? Making sure you won't need to get your praise from other men at the party tonight? Again, it's dumb and destructive to worry the compliment to death—you *know* that, and you don't want to undermine your relationship with neurotic hypotheses. But . . . *Wouldn't it be nice to know if I were really* . . . ?

Compliments from women can also make you wonder—and here I'm not talking about the frankly bitchy remark like "Oh Marie, I see your skin has cleared up." What I mean is the genuine-sounding praise that *friends* seem to offer so sincerely. When a girl friend tells you she absolutely *adores* your scarf, is she just trying to shore you up . . . grasping for *something* nice to say because she knows—and knows *you* know—that your hair looks like you washed it in mayonnaise? And if she tenders a perfunctory or obligatory comment like "You look great tonight," is she placing loyalty above truth (some loyalty!) so as not to hurt your feelings? No matter what good friends you are, her true motives for a compliment are something you'll never learn.

All right, then, the *street* compliment—the *pure* variety . . . the kind that is never rude, lewd, prolonged, or otherwise excessive—goes a long way toward filling your need for spontaneous, frank praise. (Let's forget about the other brand, which is actually nothing but an irritant; what woman, after all, *wants* to hear a stranger say, "Hey, what a pair of tits!") The kind of street compliment I'm talking about commends your *public* image . . . expresses an appreciation for *you* in the way you want to be seen by the world—and especially by men—but it never transgresses your private sexuality. Nor is it a pass or even a genteel attempt at a pickup but merely (and this is the best "merely" I know of) a tribute freely offered and meant to be just as freely accepted . . . unphony, no strings—simply one person vocalizing pleasure at seeing beauty in another.

A lyrically phrased "Oh baby, are you bea-*u*-ti-ful!" is one of the nicest street compliments you can hear. But there are infinite variations, from the simple smile and head turn to the eloquent statement. I once saw a gigantic, elegant black locomoting his way up the avenue like a twin of dancer-actor Raymond St. Jacques. All at once he stopped short and said to an attractive girl, "Man, I just *love* to see a *young . . . beautiful . . .* woman!"—then resumed his pace, shaking his head in appreciation.

Of course, street compliments don't have to be made *on* the street. A friend of mine who taught school in a ghetto neighborhood received her most flattering ego-biscuit in class. Ordinarily, she wore her hair pulled back in a matronly bun—an attempt to ward off possible disrespect from her students. But on the last day of school she arrived with her civilian hairdo, shoulder-length and free. "Oh, Miss Smith," one of her girls said, "you shouldn't be wearing your hair like that. You're a *teacher!*" But a streetwise thirteen-year-old boy countered quickly: "No, she's not; she's a *woman!*" Coming from a child, even a tough one, that qualifies as pure praise.

Although the street compliment can come from anyone, anywhere, its *classic* milieu is the construction site, particularly when the workers are on their lunch hour, sitting in a row, forming a kind of gauntlet of inspection to be run by female passersby. The men's remarks are almost never obscene but reflect instead a rather homespun quality: "I'd like to have a cup of coffee with *you!*" or "Hiyah, cutie!" (Now, what rapist worth his mug shot would say "Hiyah, cutie"?) Don't you almost feel *hurt* if they fail to throw a line at you? I remember the Broadway musical *Skyscraper*, in a number set at a construction site, had a foreman chew out his crew for ignoring two lovely pedestrians. "Where's your civic pride?" he asked, and proceeded to give the workers lessons in whistling, smiling, ogling, and verbalizing.

Civic pride aside, the street compliment is still hard for *some* women to accept—a friend of mine used to take an inconvenient detour to work every morning so she *wouldn't* have to pass a construction site and face the wolf whistles. Or the pretty girl waiting with me and about ten other customers in a hardware store. It was a chilly day, so most of us were wearing coats—except for one young man. The girl, apparently mistaking the coatless customer for a salesclerk, approached him and asked, "Can you help me?" "I don't know," he said. "If you'd like a companion, I'd be glad to oblige. You're very pretty." The other customers smiled pleasantly at this exchange—he was an appealing young man—but the girl clucked her tongue rudely and stalked out of the store. Had she been able to accept the compliment, she might have been happier, and so would the rest of us, who instead stood around somewhat disconsolately, embarrassed for the spoiler.

Then there is the famous case, retold in many books on group therapy, about a disturbed girl who was deeply upset by a confrontation with the janitor of her apartment building, whom she fancied to be a dirty old man. One day he met her in the hallway and said, "You sure are pretty." The girl, terrified of being attacked, recoiled and fled. In a psychodrama session, trying to work out her fear, she dramatized the scene over and over again, playing herself while another group member played the janitor. Finally, she discovered that when the janitor leered, "You sure are pretty," all she had to do was say, "Thank you."

Life may not always be so simple, and there are certainly enough weirdos working the streets. But the legitimate street compliment is nothing more—or *less*—than a passing, graceful appreciation of *you* . . . a tribute, if you like, to your womanliness. It can do wonders for your ego, and when a street compliment has made you feel beautiful, you can project that aura to the men who are really *in* your life and not just passing by. Accept the spontaneous panegyric, then, with joy—either inner pleasure as you walk on by (some people will *never* be able to bring themselves to acknowledge strangers on the street, so there's no point in forcing the issue), or, if you *can* react more openly, with a smile or a "thank you." The joy will reward you many times over.

Well, now that you know why street compliments are *good* for you (I think you *knew* all along), here's how you can make sure you get *enough* of them (not that you want to go about your daily routine to an unending chorus of gasps, wows, and whistles; but you do need a *little* recognition now and then):

RULE 1: Don't tart yourself up just to attract attention. You'll be going against the grain of the current nudie-freakout, get-noticed-at-any-cost *Zeitgeist*, but you don't want to attract by being a monster . . . you want to attract by being *you*. (If you *are* a monster, of course, you won't have any trouble in this department.)

RULE 2: Look *alive!* The archetypal spontaneous-compliment lure is Julie Christie in her sashay down the street in *Billy Liar*—hair bouncing, legs swinging . . . fresh, free, energetic, opened up to the world yet unselfconscious, not *soliciting* looks or approaches from the men she passes by.

RULE 3: If you *must* go out while down in the love-dumps, please try to put a pleasant face on your mood for the people you'll see. You might evoke a spontaneous compliment that will help revive *your* spirits.

The street-compliment giver, whom you'll probably never see again, holds a special place in your life nonetheless. He doesn't want anything from you or you from him, and yet for a moment you give each other the nicest presents people can exchange: his gift is praise and yours acceptance of it. A simple trade, and still so few people enter into it—even in private, let alone on the street. Now many men know how to say, "*Hey*, mama, you lookin' fine!" And, like the troubled girl in group therapy, so many women fail to respond with a simple "thank you" for one of the real boosters in life.

12. THE PERFECT TACTICIAN

You've had it happen to you. There you are in a smashing pair of "HotPants", admiring yourself in the mirror at your favorite boutique. You have the legs for it. You are, in a word, sensational! Whereupon you reach for your checkbook. And then. . . .

In an oh-so-bright voice, your companion says: "Those things look marvelous on teen-agers, don't they?"

Your alleged friend has blighted your shopping spree by implying that the longed-for ensemble is too juvenile for "ancient" (all of twenty-seven) you.

You have become a victim of *tactlessness*. And if you rationalize your companion's remark (perhaps recalling when *you* accidentally said the undiplomatic thing to her) on the grounds that she "really didn't mean it the way it sounded"—brace yourself! Many psychologists believe you say *exactly* what you intend to say—when you are tactless. A lack of tact is associated with *hostility*. If you tell Janet that her mauve draperies clash with her orange couch, you are not offering constructive criticism. You *want* Janet to suspect that she's decorated her apartment atrociously.

The difference between the tactful statement and the jibe that pierces the ego is often quite subtle. Some people seem to be *born* knowing the difference.

Can tact be learned? Yes, you *can* become aware of these subtle differences in speech that make you come off gentle and kind or bitchy and hateful. And using tact doesn't necessarily mean you must lie. Rather, to be tactful is to say or do what is *appropriate* when dealing with friends. To say things in a slightly different form—in a flattering, not a deflating way—is all that is required.

Here, then, is A PRIMER ON TACT—or: WAYS TO SAY IT WITHOUT GETTING KICKED IN THE SHINS.

BAD: (To a single girl whose shipboard reservations have *already* been made.) A winter cruise is a marvelous vacation: you'll get lots of rest. (In other words, she's wasting her money.)

BETTER: Gosh, I wish *I* were going on a cruise; they're supposed to be such fun. (Even if she doesn't meet men, she's taking a glamorous trip.)

BAD: I think she's older than you are. (Implies that your *friend* is old, too.)

BETTER: You're younger than she is. (Even if the friend is only two weeks younger, she'll be flattered.)

BAD: (To a girl who isn't married.) I think it would be dreadful to get old and live all alone.

BETTER: How lovely to be so free—you can do just as you please!

BAD: I don't think cleaning women are worth what you have to pay them. (Implies you're lazy and a spendthrift.)

BETTER: I wish *I* could find a good maid. (You're a bright girl to have located such a jewel.)

BAD: (To the obviously nervous man next to you on the airplane.) Don't worry, jets seldom have accidents—except on takeoff or landing. (He *knows* that!)

BETTER: Do tell me, why are you flying to Dallas today? (It's *not* tactless to ask personal questions; most people adore relating plans, problems, and a pleasant conversation will take his mind off the flight.)

BAD: (To a friend who's in analysis.) I just couldn't tell all my thoughts to a stranger. (Implies that she's a blabbermouth if *she* can.)

BETTER: D.B.I.U. (Don't Bring It Up.) Don't mention analysis unless she does. In that case, let her lead the way and mention it as little as possible . . . maybe something to the effect that probably most people could benefit from it.

BAD: (To your husband.) Have you called the restaurant to reserve a table for our anniversary dinner? (You thoughtless thing!)

BETTER: Have you had a chance to call the restaurant about reservations? (You've been too busy.)

BAD: (To a friend who's put a chain lock on her apartment door.) If someone really wants to break in, he'll manage to do it. (She's naive to feel protected.)

BETTER: I think I'll get one; at least it gives you time to call for help if someone tries to break in. (No false sense of security—but you've complimented her good sense.)

BAD: You look terrific in your new wig. (And don't you look awful without it!) Or, is that a wig? (The whole thing looks pretty fake.)

BETTER: Your hair looks great!

BAD: I don't think I'll take a college course . . . all the students are so *young* and liberal these days. (They'll never let *her* in the group.)

BETTER: Marvelous! Tell me what you're going to study. (Your friend is dying for you to ask that!)

BAD: (To a friend entering the hospital for surgery.) What luxury —lying there with people to wait on you hand and foot. (Demonstrates how utterly unaware you are of the ordeal your friend is facing and of what she may have to endure.)

BETTER: Do call me—or ask your nurse to—when you're *ready* for company. (I'm deeply concerned about you but don't want to intrude until you *really* feel up to seeing me.)

BAD: (Your office mate is 30 minutes late for work.) The boss was in here about 15 minutes ago looking for you. (Boy, are you in trouble!)

BETTER: Leave her a memo saying that Mr. Wells would like to see her. This keeps *you* from putting her on the spot, and is face-saving for her.

BAD: Dangling earrings always make me think of show girls at the Copa. (She dresses in a flashy way that makes her look cheap.)

BETTER: I've always wished I were tall enough to wear earrings like that. (Even if she's only a fraction taller than you.)

BAD: (Your friend's messy divorce is the topic of the day.) How've you been lately? (Any similar inane remark is inappropriate. She *knows* you're aware of her circumstances.)

BETTER: I'm sorry you've had such a rough time of it—I know things will get better soon. (Bring the divorce out in the open. Otherwise, it makes *all* conversation difficult.)

BAD: This soufflé looks absolutely marvelous and the flavor is delicious. (Falseheartedness can be inappropriate. She *knows* it looks like a *pancake* and tastes absolutely terrible!)

BETTER: Don't be upset. The first seven soufflés I made were disasters. (You, too, have had failures; you understand and sympathize.)

BAD: (To a friend who asks your opinion of the ghastly dress she's trying on.) Frankly, it doesn't do anything for you. (And, boy, do you need something *done* for you!)

BETTER: I think it's too long-waisted for you (if she's petite). Or (if she's tall): it's not dramatic enough. (Find fault with the dress, not with your friend.)

BAD: (A friend begins relating a sordid episode in her past.) You don't have to tell me about it. (You disapprove of her conduct; also, you don't really care what happened to her.)

BETTER: Do tell me about it. (Bringing it up at all means she probably needs to talk about it.)

BAD: (She's broken up with her lover.) I'm sorry, but you're probably better off without him. (Her romance was a big nothing and she was a nut even to get mixed up with the man.)

BETTER: I know it was fun while it lasted, but do you think he was really your type? (He was fine but she's even *more* scintillating.)

BAD: (A plump friend is shopping for a bikini.) Why not? All kinds of people wear them in Europe. (Even fat people like you.)

BETTER: Frankly, Sue, I don't know. Many Midwesterners just don't understand them. (Sue is a sophisticate, far livelier than her provincial environment.)

Care and Feeding of the Male Ego

BAD: (He's gone ape over a new hobby.) Are you really going to race that beautiful new car? (He's some kind of a nut!)

BETTER: Was Fangio as great as everyone says? (If you don't know the heroes in his new world—find out!)

BAD: (He wants you to spend the weekend with his family and you're not that serious.) I'm sorry, but I really can't get away for that long. (Your family isn't worth my time and trouble.)

BETTER: How marvelous—maybe a dinner-date visit would be best for the first time we all meet. (Shifting responsibility back to him and gently taming down the unattractive invitation.)

BAD: (On the dance floor, he admits he's a lousy dancer.) You're really quite good. (He knows you're lying . . . what must you think of him to expect him to swallow this?)

BETTER: It doesn't matter. I don't know when I've had a lovelier evening. (His many assets make up for this one small failing.)

BAD: (He loses his job.) We can *always* eat at my apartment instead of going out. (He's too inept to be able to start earning money again soon.)

BETTER: I think you should take your time choosing a new job. (A man of his abilities is certain to have numerous offers. Ask him to your house for dinner a week or two *after* the firing.)

BAD: (He's just been drafted.) Maybe it won't be as bad as you think. (How could anything be *worse* . . . you both read the daily reports.)

BETTER: Oh, Peter, what am I ever going to do without you? I promise I'll write. (Let him know you'll cheer him regularly.)

BAD: (You know your dinner date is having financial difficulties.) Don't order the cheapest thing on the menu. And don't ask him to choose for you (he may ask for a portion of *cordon bleu*, trying to show off).

BETTER: Select a moderately priced dinner and say, "I adore Southern-fried chicken." (Don't go *overboard* on enthusiasm or you'll give the whole plot away.)

BAD: (To your friend behind the steering wheel.) Be careful—the state police patrol this stretch of road regularly. (She's driving recklessly.)

BETTER: Wasn't that a state-police car that just passed us in the other lane?

Talking About Your Social Life

BAD: (Your luncheon companion has just ordered cherry cheesecake.) I've never really cared for rich desserts. (Anyone who *does* is a pig.)

BETTER: I had to choose between liquor and desserts—cocktails won. (You, too, are a weakling and therefore human.)

BAD: Don't bother to clean up your apartment just for me. (I know you live in squalor.)

BETTER: Please don't go to a lot of trouble—I know how busy you are.

BAD: I've never found time to join a club. (Only fluffheads bother with trivia.)

BETTER: I wish I could get organized enough to join something. (Your friend manages her time better than you do.)

BAD: (To your date who always drinks Scotch-on-the-rocks.) I just don't care for liquor unless it's diluted a little. (He must be a lush.)

BETTER: Actually, I think it's all the sweet stuff mixed with liquor that causes hangovers. (You wish *you* drank as sensibly as he does); or say nothing.

BAD: What a great party—you should have been there!

BETTER: D.B.I.U. (Don't Bring It Up.) So your friend wasn't invited, maybe, or had an *un-funny* case of chicken pox. (You may be putting her on the defensive for something over which she had no control.)

BAD: Betty, this is Mike Wayne, the man I've been telling you so much about.

BETTER: (Just introduce them.) If you've been telling her about him, she doesn't need reminding. Also, you'll embarrass *him* and this will leave them both tongue-tied.

BAD: Come over when you're ready; we won't do anything special. (You're not worth it.)

BETTER: I thought we'd play bridge tonight. Or: We'll mix up a blender of daiquiris—or whatever your guest's special preference may be.

BAD: John and I have been out every night this week.

BETTER: D.B.I.U. (Your friend may not have been anywhere for weeks or even months.)

When It's Better To Be Blunt

BAD: (Your friend has just failed at something important to him.) Forget it—you couldn't really help what happened. (He's so untalented he wouldn't have changed the outcome.)

BETTER: O.K., you blew it. There'll be another chance and you'll do it differently next time. (He's smart enough to learn from his mistakes.)

BAD: (He wears a tie that you suspect another girl gave him.) What a lovely tie—where did you get it? (Squirm out of *that*, you louse.)

BETTER: D.B.I.U. (Don't Bring It Up.) If he meant to make you jealous, he'll be thwarted. If he cares for you and wore the tie by mistake, he'll be grateful you said nothing.

BAD: (He suggests TV at your place and you'd rather go out.) Oh, let's not stay in. Television is so dull this season. (Only a dullard would suggest it.)

BETTER: I think it would be less of a strain on my willpower if we went out. (He's devastating—you don't trust yourself with him.)

BAD: (He gives you an inappropriate gift like five pounds of chocolates.) How sweet—I just *wish* I weren't on a diet. (You thoughtless creep!)

BETTER: How did you know this was what I've been craving? (You haven't said you'll *eat* it.)

BAD: (He's losing money at the races.) How about letting me pick the next one. (Particularly bad if your 17 to 1 longshot came in in the last race, and he's just lost $10 on the favorite.)

BETTER: I don't think your horse had a chance; the jockey held him back too long. (The jockey, not your date, is the one who has failed.)

BAD: (He's intoxicated, and it's time for him to drive you home.) Maybe we should call a cab. (You're too bombed to find your own car, let alone *drive* it.)

BETTER: I've always wanted to drive this car—will you let me? (Weak but worth a try. If he's really plowed, simply demand the car keys: chances are he won't remember it tomorrow.)

BAD: (He's getting amorous and you don't like him that well.) Stop that! I'm sure I haven't done anything to give you ideas like *this*.

BETTER: You're a *most* attractive man. I'm tempted, but I think we'll just give this a little more time. (Sweetness but firmness . . . the *only* answer!)

13. THE GENTLE ART
OF SELECTIVE HONESTY

This is an article on lying. When to and when not to.

You will find that we are *always* on the side of constructive lying.

If you think that is immoral or phony or compromising to your sense of truth, don't read any farther, because we are going to make the strongest case for lying that we possibly can.

Now, suppose there's this Clarence or whoever. He calls you often but you don't want to see him often. In fact, not at all. Pick the way you would handle the situation:

A. "Darling, I'm just crushed! I'd adore to go to see your office bowling team, but I've been invited to this huge dinner party and then we're all going on to the opening of a new discotheque; otherwise you *know* I'd be enchanted."

B. "Clarence, I'm a fairly honest person, and the truth is I'm just not interested in going out with you. I *don't* want to waste your time. I respect you as a person or I wouldn't be telling you this. But thanks, anyway, for calling."

C. "Clarence, I'm awfully sorry, but I'm involved with this project at work right now; it's just been keeping me all tied up like a birthday present. I don't know how long it's going to go on . . . please understand, and thanks anyway."

You have here three styles of communication, which will be discussed, along with others, in more detail later on. But just briefly: If you selected example A, you are using Super Truth. Now your excuse to him may be perfectly honest, but why egg Clarence on with a gush of enthusiasm you simply don't feel, and why, also, even worse, zing him with something that is bound to make him feel tacky and jealous to boot. If you are really a princess, you don't have to go around making the commoners feel inadequate.

Example B is the Brutal Truth. You've had it with the hypocrisy of the Older Generation and, apparently, with their *tact*, as well. However, what you are saying to Clarence is not that you're trying to save *him*, but you don't want to waste *your* time on the phone. If you *really* respected Clarence, you'd know that he'd eventually make up his own mind about when to give up. And are you so sure that you may not need a friend sometime? (If you operate like this, lady, you will.) I can't believe that any compassionate girl really finds it easy or comfortable to zap anyone like that, so then what are you trying to prove?

Now, example C, which we recommend, could be called the Mannerly Lie, or the Gentle Truth (we will see that there is often some truth in certain lies, and vice versa). And if Clarence should see you out with your "work," there's no serious harm—you didn't go barreling into a specific Careless Lie (we'll get to that one) where you embroider much more than is necessary. (Like telling Clarence that "work" is heavy dictation that will keep you stuck *in* the office next to a typewriter until way after midnight.) With this lie, he should get the gentle hint that if work is more important than he is . . . well . . . and if he doesn't you haven't hurt him. Believe me, he'll get the message, eventually, if you keep using this alibi, and still come away thinking of you as a kinder person than if you just say, "Leave me alone." (Incidentally, Clarence *may* have some interesting friends and you know how *that* works.) The main thing, of course, is you can probably live with yourself with this method of saying no. You've given Clarence a way to "save face." It's called diplomacy.

Styles of communication do *change* through the years. Maybe not as radically or frequently as styles of clothing, but they change, and most of us, no matter how we have been brought up, react. Of course, when fashions change we dash off, checkbook in hand. When *communication* changes, however, we don't necessarily stand poised in mid-conversation and think, "Everyone is telling-it-like-it-is, so I will, Right Now!" Subtly, if done the right way, we begin to put new words into our vocabulary, take others out (currently, we are exorcising "groovy" with some difficulty), and we *have* learned to speak more frankly about our emotions, our hangups, and about sex. That's all to the good. But just as we have intuitively learned to be selective about clothing ("I'll wear the see-through pajamas with Alphonse, but I'll wear my old A-line with some new chains when Tom takes me out with his parents"), we should learn to be selective about *word* choices. We don't think of clothes selectivity as hypocrisy, so why should it be hypocritical to be selective about *modes of communication* . . . giving a little less frankness with this person because he wouldn't understand, or because he might be hurt . . . shading the truth a little here and there because it won't cause any harm and might do some *good*. I believe it is possible to adapt to situations verbally without feeling like a hypocrite. At least it is the *gentle* thing to do.

Now, as I said, it's difficult to tell where truth leaves off and lying begins, at times, but there are some basic categories of everyday lies and truths we do run into, both good and bad, so here we go:

Perfectly All Right Lies

THE MANNERLY LIE

It's the same kind you used with Clarence . . . it keeps people from being hurt. Say your Aunt Jane gave you a really dreadful flower poster print for your new apartment (the kind you used to collect on trading stamps when you were a kid). What is it going to do to your integrity to say, "It's just lovely, you're a darling, thank you." You are *not* going to change her taste in art by saying it is bad. Put it in the closet and take it out, comic-strip style, when she comes over.

The same practice usually holds true for gifts from *anyone*. You must *say* you like them. A fellow gave me a sweater in emerald green, a color I've always hated. Because I loved him, I learned to love the sweater (until I stopped loving him, then I gave it to a friend). If your lover or husband consistently guesses wrong, give him specific hints before occasions come up. He'll catch on, and if not, maybe he has a different image of you—an image he enjoys. Indulge him a little; adapt your taste. It can really hurt if you reject something he thinks is beautiful for you.

You're invited to your boyfriend's parents' house for dinner. The place is awash with rose beige and ceramic swans. You say it is really nice. They think so, obviously, and so they'll be pleased by the compliment. If you're worried about what he might think of your taste, don't be—he knows your style and taste by now; he'll appreciate your manners.

O.K., these examples are fairly obvious. What do you do, however, if your friend has a party, burns dinner, half her guests don't show up, and those who do sit and glare at each other. I mean, she *has* to know it's a disaster. The next morning she calls to wail; do you go into raves like it was the best party in the world and ought to have a double-page color layout in *House Beautiful?* No, but you can find *something* right. Tell her you had some good conversations; she was too busy with the food to notice: "Really, Clarissa, we were so involved we didn't notice the food, and, you know, something like that draws people together—not that you should do it every time, but it had a wonderful informal thing about it." I know of few hostesses who *don't* think their parties are beastly. They will be only too glad to have someone try to convince them otherwise. It may be your turn next, and if something does go drastically wrong, you won't appreciate anyone else confirming your worst suspicions. Nobody ever really *does* appreciate it.

The Mannerly Lie probably covers more territory than any other aspect of selective communication. You will also use it when, say, a friend has Created Something . . . something *bad!* Let's say it's a book. Even if you hate it very much (or only a little), you must say it is wonderful! If it is something as important as a book, the *critics*, you can be sure, will lay on the truth. Criticism from friends is, believe me, not needed or appreciated. Even with advice *before* the fact, be encouraging; say, "This part is wonderful, but I'd love to see more of . . ."

Let's say a friend has just cut off all her hair and dyed it red. *Couldn't* be more awful! But it's done, isn't it? She can't *undye* it. Then tell her it's perky and cute. (It will grow back!) If she asks you what you think *before*, that's the time to say you love her hair the way it is. Afterward, just take a deep breath and be "pleasantly" surprised!

THE CAMPAIGN LIE

Here is another kind of lie an intelligent girl practices. This kind is not *entirely* unrelated to political promises or advertising claims. Used with discretion, it has its merits. You want to meet a certain fellow who loves tennis, or Camus, or harpsichord music. None of these has ever appealed to you before. But it is now proper to study up (or tell him you're interested when you first meet, vamp as well as you can, and *then* research it before you meet again). With something like tennis you say, "What a coincidence, I've just started taking lessons. . . ." Then start. If he becomes interested in you, he'll enjoy helping you with your game. Actually, what have you to lose by taking a quick cram course in any sport or other interest? It'll probably come in handy *some* time again in your life. Of course, your course may not "take," as it were. A friend of mine was mesmerized by a sailor (thirty-foot ketch). Lynn, whose experience with boats was limited to the Sausalito ferry, read all about jibs and starboard and mizzenmasts and came on for their first date dressed in natty navy and full of nautical jargon. Off they went for a weekend on the high seas where Lynn spent an enormous amount of time in the loo or on her bunk. Alone. Scroddy performance for an old sea hand. Her friend appreciated the fact that she had *tried*, however—any man worth having has a sense of humor and enough ego to be flattered. He explained that a man's hobby comes second to his interest in his lady (remember that), and afterward confined his sailing to alternate weekends.

O.K. Nobody ever said you could build any kind of gorgeous relationship on a stack of lies, but a little advance market research is not all that *lying*. I wouldn't, for instance, claim to a guy who has stated that he doesn't want his wife to work that you can hardly wait to get married and stay home and cook if you happen to be a girl who is immersed in a career. You simply cannot hope to be consistent about a lie that incorporates something as basic as a life-style. But a little dishonesty about interests or hobbies can help you get together, faster. And you never know what you may wind up being really interested in.

This extension of the truth sometimes merges with the Mannerly Lie, but generally applies to and should be used only in very close relationships. Although it is technically a lie, it is fairly gleaming with goodwill and is a *necessary* lie. It just has a way of making everyone *comfortable*.

Your best friend asks what you think of her current lover. You think he is a creep, but she looks so eager and anxious. Use your sense of selectivity. He must have *some* good quality: "He has the kindest eyes . . . and such a sense of responsibility." Or simply, "Well, I know one thing, Sally, I've never seen you so happy." Even if he should be a known philanderer, you don't need to warn her. She probably has heard his reputation, too, and anyway you can't save her. What she wants to hear from you is that maybe she is different and has a chance.

If Sally is That Close to you, and she is really thinking of marrying a man who you think will be a disaster, then take her out to lunch and say, "You are such a special girl, Sally, and Arnold is really pleasant, but are you sure he's got that kicky thing going which you've always liked in men? I'm just hoping, love, that you think about it carefully." If you are very gentle, she can't help but appreciate your concern; she may even reconsider. With this kind of approach, even if she marries Arnold, your friendship won't be destroyed by the things you *might* carelessly have said about her future husband.

Try to be sure of your motives. . . . A friend of mine once roasted a guy I was going with. "He's mean and arrogant," she said. After we broke up, she picked up the pieces. With him. Not that she influenced me to break up with him, but she certainly didn't help us stay together.

There are also times in your own romance when you may lie, in a loving way. He asks if you've ever loved any man before and maybe you aren't all *that* over the last one right this minute. Just say, "Never like I've loved you; this is very special." Actually, that isn't even a lie, is it? You can also say, and this is getting into the area of Gentle Truth, "How could I know I love you so much if I've never loved at all?" Never, never go into a description of each man or *any* man you've loved before. He doesn't *really* want to hear unless he's a masochist. Even if he asks with some persuasion, it's best to keep details to a minimum: "I went with this chap for a year or two—but nobody was *ever* like you." This is a supersafe rule. Do *you* ever really want to hear *all* about *his* girls?

Don't be *afraid* of verbal expressions of love, however, because he might take it too seriously. When you want to say, "I love you," say it, and don't think that it has to mean forever. People are so stingy with their "I love you's." Men particularly are scared to death to say they do, but it usually isn't those words that cause any grief to a girl. It's probably some things they didn't say or do. "I love you" is an impulsive expression of delight. Tell him also sometimes that he looks wonderful when he isn't all shaved and dressed. It isn't a lie, really; maybe the thought just hasn't occurred to you. Learn, and it shouldn't be hard, to compliment him when he is feeling really scruffy. He may even really look it, but watch how he brightens up.

Loving Lies are often little lies, like "I've been thinking about you all day," when maybe you've been thinking all day that you need a new dress or a raise. Loving Lies do not come easily to a Stickler for Truth, but they're awfully nice to get used to.

Hardly Ever Worth It Lies

THE CARELESS LIE

These are sort of accidental; you tell them to get around or out of a situation, and then you get more specific than you should, and WHAM! You say, "I wish we could make it tomorrow, Wilma, but we've had these tickets for . . . and . . ." Wilma calls two weeks later. "How was the . . . ?" "What?" you say. And then you wriggle for ten minutes trying to make up something else that happened. When you do cancel or switch dates because someone marvelous arrives suddenly, you probably should stay home with your later entry, and not risk being caught.

What do you do if you catch someone else in a lie? Men, often, are reckless liars. The boyfriend of a girl I know called and told her that he was wiped out, wanted to turn in early and sleep twelve hours—could he postpone their date? Sure, she said, and just happened to drive by a theatre where he was standing in line with his probable sleeping companion (in purple tights and hoop earrings). When he called the next day, I think she handled it well. "Look. I think you pick funny places to sleep . . . and I don't like to be lied to . . . so, what movie are *we* going to see tonight?" Unless you're tired of him *altogether*, and it's good-bye time, steel yourself not to make a federal case of it; you're capable of doing the same thing, aren't you?

Honesty Is Not Always The Best Policy

THE BRUTAL TRUTH

As we have said, there are *good* lies; there are also bad *truths* which are *very* popular right now. (So, in some circles, is heroin.) Say you see a friend's lover out with another girl: "Maggie! I just thought I ought to tell you; I saw Dave out with Carol last night." That's just trouble-mongering and you are secretly a hostile girl. Now, if Maggie asks you if you think Dave is going out with someone else, use the Loving Lie. "Gee, Maggie, I wouldn't know. I *doubt* it." If Maggie is insecure about her scene, she must work that out with Dave. Your role as a friend should be as a shoulder to cry on, not a gossip or a private detective.

Telling-It-Like-It-Is, imperative though it may be to group therapy, is a shock technique too strong, generally, for social or personal situations. We all know people who seem to thrive on such statements as "You look awful. What have you done to yourself?" or, "I didn't like that chap you brought over the other night." Don't *be* one of them. The expert on Brutal Truth enjoys making others feel uneasy, unhip, or clumsy; this should be left to Don Rickles or genuine-encounter operations like getting a divorce! If you play around with it with friends or lovers, you're just being hostile.

SUPER TRUTHS

You can always recognize an insecure person by the way she uses Super Truth to build herself up while she is slyly belittling you. There's a girl, Tomi, who, if you call her to invite her over to dinner, says, "I'd love to, but we're having a party for Andy Warhol and some other Very Close Friends. . . ." Although she *seems* to be explaining why she can't come for dinner, she's actually telling me I didn't rate an invitation to *her* party and giving me the guest list to explain why I didn't qualify. A simple "Thank you, can't make it . . ." would do nicely, but Tomi obviously feels so uneasy about her own specialness she must make others feel very nonspecial.

Of course, if something marvelous is happening to you, you can't wait to call up and tell your friends—part of the excitement is sharing it. That's a little different. Know the difference, and know your own motivations. Make sure one of them isn't "Oh, won't she just be jealous!"

THE GENTLE TRUTH

Here we have a Good Truth, similar in many ways to the Loving Lie. They occasionally overlap.

At one time or another we've all been in the position of fixing up a couple of friends on dates. To begin with, if you really have to lie, no matter how fond you are of each person, don't fix them up. But if you think they might like one another (although, like everyone else, each has drawbacks), then give it a little push with the Gentle Truth. Instead of saying, "She's really beautiful," when she's not very pretty, say, "No, she's not beautiful, but she has a warmth I think you'll like." He'll get the message, and if he's insisting on Leigh Taylor-Young every time, hopefully he'll have the honesty to say, "You know how I am about appearances. . . ." Warn him he's sophomoric and drop it there. Don't tell a girl a man is rich, handsome, and witty when he's just a nice Wednesday-afternoon kind of guy. Let her decide. If she finds him wonderful, let her have a thoroughly pleasant surprise.

One of the most vital areas for the Gentle Truth is in the area of sex. We've all been told to learn to communicate about our desires and our fantasies, about what is satisfying and what isn't. But even if you're not in love, sex *must* be loving, and I trust you understand the difference. Encounter-type tactics are *out*. So is lying. With one exception (and you may disagree, but think carefully): there are times when a woman can pretend to have an orgasm. Say you have managed to turn yourself off—you're worried about work; you feel fat; you're getting a cold; whatever it is, you *know* nothing is going to turn you on. Don't just lie there; be warm and responsive. He may, or may not, suspect. If he says, "It wasn't good for you . . ." or something, just to be affectionate say "I love you," or "It's lovely just to be this close." It was, if you care for him—for one thing, his pleasure should be a delight to you. There are times when things just don't work out equally. Look forward to the next time.

Naturally, if this is consistently the case, then you must gently indicate to him—without saying anything negative—just what it is that would make you completely responsive. (If you're up to that kind of helpfulness.) You can do this with gestures or words. You are cheating him, as well as yourself, if you can't learn to be honest. Say, "Next time, I'd love to try this . . ." or ". . . would you . . . ?" Guided gestures mellow the truth: use them.

The only serious lying done in bed should be lying down. But, again, closeness does not preclude tact.

The problem with lying to someone you are very close to is that the truth will come out in a fight. Don't pretend virginity; it isn't necessary if you tell a man that he is the only man you ever loved. When you fight you may just blurt out, "Gawain never yelled at me. . . ." The fight will become more serious over the issue of your lie. No one can fight carefully enough to avoid the truth coming out. If you can control your anger that well, you are probably controlling all your emotions, and that is like dancing with iron boots and handcuffs.

I know a woman who looks incredibly young to have three married children. She—amazingly—has never told her new husband about the children, or just how old she is. Obviously, and just use your own imagination, the truth is bound to come out at some point. Even if it doesn't, she lives in terror of that day. In cases like this, where there is some deep, dreaded secret, tell your man as soon as you begin to sense the seriousness of his feelings for you. Pick a time when you are calm and alone (you don't dash this one off on the way to a party), and tell him. If he really loves *you*, as you are, he will not be thrown. But the longer you wait, the more tension will develop and you will always wonder if he would love you if he only knew. . . .

In all instances, when you're not sure just how to handle the truth, the best course of action will be guided by your own gentlest instincts. Your selectivity in communication must be accompanied by an honest appraisal of your own motivations, and of the relationship. If you lie to yourself all the time, you never can be sure when you are telling the truth to others. The closer the relationship, the more frankness it can bear—and you are the person closest to yourself.

Real sensitivity toward others comes from honest understanding of oneself, and truth—and this is most important—without sensitivity has hardly more value than the worst kind of lie.

The point is that there is no strong line between the truth and the lie (it cannot be said too often); the dividing line, instead, is between thoughtlessness and hostility. Communication styles may change, but what doesn't change is that radar—call it tact—which doesn't think first, "Should I lie or tell the truth?" but which instinctively causes us to communicate with gentleness. And that instinct may well be the best of what they call "female intuition."

14. DATING EXPERTISE

Standard dating procedures are fairly predictable: dinner, movies, dancing, theatre, sports events, parties. If your partner has a good deal of money (and you'll *know* if he does), then all the above will take place at more expensive places, in better seats. Appreciation and enjoyment are all that are required from you. But, when the man in your life is broke, he may feel demoralized and act like a hermit. Coax him back into the sunshine with this treasury of inexpensive dating. A $50 night at the Metropolitan Opera is a joy, but for leisurely getting-to-know-each-other what could be more fun or more revealing than Window-Shopping . . . see "W" below. A girl with imagination and style can make her—and his—life much more fun, and infinitely more rewarding.

Alphabet of Inexpensive Dating

A. AIRPORT . . . drive out and watch the planes; carry a car picnic. AUC-TIONS. Sit in on bankruptcy, customs, post office, and art auctions, estate jewelry and furniture sales. See who's buying what, keep up with prices . . . be careful, you might find yourself buying a walk-in refrigerator or one hundred old velvet theatre seats or four dozen cracked soup bowls. ADOPT a child for the day from a friend or your community children's shelter . . . visit the zoo, the park, a kiddie show, the automat, or an ice cream parlor.

B. BARBECUE . . . at his place. Needn't be costly sirloin. Try grilled curry-scented chicken, or hamburgers topped with sour cream, and *sangría* (inexpensive red wine with slices of lemon, orange, peaches in season, lots of club soda—your treat). BICYCLE ride, rent or borrow, pack an elegant picnic lunch—your contribution. BASEBALL. See the game from the bleachers. BOWLING. BREAD . . . bake it together. The aroma of baking bread is homey and romantic . . . it stirs the domestic in a man.

C. CHINESE and other ethnic restaurants are still offering super exotica at bargain prices. CAMPUS activities. Put your name on the mailing list of the nearest college. Find out what's cheap . . . what's free in lectures, concerts, movie festivals, art shows, sit-ins. CHURCH and church social groups. CANVASS together for your favorite candidate. Hike, bike, or drive to the COUNTRY. Find a treasure for pennies at a country auction. Visit an orchard at harvesttime and pick your own apples. Some farmers will let you use their cider press to bottle your own. Other farmers offer pick-them-yourself strawberries in July. Take a winery tour in grape country, sample free.

D. DRIVE-IN movies with a snack packed by you.

E. EXPLORE caves.

F. FOSSILING. Dig for fossils in shale and riverbeds . . . great fun. FAIRS. All kinds of fairs: country fairs, the boating fair, gourmet food fairs . . . check newspaper ads or the Chamber of Commerce. FLEA markets. FACTORY visits . . . some companies have regular, organized tours. FISHING. FREE. Check newspapers for free entertainment in your town, band concerts, parades, theatre, church-sponsored events.

G. GOLF. Miniature golf or tee off on a driving range. GARAGE sale. Stage one together. Your white elephants might be someone else's treasures.

H. HORSEBACK riding. Real horses, or merry-go-round. HOME . . . yours. Pop corn in front of the fire. Read poetry aloud to each other. Invite him to dinner . . . say you have a special wine you want him to try so he doesn't spend his precious few dollars. Invite him back to your house after the movies for a snack: homemade ice cream, a puffy dessert omelette, blueberry pancakes . . . or heartier fare, chili, your fabulous fettucine, green salad, herb bread, and poached pears.

I. ICE skating. Carry a thermos of hot chocolate or hot toddies, or bullshots. ICE cream . . . make your own.

J. JEWEL shopping. I once spent a most glorious afternoon with a penniless South American student shopping for diamonds at Van Cleef et Arpels in Paris. Naturally, we didn't spend a *sou*, but I felt like a princess.

K. KICK a football. Touch football . . . it's still terribly chic. KINDLE a fire and toast marshmallows or just your toes.

L. LOVE. It's free.

M. MUSEUMS . . . museum restaurants are inexpensive too. MOUNTAIN climbing.

N. NIGHT court . . . fascinating. Federal court or State Supreme Court . . . intricate puzzles.

O. OPERA, the cheapest seats. You meet marvelous people in the standing-room section.

P. PICNIC. PRESS PARTIES. You're invited . . . bring him along. Bold folk even gate-crash.

Q. QUAFF a drink at a bistro that offers free hors d'oeuvres. That takes care of dinner.

R. ROLLER skating. REVIVALS of cinema classics at museums, film societies, etc.

S. SQUARE dancing. Pack an old-fashioned box supper. Almost all campuses have some kind of folk dancing.

T. THEATRE. Give him two tickets for his birthday . . . share your free passes. Duck into the theatre free with the intermission crowd. Get on a TELEVISION quiz show. Have an orgy of old movies all day on the TELLY, nibbling imported goodies out of cans (your treat . . . smoked mussels, Greek olives, pickled eggplant, artichoke hearts, quail eggs, truffled foie gras, babas au rhum . . . fresh, strong espresso brewed in your tiny Neapolitan coffee pot. TOBOGGAN. Or plan a party around a TV cultural special.

U. UNWIND at a Yoga class. UNDERGROUND movies . . . film one. UNDER covers . . . nice. UNDRESS . . . skinny-dip.

V. VEGETATE . . . it's great to do nothing together . . . just lie in the sun, read, snooze. VEGETABLE garden . . . plant one.

W. WEIGHT WATCHERS . . . it's good for you both. WINE tastings . . . free, if you can get on somebody's list. WINDOW-shopping . . . pretend you each have to spend $10,000 in the next two hours . . . keep a list.

X. EXPEDITION . . . plan one . . . collect folders from consulates, tourist offices, airlines, and travel agents.

Y. YMCA . . . co-ed swimming and all kinds of inexpensive busyness here.

Z. ZOO and lunch at the zoo cafeteria.

39 Ways To Be A Great Date

FOR STARTERS: HIS ARRIVAL

1. Be ready. It means you looked forward to the night. Wear a taffeta slip that *who-o-shes* and *crackles* when you move. This makes men delirious.

ALTERNATE: Rub your thighs together when you walk. The *squish-squish* sound of nylon also has a frenzying effect.

2. Dunk yourself in man-tested perfume, the proved stuff that has caused rapturous comment from cab drivers, strangers in elevators, and your boss. Use lots. Men's senses differ from girls', so don't ask your girl friend's advice.

3. Ask him to finish zipping your dress. If it's a back zip, you needn't know him well. If it's a front zip, the propriety of the confrontation is up to you. Suffice it to say, zip-ups tend to draw people together.

4. Use the squeeze ploy to show him you're glad to see him. Exhibit

a bit of tactile enthusiasm for his person with a happy pat or grabby hug at the very sight of him.

5. Tell him he looks splendid. Straighten his tie or fertility medallion or any other part of his attire that may properly be handled, assuring him of your interest in and approval of his appearance.

ALTERNATE: If needed, provide emergency-valet service. Should you see a button hanging and know how to sew it on without impaling his wrist, do so—if he has achieved any level of emotional maturity, he will love being looked after.

CAUTION: Save the coy little-homemaker looks or he may leave his jacket and scamper.

6. Break out the ice and nibbles before he arrives, a sign of preparation that will surely warm a man's ego.

7. Let him fix the drinks, even if you are ace champion gimlet maker of the entire world. It's a ritual men like to perform.

WARNING: If *his* gimlet tastes like furniture polish, *shut up*. New Chinese proverb says girl who insists on making perfect cocktail winds up drinking it alone.

PICKING UP SPEED

8. Tune in on his special interest early in the dating game, but be subtle—no avalanche or he'll feel snowed. For instance, mention seeing the golf match on TV without reciting it play by play. If philately is his thing, at least know enough to realize it is not some new sex perversion. Do not save used air-mail stamps for him. Should you read about a stamp auction, however, casually mention it might be fun to go.

9. Compliments: Learn to accept them with good nature, whether they come early in the evening or close to the goodbye kiss.

Bad example:
HE: You have nice, green eyes.
You *(tight-mouthed and snippy)*: They happen to be gray.

Good example:
HE: You have nice green eyes.
You *(provocative smile)*: When I'm kissed, they look gray.

10. The Dreaded Question: "Where do you want to go?" The world's leading lovers will at some point ask this dumb question. Don't shrug. Have some answers ready.

Bad example:
HE: Where do you want to go?
You *(sullen)*: I don't care.

Good example:
HE: Where do you want to go?
You *(bubbling)*: I was hoping you'd ask . . .

11. When you order a drink, drink it. Don't *ever* drink some of his.

12. When you order food, eat it!

(If either of the above is not as ordered or tastes as though it might cause ptomaine poisoning, say so. Otherwise, a man feels you are wantonly wasting his hard-earned gelt.)

AVOIDING DISASTERS

13. If your shoes are uncomfortable, don't wear them. You'll be miserable and so will he. If you think it's going to rain or that you'll have to wade through a muddy lawn to get to the party, don't wear the blue satin pumps with dissolving soles. If you do wear them, don't complain. If they get ruined, so be it. To behave otherwise is to suggest to a man that your shoes are more important than he is.

14. Feeling crummy? If not your usual adorable self because you had a tooth removed or your rent doubled or your throat's about to turn magenta, tip him off. If you suffer silently, he'll think you're acting touchy because of some lousy, sneaky thing he did.

15. Need specs for the flicks? Then *wear* them.

16. Booze make you snooze? Set your personal booze-o-meter at your own capacity level.

17. His jokes make you choke? The *tedium* of the ill-told jest is second only to the strain of your having to *react* to it. Philosophical thought: Man's compulsion to provoke laughter is one of courtship's mysteries. If you can't laugh outright, smile. Eventually, joke prevention may be worth a try. Groan lovingly and say, "That's the worst joke I ever heard." Or, tell him how much you love his jokes but how much *more* you love to hear his serious thoughts . . . his ideas are so *profound.* (Take heart with first-time jokesters. Often, it's a nervous tic that disappears once confidence sets in.)

18. Beauty insurance. *Always* take along necessary tools of the dating trade. If romping in an open car or through a damp night, take a scarf for your hair so you won't want to hide your head on arrival. If it's cold, dress warmly. Sun blinding? Wear goggles. Muddy? Wear boots.

THE OLD CHIVALRY YELL

Chivalry is dying from a bad case of the cools. Men are afraid of showing courtesies lest it reflect badly on them. This deprives both sexes of certain cozy and stimulating rituals—unless you know how to throw the right cue.

19. When you want him to light your cigarette . . .

Bad example: "If you had any manners, you'd light my cigarette."

Good example: Lean toward him with the cigarette up to your lips. Smile (very important: men say girls don't smile enough). Murmur. "Do you have a match?"

When you want him to help you with your coat . . .

Bad example: "A gentleman is supposed to help a lady on with her coat."

Good example: Hand him your coat with a big smile (yes, again), and say, "I have trouble getting dressed by myself. Would you mind helping me?" (This is especially effective when wearing a barebacked dress.)

HERE COMES THE GRUDGE

20. Don't crab all night about people he doesn't know—your boss, hairdresser, other men, or your spiteful sister-in-law.

21. Pay back even small sums. Don't ask for ladies'-room money.

22. Return borrowed books and records.

FIGHTING THE BORE WAR

23. When you're out with his business associates or plunked in the middle of a reunion with his old barracks chums, pay attention—no matter *what.* To him and to *them.* However paralyzed with boredom you may be, it can't be helped—so you might as well fight the good fight. Most men know when a girl has been a good little trooper and they're grateful.

WATCH OUT

24. If, as a surprise, he takes you to a restaurant that turns out to be more Delhi than delish (and curry makes you curdle)—tell him sweetly and laughingly. Don't eat up and *urp,* or it will be a bad scene for you both. There'll be *something* you can nibble.

25. If you are out with his friends and one of them wigwags you a smoky signal, file it and forget it—at least for now. A great date sticks with the chap who brought her.

BITE TONGUE

26. Before criticizing your family.

27. Before criticizing *his* family.

ADORABLE THINGS TO DO

Think the adorable thought and act on it. It's possible to be considerate without being a doormat. Examples:

28. SCENE: BUFFET PARTY. He's engrossed in conversation. Fix him a plate of goodies or recharge his drink. Serve him with sweet ceremony. This not only demonstrates to others that he is with a woman who is concerned for his comforts but also gives you an excuse to circulate instead of sitting like a lump.

29. SCENE: THE EARLY-EVENING DATE. The timetable is running close. He gets home from work later than you, so why not suggest you pick up a cab and collect *him* en route? This gives him an extra twenty minutes to get prettied up and into a loving frame of mind for the evening ahead.

30. SCENE: HIS SAILBOAT, COCKTAIL PARTY, OR THE SKI HUT HE SHARES WITH NINE GUYS. You're not only his date but his guest. Do the best-guest thing: bring a tiny offering—some deviled eggs, a bag of canapés, a bottle of wine.

31. SCENE: HIS CAR. If traffic's tricky, offer to light his cigarette for him. If traffic's insane, suspend all argument. Watch his hands on the wheel—if his knuckles turn white, shut *up*.

NOBODY LOVES A KNOW-IT-ALL

32. Don't correct his grammar. If he's old enough to take you out, his speech habits are set. Rocky Graziano is not going to turn into Rex Harrison.

33. If he's crude enough to spear the asparagus with his fish fork, cover your profound distress with the thought that it's not the fork but who's at the other end of it that counts.

ARGUE WITH A LITTLE STYLE

34. There's nothing sexier than a sizzly discussion. If you know the facts, say so. If he proves you wrong, be gracious. (Also be gracious if *he's* proved wrong.) If you feel passionately about something, try to persuade him with fire and logic. No crying. No calling names.

FACE-SAVERS: HIS AND YOURS

Learn to "telegraph" signals to him, so as to avoid a direct discussion when signaling seems more tactful. The smartest girl in the world can be told things without having to be told.

Example:

35. *He* wants an early night. He's grumpy, has a report to study, or needs quiet time alone. His signal may be to apologize for being droopy or just kiss you good night at the door and murmur about its being late. When this happens be charming, however you may feel. Sure, it's possible to strong-arm him into staying—once. But tender as his feelings may be, he'll resent it.

36. *You* want an early night. For reasons of cycle or psyche, you're zapped out and want to turn in. Don't wait until he's comfy on the couch to tell him to scat. No later than on the way home, send up the signal flare that the game is being called because of lateness and can you please give him a raincheck?

BEST FOR LAST

37. Kiss him unexpectedly.
38. Cook him a delicious meal "just because."
39. Never, no matter what, even if you're playing *Camille's* death scene, ask him to take out the garbage.

15. EATING OUT IN FRENCH AND ITALIAN

O.K., you've mastered *omelette aux fines herbes* for lunch. You know it has something to do with eggs, it usually tastes good, and you can almost even pronounce it (ahm-lett oh feene surb). For dinner there's that old friend, *coq au vin* (coke oh vahn), although you can get a bit surfeited with winy chicken all over your plate (this is the fifth year you've been *coq-au-vin*-ing and *omelette-aux fines-herbes*-ing) when friends with a better knowledge of French have all those interesting dishes that seem to contain beef, lamb, or lobster. You've always known you could do something about it if you *tried*, but you *forget*, until there you are again in an elegant French restaurant, with a man or woman companion you wish you didn't have to show your ignorance to, and a haughty captain who ought to be able to help but is so intimidating. You can change all that. Get busy and start learning French Restaurant Basic.

Learn Your Crêpes from Your Coquilles

The old Hollywood notion that snails are the necessary prelude to dinner in a French restaurant is not bad at all. If garlic is no object and *escargots* (ess-kar-goh) are on the menu, pronounce everything but the *t* and last *s*, and snap off an *h* sound. Don't worry about looking gauche as you extract the snails from their shells: there's only one way to do it. Your way.

Pâté—usually followed by *maison*, but just order the pah-teh (and swallow the *h*) to the waiter—is another old reliable. It's a slice of ground, seasoned liver "paste." *Maison* means house: the idea is that the *pâté* was made on the premises, according to the chef's own recipe. *Pâté* sometimes comes with an outside coating of fat—forget *that*—but, it may arrive with a gelatinous coating of aspic. *That's* edible, but you won't be hurting anybody's feelings if you don't respond. You're supposed to eat the *pâté* spread on the thin toast that's supplied with it, but it's perfectly acceptable to eat it with your fork. (If they don't give you thin toast, you're not in a truly elegant restaurant.)

As an alternative to *pâté*, have the *oeufs à la russe* (erve-sahlah roose—but slide over the *rv*): hard-cooked eggs with Russian dressing.

Too fattening? Choose *crevettes* (shrimps, pronounced kreh-vette). You're skinny? Try *coquilles de fruits de mer* (coh-key duh froo-ee duh maihr), a clamshell, or a shell-shaped dish, filled with sea food in a cheese-and-cream sauce. (The cheese makes it *au gratin* or *gratiné*, but you don't have to say it.) In a *coquille St. Jacques* (sahn-zakh), the sea food is strictly scallops, but the sauce is the same. *Crêpes farcies* (krepp fahr-see) are pancakes stuffed with much the same cheese-and-cream mixture, although the major ingredient might be chicken instead of fruits of the sea. Most men love crêpes (in fact, it might be wise to learn how to fix them yourself). Or: order melon—just say melon—or maybe *melon au jambon* (mell-ohn oh jawm-bohn), if you like ham with your melon. That way you can save your calories for dessert.

"What is the *soupe du jour?*" (zouph doo zhoor) is an acceptable question, since, obviously, it changes every *jour*, or day. The waiter will probably explain automatically. If the answer is *petite marmite* (p'teet mar-meet), it's a vegetable soup. But you are expected to know that *soupe aux champignons* (sham-peen-yonh) involves mushrooms, and that *vichyssoise* (vee-she-swahz—don't lose that *z*) is made of potatoes and leeks and cream. *Soupe à l'oignon* (lohn-yohn) is something so familiar that you can ask for the onion soup without losing caste. If the waiter forgets, be sure to ask knowingly for some cheese; grated Parmesan should, of course, accompany this soup.

Now, you'll never remember any of this unless you practice! I'd suggest when you get through reading each section, get a pencil and paper and write down the names of the dishes—and the pronunciation—you've just read about (and say them *out loud*). There is a master list at the end of the chapter, but that's not nearly so good as writing them down yourself; this helps jell them in your mind. If you're really *serious* about never being ill at ease with a French menu again, this is what you must do. Otherwise, you'll read this and forget.

MAIN COURSE
Lunchtime menus often include an *omelette* (ahm-lette). There are many ways of preparing an omelette, but the two most popular are *aux fines herbes* and *aux foies de volaille*. *Aux fines herbes*—chopped herbs, in English—is light and subtle. You already know about it. *Aux foies de volaille* (oh fwah duh vol-eye)—made with chicken liver—is more substantial. *Foie* and *volaille* are handy words: *foie de veau* (vo) is calf's liver, and *suprême* (pronounce the word as if it did not have an *e* at the end of it) *de volaille* is chicken.

Caneton and *canard bigarade* (kahn-uh-tonh; kahn-R-beeg-R-adh) are both duck—the second is served with orange sauce. *Canard Montmorency* (kahn-arrh mon-mohr-on-see) isn't available everywhere, for it is served with a certain amount of fanfare. It's a duck bedecked with Bing cherries. There are other duck dishes, too. Just say "I'll have the *caneton.*" If the waiter asks which kind you prefer, ask *him* to recommend whichever the chef does best.

Poulet (poo-leh) comes in many forms: it's only chicken. If it's *à l'estragon* (said as it's spelled), there will be a tarragon-flavored sauce; if it's *chasseur* (shass-uhr), it will be cooked with onions and garlic—maybe mushrooms—and, indispensably, tomatoes.

Escalopes (ess-ka-lopp) are scallopini—thin slices of veal. They might be *sautées* (so-tay)—almost anything can be sautéed, actually; this means browned in very hot fat. *Escalopes de veau sautées au madère* (oh ma-dair) is a French version of veal scallopini.

Veal also comes in *côtes* (the closest sound is koht), which are chops, and so does *agneau* (ahn-yoh), which is lamb. *Fricadelles de veau* (you say that the way it looks except for omitting the final "s" sound: free-ka-dellh duh vo) are ground veal patties. *Selle* (sellh) and *carré* (car-reh) and *noisette* (nwa-zette) refer to cuts of roast meat—saddle, breast, tenderloin—of *veau, agneau,* or *boeuf* (buef), or maybe even *porc* (por-kh)—exhale gently on the (kh)!

But with *veau*, never assume! *Les cervelles* (leh ser-vel) *de veau* is not just another cut of roast veal—it's veal *brains*! *Rognons* (rohn-yohn) *de veau* are veal kidneys; *ris* (ree) *de veau* are sweetbreads, and you already know about *foie de veau* (liver). *Ris* means thymus—a part of the neck—whereas *riz* means rice; *riz sauvage* (ree so-vazh) is wild rice.

FISH

Fish, *les poissons* (lay pwas-zohn), in French restaurants is *merveilleux* (muhr-veh-yeuze). *Homard* (ohm-R) is lobster—you can tell from the price; *moules* (mool) are mussels; you'll be able to figure out most of the rest. Two exceptions: *cuisses* (kweess) means thighs; now *that* might be useful, but *cuisses de grenouilles* (duh grun-oo-E) are frogs' legs. Expect the dish to taste like chicken laced with garlic.

And now, a very chic number: *quenelles de brochet à la Nantua* (kuh-nell-duh-brosh-ay ahla Nahn-too-wuh: but all you have to say is kuh-nell). This is ground-up pike mixed with a delicate batter and heavy cream, then formed into balls that are poached in fish stock. *Nantua* describes the accompanying sauce: it's basically creamy, but mightily dressed up with *écrevisses* (ay-krehvisse)—crayfish, a kind of mini-lobster. Well, it may not appeal this minute, but it's something you should know about.

You won't save many calories if you choose, instead, a sea food accompanied by the word *mornay* (more-neh)—that's another creamy sauce, with grated swiss cheese added. *Bercy* (bare-see) is similar, but even richer. *Meunière* (meuh-nyair) might appeal: just a smidge of butter and lemon juice. A real self-disciplinarian? Look for something *grillé* (gree-eh) or *pouché* (poe-sheh)—that's grilled and poached: but you knew that, you slender, iron-willed creature.

Légumes (leg-gewm) are vegetables. If you must have one, pick *broc-oli* (broak-oh-lee) or *carottes* (kar-*ott*) or *artichaute* (arti-shoh)—nothing to remember and you ask for them by their English names. Skip the *pommes de terre* (pawm-duh-tehrre)—potatoes. And just ask for a mixed green salad in English. If the waiter repeats your request as vairt meh-lahn-jeh *(verte mélangée)*, you've connected.

DESSERTS

As in any other restaurant, the reward of virtue is dessert. Sometimes it's called *les entremets* (lez on-trayh-may), but it's still dessert. Let the saints be your guide: *coupe St. Jacques* (coop-sahn-zahkh) is vanilla ice cream with fruits strewn carelessly about it; *gâteau St. Honoré* (gah-towh sahn-ton-or-eh) is for esthetes—a whole *St. Honoré* cake is an unforgettable visual experience: layers and rosettes of whipped cream. Chocolate cake? Try *le gâteau reine de Saba* (leuh gah-towh wren *duh* sa-*baa* means Queen of Sheba cake). Its delicate, undefinable taste comes from finely ground almonds. *Tartes* (tahr-teh) are like U. S. pies, at least to look at. Sometimes they're better and sometimes they're worse to taste. *Aux pommes* (oh pawm) is apple-filled: *aux pêches* (oh pesh) is made with peaches.

Ask to see the pastry cart. When the waiter rolls it around, you can see *le gâteau St. Honoré* but order *fraises* (strawberries)—just by indicating their serving bowl. (If you say it, it's freh-zeh—to rhyme with a drawn-out fez.) Casually cast your eyes at the *mousse au chocolat* (moose oh show-ko-lah), that lighter-than-meringue confection of chocolate, eggs, and cream; or consider the *oeufs à la neige* (erve-sahlah na-ezh)—floating island.

A host with more foresight might have thought to suggest a *soufflé au chocolat* (soo-fleh oh show-ko-lah) or *au Grand Marnier* (oh grahn marn-yay)—an orange liqueur—when the waiter brought the *pâté*. This takes a while to bake and *must* be served as soon as the egg whites have finished puffing it up like a popover. If he forgot, try *crêpes* (krepp)—nobody adds the *suzette*—little pancakes drenched in orange liqueur, butter, and sugar, prepared and flamed right before your eyes. *Cerises jubilées* (seh-riiz zoo-bee-lay) is another flaming dessert; while the alcohol flickers, cherries and brandy are ladled onto ice cream.

CHEESES

No dessert at all? To choose a *fromage* (froh-mahz) instead of a sweet demands a little skill. If you don't feel comfortable in the presence of cheeses, you may be in trouble as the large cheese board is presented. Just ask the waiter for something mild or something sharp. If there are specific cheeses listed on the menu, you're safe with mild *Gruyère* (grew-yair).

Well, now, you're ready to dine at La Tour d'Argent, if anyone should invite you to Paris for the weekend. If that happens sooner than you expect, and if the menu in your hands suddenly melts your *expertise* (X-pair-tease), remember you're entitled to one (just one) discreet question of the waiter or captain. Once, a stylish fashion photographer in Paris did not ask the waiter to define *fraises des bois glacées*. He thought he was ordering iced wild strawberries. Turned out to be strawberry ice cream.

Finally, if you want to expand your French Restaurant Basic, ask a French friend to snaffle an authentic French menu, preferably from France—many restaurants are enchanted to give them away—buy yourself a *dictionnaire*, and start translating. It may be *hamburger* to you, but it's *biftek haché* (ah-shay) to them. Bon Apetit!

addition, l'—the check

agneau—lamb

ail—garlic

amande—almond

anchois—anchovy

anguille—eel

apéritif—any drink before a meal

artichaut—artichoke

asperge—asparagus

assiette—platter

baba au rhum—rum-soaked cake

barquette—a boat shaped pastry

béarnaise sauce—buttery, egg-thickened sauce scented with shallots and tarragon

beignets—fritters

beurre—butter

bien cuit—well-done (as in steak)

bière—beer

bigarade sauce—roast duck drippings blended with orange rind, juice and a squeeze of lemon

bisque—a purée, more particularly of shellfish served as a thick soup

blanquette—a white ragout made with egg-yolks and cream

blanquette de veau—veal stew in cream sauce

bleu—very rare (steak); a blue-veined cheese

blini—thin, unsweetened pancake

boeuf—beef

bouillabaisse—a soup or stew of varied fish and shellfish, usually garlic and saffron-scented, with tomatoes and parsley, etc.

bourguignonne sauce—dark, herb-scented red wine sauce

brie—a creamy dessert cheese

brochet—pike

brut—dry

café complet—continental breakfast: rolls, coffee, butter and jam

café noir—black coffee

camembert—soft runny dessert cheese

canard—duck

caneton—duckling

carré d'agneau—rack (ribs) of lamb

cassoulet—a white bean stew, cooked with lamb, and/or goose, sausage, etc.

céleri rémoulade—celery root, cut in matchsticks, in a cold zesty sauce; an appetizer

cerise—cherry

cervelles—brains

champignon—mushroom

chaud—hot

chou—cabbage

choucroute—sauerkraut

citron—lemon

coq au vin—chicken braised in wine sauce with onions, ham or bacon and mushrooms

coquille St. Jacques—scallops, also the name for scallops in a white wine sauce

couvert—cover charge

crêpes—thin pancakes

crêpes suzettes—pancakes in a sweet orange sauce spiked with Curacao liqueur

cresson—watercress

croque monsieur—fried cheese and ham sandwich

croûte—breadcrust; *en croûte*—in pastry

dinde—turkey

emincé—leftover meat, minced, served with a sauce

entrecôte—rib steak

épinards—spinach

escalopes—thin slices of meat

escargots—snails

farci—stuffed

fenouil—fennel

fines herbes—chopped mixed herbs

flambé—flamed with brandy or liqueur

florentine—served with spinach

foie—liver

foie gras—literally, a fat liver; usually goose, or duck or the minced spread made of liver

fraise—strawberry

framboise—raspberry

frit—fried

froid—cold

fromage—cheese

fruits de mer—sea food

fumé—smoked

gâteau—cake

gigot d'agneau—leg of lamb

glace—ice or ice cream, *glacé*—iced

gratin, au—baked with cheese

grenouilles—frog legs

grillé—grilled

hareng—herring

haricots—beans; *verts*—green beans

hollandaise sauce—thick, rich sauce of egg yolks, butter and lemon

homard—lobster

huîtres—oysters

jambon—ham

jus, au—with natural pan juices

jus de fruit—fruit juice

laitue—lettuce

langue—tongue

maître d'hôtel sauce—butter, spiked with lemon and parsley

maquereau—mackerel

marrons—chestnuts

moelle—beef marrow

mornay sauce—cream sauce with cheese

moules—mussels

mousseline sauce—cream-enriched hollandaise

niçoise—in the style of Nice, usually means onions, olives, tomato, garlic

noisette—hazelnut, also refers to a heart or round of meat—*noisette de veau*

oeufs—eggs

oeufs à la gelée—poached eggs in aspic

oeufs sur la plat—fried eggs

oignon—onion

omelette norvegienne—baked Alaska

pain—bread

palourde—clam

pamplemousse—grapefruit

parmentier—a dish prepared with potatoes

pâté—finely minced or ground

pâté maison—fine ground meats in a home-style; an appetizer

pâtisserie—pastry

pêche—peach

périgourdine—in the Perigord style, usually with truffles

persil—parsley

point, à—medium (steak); ready to eat (cheese)

poire—pear

poireau—leek

pois—peas

poisson—fish

poivre—pepper; *au poivre*, with fresh-cracked peppercorns

pomme—apple

pomme de terre—potato
  au four—baked, *frites*—fried, *parisienne*—small potato balls, *soufflés*—twice-fried into balloon-like puffs

potage—soup

poulet—chicken

poussin—a very young chicken

primeur—the first of the season, usually the earliest of a fruit or vegetable crop

prix fixe—price fixed meal

purée—mashed or sieved

quenelles de brochet—oval dumplings of fine ground pike enriched with cream and egg white, usually served in a rich cream sauce.

quiche lorraine—a custard pie of bacon and sometimes cheese

ratatouille—a vegetable stew—egg plant, tomato, green pepper, onions, zucchini—served hot or cold

rémoulade—a piquant mayonnaise-like sauce served with seafood or celery root

ris de veau—sweetbreads

riz—rice

riz sauvage—wild rice

rognon—kidneys

rôti—roast

saignant—rare (steak)

salade nicoise—a Mediterranean salad of greens and variously, tuna, anchovy, boiled potato, string beans, olives, hard-boiled eggs, capers

salade verte—green salad

saucisson—sausage

saumon fumé—smoked salmon

sel—salt

service compris—service charge (tip included)

sorbet—sherbet

soup a l'oignon—onion soup

supplément—additional charge

suprême sauce—a rich cream sauce

suprême de volaille—the choice fillet of poultry breast (two of each bird) removed in one piece

tarte maison—a tart or open pie prepared in the house's own style

terrine—an earthenware casserole. Also refers to the pâté in the casserole

timbale—a turban shaped mold

tortue—turtle

tournedos—small fillet, filet mignon

truffle—a rare and costly variety of fungi that grows underground in the roots of certain trees, used for flavor and texture

truite—trout; *au bleu*—trout is kept alive until cooking

veau—veal

vin—wine

vinaigrette—a tangy sauce of oil, vinegar, mustard and herbs

THE INDISPENSABLES

s'il vous plaît—please

merci—thank you

au secour—help!

Learn Your Calamari from Your Ceci

Red-and-white checkered tablecloths, a cellar dimly lit by multicolored candles melting down the necks of straw-wrapped Chianti bottles, spaghetti, veal parmigiana, biscuit tortoni with espresso. The setting is so delicious that what you're eating hardly matters. But it *should* matter! Fortified by the expertise you're about to acquire, you and the man you dine with may want to undertake some *gourmet* adventures during your next Italian evening.

Should you begin with the antipasto (on T pahs' toe—literally "before the pasta")? In *most* restaurants this appetizer is boringly predictable—tuna, anchovies, chick-peas, black olives, pimientos, artichoke hearts, stuffed eggs, scallions, pickled mushrooms, slices of salami, either right out of the container or dressed up in a flavored oil and vinegar. Even at its best, antipasto is too filling for the American appetite and will keep you from enjoying the chef's best dishes.

Since the pasta course, entrée, and dessert are still to come, think for a minute about a lighter beginning, *prosciutto e mellone*—Italian ham with melon. No ham can compare with prosciutto; with a slice of ripe melon, it's *magnifico*. Ask for "melon with pro shu' toe." Now is the time to commit Rule One of pronunciation to memory: *sci* or *sce* in Italian is pronounced *sh* as in prosciutto, and *ci* or *ce* becomes *ch* as in *ciao* (chow).

Take note of minestrone (min uh stroh' nee), which can be a one-and-only, truly incredible vegetable soup if the chef is worth his seasonings (and knows his onions, lentils, spinach, and beans). But note it only in passing—save yourself for the pasta.

Don't be put off if the menu says "Farinaceous" (fair on A' shuss) where you expected to see a heading that says "Pasta"; farinaceous is simply the adjective for farina and farina equals pasta and pasta means noodles. Ask the waiter whether you can order a half-portion—he probably doesn't like fat women either, so he'll understand. But a half-portion of what? The appetite boggles at the multiple choices of just spaghetti—*spaghetti con pesto* comes with a green sauce made of ground parsley, basil, and nuts; *alla vòngole* (von go' lay) *in bianco* is white clam sauce with lots of garlic; *al burro* (pronounced like the Spanish donkey) is a sauce of plain butter; *alla bolognese* (bolo nyay' zay) is spaghetti with a tomato-meat sauce, the kind most of us think of when we think of spaghetti.

But pasta isn't *always* the usual creamy spaghetti color. It may be *verdi* (vair' D)—green—and not from U.S. certified dyes but from spinach. The taste is just a touch different from plain pasta, sort of healthy but by no means spinach-y.

And pasta doesn't always have to be the usual elongated spaghetti *shape*. The same farina, formed into squat, ridged, slant-ended tubes becomes ziti (Z' T) or the slightly larger rigatoni (ree gah toe' nee). New York's Italian Pavilion offers a rare and beautiful *ziti pasticciati* (che ah' T—*ci* equals *ch* as in the *ciao* rule). The ziti are baked in a sauce of heavy cream and tomatoes; then cheese is sprinkled over all and the dish is run under the broiler to melt the cheese.

Lasagne (la zan' yuh) is a sublime pasta casserole—cream sauce, meat sauce, lots of cheeses, layered alternately with fat, flat ribbons of noodles. (The *al forno* that may follow the word lasagne on the menu freely translated just means "baked.")

You were thinking of a bit more subtle pasta? Fettucine (fet too chee' nee) Alfredo is your dish. Fettucine is the aristocrat of spaghettis and somehow seems to *absorb* the sweet butter, heavy cream, grated cheese, and yolk of egg with which it is so lovingly tossed right at your table. Try just one twist of the pepper mill when this delicate dish is set before you.

If you want something that doesn't even *look* like the spaghetti you're familiar with, consider cannelloni (can alone' E). Cannelloni are pancakes rolled around a meat filling and then adorned with either a creamy sauce or tomato-meat sauce that is spaghetti's customary embellishment (the latter version is *bolognese*).

Try tortellini (tor tell E' nee) if you're in the mood for bite-size morsels. These are little round meat-stuffed dumplings. Sometimes they come *in bròdo* (in broth), and sometimes *they* come *bolognese*, too.

How about an unassailably sophisticated dish? Gnocchi (naw' key) are dumplings that come mainly in two varieties: *gnocchi alla romana*—baked from a dough of semolina (wheat flour) and eggs and served with cheese and butter or with gravy. *Gnocchi alla piemontese* (p'yay mont A' zay) are made of mashed potato and flour, generally served with tomato sauce and mushrooms.

Of course, if your next-to-no-starches life-style was dented the minute you sat down and saw those breadsticks on the table, you may want to pass up the pasta (sob!) and press on to the *piatti del giorno* (P ah T dell G or' no)— today's entrées.

A main ingredient of many Italian entrées is *scaloppine di vitello* (scallo P' nee D V tell' O—all you need say is scallo P' nee), which are thin, boneless slices of veal, delicately flavored and as near as meat can come to being calorieless. Simplest and subtlest of the scaloppine dishes is veal *piccata* (peek ah' tuh). The scallops of veal, as cookbook authors call this cut, are cooked quickly in butter, then served with parsley and lemon slices. That's it!

Piccata alla milanese (me lahn A' zay) will arrive at your table accompanied by a saffron-flavored rice. Rice accompanies almost anything *alla milanese* except *risotto* (ree zoh' toe) *alla milanese*, of course, which is simply rice *alone*—cooked till creamy in broth and white wine, seasoned with saffron, and probably embellished with marrow, that soft, meaty interior of good soup-bones. You may have noticed *risotto alla milanese* tucked away under Farinaceous.

Scaloppine al marsala (no trouble reading *that* aloud) is also cooked quickly in butter, but then marsala wine is added to the skillet so the dish arrives with a gentle but perceptibly winy sauce.

Scaloppine cacciatora (kah chee ah tor' ah) begins, like all scaloppine dishes, with quick cooking in butter. Then white wine, mushrooms, and tomatoes are added. The tomatoes are the clue to the name—*cacciatora* means hunter's style, and hunters' caps (like tomatoes) are red, right? (In French, *chasseur* means hunter—and now you know what veal *chasseur* is in a French restaurant.)

Rollatini (roll a T' nee) *di vitello* is a rolled-up veal scallop, concealing a filling usually of prosciutto and Parmesan cheese, or possibly finely ground pork. The same fillings stuff *costolette di vitello alla magènta* (pronounced like the color). Veal *magènta*, as it's sometimes listed, is a veal chop, split in the middle to accommodate the prosciutto and cheese. These two dishes are rich and complicated blendings of flavors and textures—you *owe* yourself the experience!

Saltimbocca (salt im bock' uh) doesn't read like the other scaloppines, but basically that's what it is. A slice of prosciutto is tooth-picked to the veal scallop. After a quick browning, the meat combination is basted with white wine and sometimes seasoned with sage. *Saltimbocca*, by the way, means "jump into the mouth,"—in other words, delicious.

Osso buco (oh so boo' coe) translates as "hollow bone," but, happily, a dish of *osso buco* is much more than that, namely pieces of veal shank cooked with white wine and tomatoes, plus the refinements of parsley, garlic, and lemon peel. There *is* meat on the shank bones, but the joy of this lovely dish is the marrow inside the bones. An oyster fork is given you to dig it out.

Now that you know the basic veal styles, *pollo* (polo) dishes, which means chicken, are practically self-explanatory. *Pollo saltimbocca* is boneless breast of chicken plus a slice of prosciutto, quickly browned in butter and basted with white wine and perhaps a touch of sage. *Pollo alla cacciatora* (the red-capped hunters) and *pollo alla bolognese*, with tomato-meat sauce, are prepared basically the same way as their veal counterparts. *Pollo alla fiorentina* (fee or N T' nah), like anything *fiorentina*, signals a spinach accompaniment; *pollo alla parmigiana*—but you *know* that.

Fegatini di pollo (hard *g* in *fega*, *tini* is pronounced T' nee) is *not* another kind of chicken but rather chicken livers; similarly *fegato di vitello* (hard *g* again) is calf's liver. *Fegato di vitello alla veneziana* will arrive in finger-sized slices, will have been quickly and tenderly browned, and will be accompanied by the onions cooked in the same pan.

One word to beef-eaters: forget about steak and try *braciole* (bra chee O' luh), a fillet of beef rolled around a filling of finely ground pork or veal or of parsley and cheese. The beef roll is seared and then simmered, usually in a tomato sauce.

Shrimp scampi (skahmp' E) are pretty firmly entrenched in the American Way of Life. On an Italian menu they are called simply "scampi"; chefs' recipes vary—some include tarragon, others shallots—but garlic is always present, by definition. And if garlic should happen not to be on your most-wanted list, you will miss not only scampi but also *scampi alla marinara*. And everything else marinara, too! Marinara sauce makes up for *no* meat with a plentitude of garlic, tomatoes, onions, and oregano. It's most often on the menus of restaurants Southern Italian style where all the cooking is spicier, more peppery, and more replete with garlic. If lots of things on the menu are *alla marinara* or *alla napoletana*, another designation for this Southern point of view, expect even more delicate pastas to be peppery.

Aragosta fra diavolo is a beautiful Southern Italian specialty. *Aragosta* (ah rah goss' tah) is lobster; *fra diavolo* (frah D ah' vuh loe) means "brother devil," which should give you some idea of the hotness. So will the sauce ingredients: tomatoes, garlic, vinegar, and quite a few crushed red-pepper flakes!

If you've begun with a pasta or chosen a dish amplified with spinach or rice or a sauce, you probably won't have *room* for the *legumi* (lay goom' E) or vegetables. For the sake of education, however, note that *melanzane* (melon zahn' A) is eggplant; the Italian words for most other vegetables are easily deciphered.

There's always room for "a mixed green salad, *per favore*" (pair fahv or' A means please), which the menu may call *insalata mista* (the *i*'s are long E's, remember). The salad will contain the usual American greenery and, with luck, rugula, a peppery leaf that looks like dandelion leaves. The house dressing will be oil and vinegar and, most likely, garlic.

Ready to assume the responsibility of choosing a wine? Italian wine is well worth knowing about—and not complicated—even if all you ever do is *discuss* it with somebody. Between us, Chianti is every bit as acceptable a choice in an elegant Italian restaurant as in a neighborhood café. There is a white Chianti, of course, as well as a red . . . just about as dry and as strong. An excellent dry white wine is Soave (swav A). A less dry, more soft-tasting white wine? Try Verdicchio (vair D' key O). Now, if you're put off by *any dry* wine, practice saying, "You know what I'd really like? Abbah cot' O or V eh' toe" (that's *abboccato Orvieto*), and your waiter will produce a rather sweet, pleasant white wine. You prefer a red, but not Chianti again? Suggest a Bardolino (lee' no), a light red, fruity wine, or Valpolicella (val pole E chell' a), a velvety red wine, more intense than Bardolino and less apt to be overpowered if the entrée you've chosen is strong-flavored.

Your planning ahead now pays off; it's time to order the dolce (dole' chay, as in *La Dolce Vita*). Italian ice cream, *gelati* (jell ah' T), is rich and also comes in a rich *variety*, like the rum-flavored, crumb-be-decked cups of *tortoni*, or the variously combined flavors of *spumoni* (pistachio, chocolate, and vanilla, molded in layers, with nuts in the center). But save this experience for your trip to Italy. Italian ice cream (U.S. style) is often only a pallid imitation made in a U.S. factory. There are other delicacies to be sampled.

When the pastry tray comes round, you might point to the delicate horn of plenty, filled with a creamy cheese, and ask for the *cannoli* (can O' lee). And you'll recognize the Napoleon—layers of puff pastry filled with custard. Its official title is *sfogliata Napoleone* (s'foley ah tuh na pole E own' A), but you may dispense with the formalities.

If the restaurant is Southern Italian and luck is with you, *cassata alla siciliana* (kah sah tuh ahl ah C cheel E ahn' ah) will be offered, and if your diet allows, it shouldn't be missed. Layers of pound cake are filled with a creamy cheese, flavored with orange liqueur and studded with candied fruit and chopped chocolate.

A still richer cake is the formidable *zuppa inglese* (zoopa in glaze' A)—English soup! According to Roberto, maitre d' at the Italian Pavilion, *zuppa inglese* was invented by an English pastry chef in Rome. Why call it soup? Because the cake contains—like a good soup should—a little bit of everything . . . in this case rum chocolate bits, chopped candied fruits, and cold *zabaglione.*

Ah, *zabaglione* (zah bah le own' A)! Rich but not gaudy, *zabaglione* is a warm, thick custard sauce of egg yolks whipped with sugar and mar-sala wine. Often it's concocted right at your table to be served at once. If diet discretion dictates fresh strawberries for dessert, at least accept the *sauce* the waiter proffers with them—it's cold *zabaglione* and de-licious!

Should the egg yolk in *zabaglione* not satisfy your dedications to pro-tein, then it's *formaggi* (form ah' G)—cheese—for you. Try a mild, some-what smoky provolone (pronounce the final E), a rather more pungent and softer Bel Paese (pay ease' uh), or stronger still, the blue-veined gorgonzola. If cheese is presented as an assortment, the provolone is the pale, firm, spherical one.

With the espresso but before presenting *il conto* (eel con' toe), the bill, some restaurants may also present you with a plate of individually wrapped *amaretti* (ahm uh rett' E), lovely, light-textured little almond-flavored macaroons. Say *grazie* (grah' tsee) and try one. If even one *amaretti* is more than you can manage, then you've learned the prin-ciple rule for ordering in Italian restaurants: ask for a half-portion of pasta and keep *away* from those breadsticks! Buon' Appetito!

Instant Italian Alla Carta

abbacchio—baby lamb

acciughe—anchovy

aglio—garlic

agnello arrosto—roast lamb

al burro—with butter

al dente—literally, to the teeth, pasta with a bite to it, cooked till just firm

alla griglia—broiled

al sugo—with sauce

anguilla—eel

birra—beer

bistecca—steak

bollito—boiled

brodo—broth

bue—beef

burro—butter

calamari—squid

caldo—hot

cannelloni—large flat noodles stuffed with meat and baked in a sauce

capellini—small thin noodles

ceci—chick peas

cervello—brains

ciliege—cherries

colazione—lunch

costolette—cutlet

cozze—mussels

crudo—raw

dolci—sweets, dessert

fagiolini—green beans

fegatini—chicken livers

fegato alla veneziana—calves' liver and onions

fettucine al'Alfredo—egg noodles with butter, cheese and sometimes cream

filetto di sogliole—fillet of sole

finocchio—fennel

formaggio—cheese

fragola—strawberry

freddo—cold

frittata—omelet

fritto—fried

fritto misto—mixed fried foods

frutta—fruit

funghi—mushrooms

gamberi—shrimp

gelato—ice cream, ice

gnocchi—potato or semolina dumplings

gorgonzola—a sharp, veined cheese

granita—frozen iced drink, sherbet

insalata—salad

involtini—meat rolls

lasagne—wide noodles layered with cheese and tomato sauce and baked

latte—milk

lattuga—lettuce

legumi—vegetables

limone—lemon

linguini—skinny noodles

maiale—pork

manicotti—large flat noodles stuffed with a meat and cheese mixture, baked in tomato sauce

manzo—beef

marinara—spicy meatless tomato sauce

mela—apple

melanzana alla parmigiana—egg plant, sautéed, then layered with cheese and tomato sauce

minestrone—thick vegetable soup

115

mortadella—soft salami

mostarda—mustard

mozzarella in carrozza—a fried cheese sandwich

noci—nuts

olio—oil

osso buco—braised veal shanks

pane—bread

panettone—the fruit-studded Christmas cake of Milan

panna—cream

patate—potatoes

pecorino—goat's milk cheese

perciatelli—long macaroni

pesca—peach

pesce—fish

pesto—green sauce of basil, parsley, oil, pine nuts. . .and garlic

pignoli—pine nuts

piselli—peas

polenta—corn meal mush

pollo—chicken

polpette—meat balls

pomidoro—tomato

pompelmo—grapefruit

pranzo—dinner

prima colazione—breakfast

prosciutto—smoked ham usually served in paper thin slices, often with melon or fresh figs

provolone—a mild hard cheese

ravioli—noodle dough stuffed with chopped meat, cheese or spinach

ricotta—mild white curd cheese

riso—rice

risotto—rice dish

rognoni—kidneys

sale—salt

saltimbocca—veal and ham (or pork) cooked in butter with wine and herbs

scampi—large shrimp

scungilli—conch

semolino—fine wheat flour

spezzatino di vitello—veal stew

spiedino—fried cheese with a piquant anchovy sauce

succo di pomidoro—tomato juice

sugo—gravy

tacchino—turkey

tagliatelle verdi—flat green noodles

tartufi—truffles

tonno—tunafish

torrone—nougat candy

torta—cake, tart, pie

troto—trout

uova—eggs, *affogate*—poached, *al guscio*—boiled, *al tegame*—scrambled, or fried

uva—grapes

vermicelli—very thin spaghetti

vino—wine

vitello—veal

vongole—clams

zabaglione—marsala-wine spiked egg yolks whisked to a froth

zeppole—a kind of doughnut

ziti—fat, long macaroni

zucchero—sugar

zucchini—green summer squash

zuppa di cipolle—onion soup

zuppa inglese—liquor or rum soaked cake with custard and whipped cream

zuppa pavese—soup with a poached egg floating, served with cheese and fried bread

THE INDISPENSABLES

prego—please

grazie—thank you

aiuto—help!

16. MEETING HIS MOTHER

A day will come, inevitably, when he announces—"I want to take you home to meet my mother." Panic! Suddenly blood seems to have stopped circulating to the outer regions of your toes. You're numb . . . a condition you feel will become permanent unless you can hire someone to take your place. No way! If you want *him*, it is essential to face *her*.

Calm down! To refuse, or even invent a reason *not* to go, is insulting to your love and his family. There is an etiquette for meeting his mother (father, sister, brother, business partner, secretary, ex-wife) and its basis is essentially what makes any first-meetings successful . . . self-confidence and some forethought.

Your man plays a large role in providing the confidence—he can complain about your appearance all the way to his parents' door *or* assure you that freckles do *not* make you look thirteen. Here are some suggestions on pre-planning:

1. Fix hair the day before the visit so it feels natural.

2. Don't buy a new dress. Wear a tested favorite . . . something he likes and that is comfortable to *move* in. If a particular color makes you feel cheerful, wear it. Avoid clanky jewelry.

3. Ask your love about his parents' likes and dislikes so you'll know what subjects *not* to bring up.

4. Bring a hostess gift if at all appropriate (see Part Two, chapter 19, for specific suggestions), and remember that something you made—food or handwork—will show how home-oriented you can be.

5. If the occasion is dinner and his mother doesn't have help, ask if you can lend a hand in the kitchen or clear the table. (It will help if you don't break anything.)

6. Love her veal paprikash, crewel draperies, streaked hair, anything

you can admire without sounding like an idiot.

7. Disagree (politely) on one *minor* point (pantsuits, a TV show) so she won't think you're playing up to her. Don't talk *too* much or momma-in-law will decide you're pushy.

8. Don't act possessive about *their* son; you've won him, no need to irritate her by flaunting it.

9. Do say something sweet about him he'd like his mother to hear.

10. Remember . . . she knows you wouldn't be there if you weren't important to her boy . . . that makes her as scared as you are, at least. Think about putting her at ease, and your tensions will vanish too.

17. OFFICE ROMANCE

"There is no time for cut-and-dried monotony," the great Coco Chanel once said. "There is time for work. And time for love. That leaves no other time." How splendid then when work and love overlap. How splendid but sometimes a little dangerous.

A ton of impressive words have been written about the pitfalls of intraoffice romance. "Don't sex around in your bread-and-butter bailiwick," cautions promotion wizard Letty Cottin Pogrebin in her wise and candid best seller *How to Make It in a Man's World.* "Define the perimeters of your professional circle and draw the line on sexual adventures right there," Letty urges, flatly placing off limits: your darling boss, married or otherwise, your co-workers and staff, the mail boy, the salesman you meet, account executives who create your firm's ads . . . all the men you sell, talk money with, negotiate and sign contracts for, all the men you pay and compete with directly.

Oh Letty, *what a bore!* A large number of accomplished women would have missed their best opportunities on *that* advice!

I agree that the path of office sex is sometimes booby-trapped with tears, trauma, tragedy, lost jobs, missed opportunities, and professional setbacks. But the working world is where men are! The ones you encounter between nine and five are often your prime source of love and adventure. It would be neater and more circumspect to be mad about a radiologist, an airline pilot, or a sweater importer, all of whom never will be in a position to get you fired. (Actually, all those men are part of *some* girl's office or professional bailiwick.) But life is not neat. Yes, you may have a peripheral interest that helps you meet interesting men—rock collecting, skiing, night school—but the odds are against hordes of them turning up that way.

With a measure of good sense, good manners, and old-fashioned consideration you can sidestep the booby traps and soften the potential

119

for trauma that may exist in office romance. For as sure as gender (and what could be surer) you *are* going to flirt with the men you meet professionally. You'll lunch with them, go to bed with them, fall in and out of love . . . maybe even marry. If you are not this very moment involved in some kind of work endeavor that is *populated* with likely specimens, that may be why you mope so much!

Go where the men are. Go where *your kind* of men are. If your company forbids intraoffice dating, it's the wrong office for you. If dating is merely frowned on, ignore the frowns . . . but don't flaunt your defiance. Some guidelines:

1. You can always have men as friends, just friends . . . as long as you both have other romantic involvements.

2. Say no when you don't want to. Don't let loneliness or revenge propel you into bed with the wrong man. Sex-by-default leaves a bitter aftertaste.

3. Certain girls *do* work their way near the top by going from bed to bed to bed, but do you *want* to? It's not the only or even best way to reach Everest and it's *NOT* the way to stay there. (You have to have talent to remain.)

4. An office affair need not undermine office morale. It's quite probable anyone who knows and everyone who suspects will be delighted . . . except the girls he used to go with and the men who have their eye on *you. Underplay it.* Don't talk about your affair with office friends. Don't hint. Do not flaunt or brag.

5. You are going to be so polite and restrained when you meet your love at the morning office conference no one could possibly guess the two of you fell out of the same bed and were sipping coffee in your sunlit breakfast nook exactly two hours ago. Don't be too cool though. That would be obvious.

6. Nuzzling, pinching, tickling, and other touching messages of affection at the office should be avoided. Love notes by interoffice memo are not recommended. Do not arrive and leave together.

7. Mooning, long intraoffice phone calls and lunch hours that last till 3:00 P.M. are unfair to your employer—and a good sign you're sabotaging yourself.

The Matinee

Many romances—*especially* between people who work and who are both married—are conducted almost entirely at lunch. The twosome may simply hold hands through long, heady meals at small French bistros or indulge in a more passionate scene. Whether or not you choose to spend this time making love is *your* decision (we aren't for or against), but whatever you do should be managed with taste and consideration.

Where is this affair conducted? If he is rich, a small *pied-à-terre* or a permanent suite at a hotel affords discreet anonymity. For a single girl, there is your apartment, of course . . . always neat, the bed immaculate, curtains drawn to filter the light slightly, martinis chilling in the refrigerator, and the makings of a light, fast lunch all ready. (When two people return to their respective offices from a two-hour lunch with stomachs rumbling, frayed tempers and possible disaster may result.)

Your noontime love is quite likely to be . . . a married man. In that case you are a *considerate* adulteress. Such a stance isn't easy, but you need your instinctive thoughtfulness and ladylike manners to weave a protective cocoon around your affair. *Never* make nasty cracks about his wife . . . let him do it. Never *ever* call him at home even if you have twenty-two *practically* legitimate excuses. Try not to pressure him with guilts . . . he has enough of those without your help.

You also don't sit home waiting forlornly for him to call. Your life is filled with work, Italian lessons, needlepoint, twice-a-week tutoring of inner-city children with reading problems, tennis, and men! Don't cut out all the other men in your life.

If *your* image of yourself is in conflict with your actions and you are suffering keenly, seek professional help.

When the day comes that you realize you are giving *much more* than you get, take a stand. And let go. Kindest of all is to provoke him into the break.

It's over now and you cannot bear to see him. But if your job still brings you together, or you both work for the same company, *then* what do you do? You can quit, or, if you are strong and brave and resilient—and your whole affair is not general office gossip—you may both be able to survive still working as colleagues, without a painful exile.

THINGS THAT ARE TACKY

Indiscretion.
Tattletales.
Tears.
Mushy love notes.
Winks and sighs, pinches, grabs, soul kisses, meaningful glances.

18. CAVIAR AND CATNIP: INSPIRED GIFTING

"I love the Christmas-tide, and yet,
I notice this, each year I live;
I always like the gifts I get,
But how I love the gifts I give!"
CAROLYN WELLS

Gift-giving can be an absolute drag or a genuinely creative experience. Some people are wizards . . . popping in out of nowhere with a gem of a wicker sewing-stand . . . no reason at all except, "I know how you're mad for wicker." The unbirthday gift—an Erte sketch from an old *Vogue*, exquisitely framed, with a note: "Your bathroom walls are positively naked . . . and aren't these your shower curtain colors?" Or a jar of organic peanut butter with a card that says, "I was in this health food shop and I suddenly remembered peanut butter is your soul food." Emeralds from Cartier's warm a girl's heart, but superthoughtful gifts make you glow.

Most of us give the gift *we'd* like. Or we choose the status label—anything from Tiffany's "under $15" selection. Sometimes we're so overwhelmed with doubts as Christmas or a birthday nears, we settle for the cliché gift of the year—signature scarf, a gaudy book to grace the cocktail table (unread), extravagant chocolates sinfully overpriced . . . or we go the other direction and are downright *cheap* (ugh!). Going broke is *not* the answer, of course. To go into debt for gifts is a sign of insecurity. And resorting to a gift certificate is, conversely, a confession of disinterest and total lack of imagination . . . unless you earmark the certificate *for a specific present*, but one the owner must select himself. For example: you know he needs a new golf club . . . but you don't know anything about how a man picks one that is the right length and weight for him. Give the gift certificate from the best sports store in town with a card that says: "Let's pick out your golf club together."

If you're buying yourself, how *do* you pick the right gift?

You write down clues all year long. Talk to people about their personal interests . . . and really *listen*. You'll discover your cleaning lady grows roses; select a rare new specimen for her. Your psychiatrist is a wine connoisseur; ask the best wineshop to recommend a lovely but not devastatingly expensive white wine—Sancerre or a Château Olivier perhaps. Your building superintendent, you learn, is daffy about his twelve-year-old son, the camera-freak. Wrap a self-mounting photo album in pages from a photography magazine for *Junior*—to give along with your super's Christmas check.

Shop all year. Haunt the sales. Buy while on vacations . . . it's easier to find unusual presents then, and friends appreciate your thinking about them while you were having fun. When you spy the Bosch volume—half price—your sister has been mooning over, buy it! Sometime in May you stitch your way through a lion needlepoint pillow for your chic Leo boss.

Manhattan's genius hairdresser, Marc Sinclaire, is deluged annually with precious baubles from the grateful ladies whose manes he tames, yet there is one gift-giver he never stops raving about. Even though this past Christmas was a dreary holiday for Phyllis Cerf with her publisher-husband Bennett in the hospital, Phyllis arrived at the hairdresser's with bulging shopping bags of goodies, individually selected, for *everyone*. She had discovered the shampoo girl painted; for her a ceramic-frog brush-holder. For proprieter Marc, a mad dandy's shirt and tie in his favorite color. It would have been easier—and no strain on the Cerf budget—to dispatch a secretary for a dozen of this and a dozen of that from Saks, but Phyllis gets too much fun out of creative gifting. So can you.

Coals to Newcastle

What can you possibly buy for disgustingly rich friend, the breakfast-food heiress—you, with your nonelastic $92.80 a week after taxes? Even if you splurged $50 what could you select she doesn't already *have?* The answer is finding something unique—a rare, out-of-print cookbook you found covered with dust in a secondhand book shop; an unusual chocolate mold shaped like a monkey, catnip for her pampered feline in a box you hinged out of shell. Jeanette, a pragmatic-realist Cosmo girl, looked around the country house loaned to her by wealthy friends and despaired. On every table were a dozen exquisite antique bibelots . . . what could they possibly give *those* people? Jeanette's husband, the camera-fiend, came up with the solution: he brought tripods, lights, and cameras out to the estate and photographed the whole place, *House Beautiful* style. Jeanette selected the best shots, had them mounted on heavy white board and presented as a portfolio to her friends, who were absolutely overwhelmed—and haven't stopped raving.

The gift you *make*—tarragon jelly, that special tomato pudding, the tiny jewel box paved with brilliantly dyed feathers—is *special*. Of course there *are* girls who cannot paint, stitch, cook, glue, or sew . . . poor dears. And if you can't, then *don't*. A ribbon-handbag that looks as though it was put together by a kindergartener is sweet . . . but something you'd really prefer to drown!

Perhaps your answer is to *assemble*. Find a chunk of polished turquoise and have a jeweler set it into a belt buckle dredged out of a thrift-shop barrel. Buy five pounds of good fresh jelly beans and present them in an old-time tin candy box, or antique glass jar. For a man who appreciates his Irish heritage, find a handsome old map of Ireland; have it imaginatively framed. You do get the idea.

I.O.U. Me

Your *time* can be a precious gift. Imaginatively wrap a "certificate," mock contract, or promissory note with a gift of: twelve evenings of baby-sitting, one month of apartment-watching and plant-tending, your services as a hem-letter-downer, "one herb garden to be planted" (by you in spring). You might offer poodle-grooming or bathroom-wallpapering, or a cocktail party for twenty to be catered by you (you promise to fill the beneficiary's freezer with your justifiably celebrated hors d'oeuvre).

One of the most precious *wedding* gifts my friend Ruth received was an album from her mother . . . all the scattered photos from Ruth's childhood collected, dated, and pasted into a leather-bound book. And Ruth, a marvel in the kitchen, once responded to a friend's lament, "We never get a decent breakfast," by arriving one morning with six tender little squab—boned, stuffed, and roasted—and a magnum of champagne. "Don't say you *never* get a decent breakfast," she announced.

The Gift of Green

Do give money! (See Tipping.) Money can often be *the* most thoughtful present. It fits . . . needs no alteration . . . is always the right color. All the hands that serve you—doorman, secretary, baby-sitter, newspaper delivery boy, janitor—will welcome such a gift, but *never naked* money. Always present crisp new bills in a gift envelope with special personalized note of thanks . . . preferably accompanied by a small thoughtful gift, perhaps a luxury edible. Or slip the money into a handsome wallet or plump Italian change purse or into a practical tapestry handbag. You might hint there's something inside. My aunt once bought a bag at Hudson's in Detroit and found a $20 bill tucked into the zipper pocket . . . someone had returned a gift purse without discovering the hidden bonus.

The one New Orleans jazz album missing from his collection.

Language records—for his trip to France.

Six superb imported cheeses and a box of Carr's water biscuits.

A Hermès tie.

Sweater you knit yourself with your personal label inside.

The most expensive chamois for his car and a promise to help Simonize it.

Homemade cookies or candy, nicely packed.

The new book by his favorite author.

A giant bath sheet with his monogram on it in a color he likes.

Eskimo carving or pre-Columbian figure from a museum gift shop.

Butcher-paper memo-pad with his name imprinted.

The *Whole Earth Catalog* (if he's a woodsman or ecology disciple).

Some special stamps to fill in his collection.

GIFTS FOR YOUR HOSTESS
(OR HIS MOTHER)

(Send them ahead, bring along with you, or ship afterwards . . .)

One long-stemmed rose every Friday for a year. Arrange with her local florist.

A quart of shallots because she's a serious cook.

One dozen bulbs for her garden and a handy new bulb planter.

Place mats and napkins you cut and fringed yourself.

Handsome bird feeder and seed.

The best Italian pepper-bread baked in your town.

Irish-wool pillow, any needlepoint items . . . door stop, eyeglass case, key-holder.

Crock of fine-ground, chicken-liver *pâté* made from Michael Field's *Cooking School* cookbook.

Whirligig wire salad basket because they're fabulous and she doesn't have one.

Everything she needs to make the most perfect salad dressing—from a fine gourmet foods shop: French olive oil, imported peanut oil, tarragon vinegar, mustard from Dijon, a bag of telicherry black pepper, basil, dill, celery seed.

Sesame Street records for her children. Or the latest Newberry or Caldecott Award book.

MORE GIFTS FOR THE MAN

Antique cuff links: find antique coins and have them made.

Twenty-five felt-tip pens (he's always losing them).

A haircut from the best local barber.

A case of good '66 wine; won't be ready to drink for years and he'll want to share it with you.

A nude sketch of you by the best artist you can afford.

A sketch of his boat . . . by you.

All the shells you collected at Martha's Vineyard last summer glued to a small box for his collar stays and tie bars.

Copy of *Stalking the Wild Asparagus* by Euell Gibbons and a wish to go stalking together.

Promise of fifty-two super-magnifico back rubs.

Elegant pipe and tobacco selected from your city's best tobacconist.

One shiny red apple.

Sunshine highlights in her hair . . . frosting . . . you do it *for* her.

Crocheted bikini—make it yourself.

Floor-length denim apron to wear (with nothing under it) at her next dinner-for-two.

Gold hoop-earrings that look pierced-ear but aren't (because she's too timid to get hers pierced).

That old boyfriend you weren't willing to give up altogether but now you *are!*

An elegant accessory—tortoise bracelet, tie-dye scarf—she wants but can't afford.

Wicked underwear.

A haircut by your town's genius hairdresser.

Fur vest you tailored out of second-hand fur coat.

Try to get an autographed picture by a celeb because she's nuts about him . . . even if you just can't see it.

Silver key chain or letter opener because she's wowed by *anything* from Tiffany's.

Bounty for the Boss

If your boss is your best friend—an angel and your contemporary—gift her as you would a *friend*. But when your boss is a dignified, distant gentleman, a present for him is something *else*. Even when nothing *seems* expected, it's a warm and thoughtful gesture to find him a special bauble. It may cost only a dollar or two—one Havana cigar smuggled in from Geneva by your roommate the stewardess, a ceramic eggcup because he *loves* soft-boiled eggs, a pound of Louisiana coffee with chicory (he loves that *too*), one jar of candied walnuts (you made them once and he hasn't stopped hinting), an efficient desk accessory, nonfiction book on a subject of deep interest to him. *Clever girl!*

The Art of Getting

Old-fashioned etiquette insists a lady will never accept anything but a modest, impersonal gift from a man. Nonsense! Times and codes have changed. *No* gift from a man is too extravagant (well, *maybe* a Bentley from a *stranger*). Of course, if there is an implied intimacy or proposition built into the gift—and there often *is*—and your instinct says "no," then that gift you must refuse.

Never, *never* exchange or return a present from a man you love even if you hate it—unless you can plead "wrong size." You must also use or wear this offering in his presence . . . just forget it isn't *you!* A man who is learning your likes—an apprentice of taste—can be transformed into a paragon of giving if you offer *encouragement.* And hints. Write a letter to Santa Claus—with pictures cut out of catalogues and sizes, leave it on a coffee table where he can see it. Or ask him to mail the letter for you.

Thank You

Say thank you immediately when you receive a present, then send an enthusiastic note later with a specific reason why you adore it. *Mention* the gift months later. Wear it when you know you are going to see the giver . . . or have it on display when he comes to call (even if you have to dig it out of the attic!).

Five years after the wedding I reminded two of my mother's friends about the deliciously wicked red nightgown they'd given me at the bridal shower. . . . They were astounded I remembered. Well, it *was* deliciously wicked.

Never *never* neglect a thank you. If the gift has been delivered, it may be the sender's only way to know you received it. Don't leave him or her "unappreciated" and anxious, even if his selection wasn't a masterpiece.

If someone gives you a Christmas gift and you have none for her, don't dissolve into fits of apology. Just say thank you and think up something special for her in the months ahead. *Never* say "Oh you *shouldn't* have . . . I don't have anything for you." You can't decide present-giving for others and shouldn't spoil *their* pleasure in giving. Be grateful, appreciate. That in itself is a lovely gift in return.

THINGS THAT ARE TACKY

Passing along to a friend a hideous white elephant you received for Christmas, unless you really truly *know* she would love it.

Wholesale-by-the-dozen junk. Wholesale *treasures* are fine, but non-returnable gifts are not thoughtful. And junk-anything is an insult, unless it's a joke.

The put-down gift—a baggy granny gown to an old maid girl friend . . . chocolates to your chum, the unsuccessful dieter.

Cash or gift certificate to a *good* friend suggests you didn't care enough to make an effort.

Asking your friend why she never wears the heliotrope vest you crocheted for her . . . maybe she hates it.

Forgetting. Keep a record of the birthdays and anniversaries you want to remember . . . check it the first of each month.

That little glass bell from Tiffany *is* precious, but not if you gave it to Edna last year *and* the year before. (If you have a favorite little thank-you item, be sure you write down whom you've gifted with it.)

Giving presents without bothering to wrap, or failing to enclose a card.

19. BEING A HOSTESS

Money and a staff of twelve certainly make spectacular entertaining a lot *easier*. But a born-great hostess or a spirited, determined beginner can manage on peanuts (a barrel of peanuts, a keg of beer . . . the beginning of a great Late Late Show-watching party!).

The warm genuine welcome, your poise, something good but simple to eat and drink, a fascinating crew of guests mean more than *elaborate* food or vintage wines. A loving hostess manages to make guests feel pampered, comfortable, and very special. But you must try not to let the strain show. It's no cinch putting together a Lucullan dinner for eight, but the successful hostess seems to manage it without the tiniest effort.

Single women—and illicit-lover roommates—are not expected to entertain often, but you *do* want to show off your super apartment, your genius in the kitchen, best friends from out of town, your brother's new fiancée . . . also to entertain the married friends who indulge and match-mate you. Add to those the loyal office helpers you're anxious to reward for their efforts on the latest Krispy Krackers campaign . . . or the fact that you have simply run out of men in your life and would like to gather a dozen or so candidates you really don't know too well just to show them you're alive! If *nothing* moves you to crack out a welcome, something is wrong with you. Which of these is your excuse?

1. My apartment is depressing.

2. I can't cook.

3. I want to be alone with my sorrows.

4. I'm too poor.

5. I don't know anyone to invite.

None of these are really legitimate reasons for misanthropy. It's time you took care of excuse number one. Excuse number two isn't crucial.

Excuse number three sounds bad indeed! . . . you may need a little psychiatric counseling. Excuse number four—see Part Two, Chapter 22, on how to be blissfully broke. Excuse number five . . . come now! Even in a convent this couldn't be true!

What Kind of Party to Give

Cocktails . . . fine. But here are a few get-together ideas that break the cocktail party cliché. Why not have a

SUNDAY BRUNCH. Serve brandy milk punch or clam diggers (vodka and clam juice), beautiful breads, plus crêpes, quiche Lorraine, or a melting lobster-cheese soufflé . . . all easy to do for four people. Or try these: just-beautiful scrambled eggs flecked with minced parsley and snipped marigolds (yes, marigolds . . . taste good, look beautiful, too). If you become a brunch genius, don't wait for Sunday . . . serve your successful brunch recipes at an after-theatre supper, postelection feast, or midnight munch.

CHRISTMAS EVE AT HOME. A tree-trimming party with buffet supper —curried shrimp kept warm in a chafing dish, saffron-colored rice, crisp greens studded with grapes, avocado, walnuts, and chunks of Gorgonzola; hot buttered rolls, and flaming plum pudding. Ask everyone to bring one bauble for the tree.

A WHITE ELEPHANT PARTY. Everyone brings the *worst* gift he can find . . . all wrapped . . . for the party grab bag. Perpetrator of the most atrocious item gets a prize—something *equally* awful you've wanted to throw out! This kind of happening makes it easy for shy guests to talk to strangers . . . then everyone helps himself at buffet: ham basted in a blend of red-currant jelly, port and dried mustard, cold rice salad flecked with minced pimiento, green pepper, white raisins, and toasted almonds, dressed with a blend of mayonnaise and sour cream, spiked with cider vinegar, homemade hot applesauce, crusty French bread, an assortment of cheese, and later a moist chocolate roll and demitasse with liqueurs.

PICNIC-SUPPER AUCTION BENEFIT. After the game or following an afternoon of touch football or a day at the beach, each girl brings a picnic supper, creatively wrapped, to be auctioned off to the men—everything strictly anonymous. Money goes to a favorite charity. Your creation: tender deviled duck—duckling quartered and baked with a dressing of mustard, herbs, butter, and breadcrumbs, *petit pains* from the best French bakery in town, hearts of artichoke vinaigrette with salted love apples (cherry tomatoes), a wedge of runny Brie cheese with fresh grapes or pears. Have Chablis on ice in an old copper or tin washtub or in individual beach pails from the dime store.

HOME SCREENING—Rent a film and projector (see the Yellow Pages under "Motion Picture and Equipment Rental") . . . show film on a portable screen outdoors in summer (after dark) or against white living room wall or bedsheet. Pass around candy bars and popcorn, or picnic suppers in school lunch boxes.

AFTER-ANYTHING SUPPER—Serve omelettes because you're a demon omelette-flipper, all kinds of fillings—sour cream and red caviar, strawberries and sour cream, *fines herbes*, mushrooms. Serve with champagne (two very good California brands: Almaden Blanc d Blanc, Korbel Natural) and choice of dazzling desserts: cold lemon Bavarian, pecan pie, *tarte tatin* (upside-down apple pie).

DO-IT-YOURSELF SUNDAE ORGY—Another mad, marvelous, after-anything entertainment. Set out an assortment of ice-cream flavors, a range of sauces, sprinkles, nuts, toasted coconut, plus some exotic embellishments: *marrons glacés*, sliced, toasted macadamia nuts, nesselrode. Adults *all* nurse a streak of ice-cream gluttony.

Or How About . . . A MAKE-A-MOVIE PARTY, produced by your boyfriend the amateur moviemaker, A TAROT FORTUNE-TELLING FIESTA over glogg and holiday cookies . . . or a TREASURE HUNT followed by cooked-the-day-before paprika goulash with green noodles, carrots in lemon-butter, garlic bread, and apricot ice (from an Arabic market or easily made yourself) on stewed apricots.

Cocktail-Party Countdown

The time finally comes in every girl's life when only a bona fide cocktail party *will* do. If you have a great loyal friend to help . . . wonderful. Enlist him. An ex-flame or your best friend's brother might also be delighted to tend bar. Otherwise, *consider* hiring a bartender. Try your nearest college job-placement office or enlist a reliable youth from the office mail department . . . ask *friends* who give great parties. If this fling is on your expense account, consider turning the entire project over to a reliable caterer who will handle all food preparation and provide bartender, glasses, trays, etc . . . anything you want.

Here's a countdown on party planning:

1. The guests. Invite them at least two weeks ahead by phone or note or *draw* your own slick invitation. Try for a good chemical mix—the beautiful young, the fascinating old, extroverts *and* good listeners, lots of men . . . hopefully a ratio of two to one, and encourage them to come stag! Be brave and invite a few *femmes fatales* you'd just as soon do without . . . they'll add to the *ambiance* you're after. Include men you really might never see socially. And if you have your eye on an interesting *stranger*, find someone who knows him and invite the two of them.

2. Never ever ask *just* married people. A lively party is sprinkled with unattached singles for intrigue and drama.

3. Invite someone who plays guitar, or a small rock trio.

4. Don't leave major interior-decorating overhauls for the last minute

. . . first guests may arrive to find you cutting out a bathroom rug. Get the house ready *weeks* before; do a thorough cleaning several *days* ahead and then a quick last-minute dusting is all you'll need. Should you have a once-a-week cleaning lady, give the party the day she cleans. Spotless house—kitchen and bath—plus polished silver are what you want.

5. One week ahead, make a master shopping list and schedule. Cross off as you go.

6. Pull together a devastatingly sexy outfit for yourself considerably ahead of time so you don't have to worry about old pizza spots or falling hems at the last minute. Arrange a party color scheme that complements *you.*

7. Cook everything you can days ahead and freeze; if not possible, at least cook the *night* before.

8. Consider mainly "finger foods"—cold roast beef and ham sliced small enough to be piled into manageable sandwiches at the buffet table, plus piquant mustard sauce and a blend of sour cream and horseradish . . . miniature pizzas and puffs you bake and pass . . . tiny quiches . . . cheese to cut . . . and salty things to munch. Or if you're serving supper, make it a hot main dish that requires only a fork to eat (that's true for salad and vegetable as well). You can't use a knife standing up!

9. Have enough ashtrays and fresh flowers or luxurious gobs of leaves piled in tall urns. Make napkins giant size . . . they serve as lap protectors as well. In the bathroom: a pile of paper towels or enough terry-cloth fingertip towels to keep guests from wiping fingers on *your* bath towel. Make sure towels are *fresh!*

10. Near neighbors deserve a small warning and possibly an invitation to drop in for a drink.

11. Your liquor dealer will agree to take back all unused bottles (and any unchilled champagne); to be safe order *more* than you need. Figure three to five drinks per person depending on the tippling habits of your crowd. (You'll get about seventeen drinks per fifth of liquor.)

12. You have devised a workable traffic plan . . . setting your buffet at *one* end of the room, the bar in another. (You don't want *all* the guests congealed in one area.) If serving punch or eggnog or glogg, all you need is a table—handsomely draped—large enough for a punch bowl surrounded with glasses. For liquor you'll need a sturdy, roomy surface for glasses and supplies. You might set aside a kitchen cupboard, cleared of dishes, stocked with glasses, bottles, mixers, openers, a pitcher of water, lemon peel, and bucket of ice. Or empty a closet or buy a few cheap pine boards and used bricks and make two temporary shelves. Cover with Contact paper if you like. Or fill a small washtub with ice and stud it with a good assortment of convenience cocktails in pitchers—daiquiris, margaritas, manhattans, martinis—already made,

chilled, and labeled . . . guests can pour their own . . . glasses are on emptied bookshelf. Washtub is set on a sturdy box, oilcloth-camouflaged, in an accessible corner.

13. *After* you've emptied all the debris—you are going to start *clean!*—and a few hours before the guests arrive, have a nap and a bath . . . a long unjangling soak . . . then make up and dress. Spray the bathroom light bulb with the same perfume you're wearing. You're *on!*

What does a hostess do at her own party?

1. Greets everyone at the door in the warmest way possible . . . a hug, a kiss, a smile . . . anything to tell the guest you really are delighted he came. Why not give everyone a daisy at the door when they arrive, or a favor when they leave (a caricature, homemade jam, a personalized shopping bag)?

2. Tell guests where the bar is, and whether to help themselves or ask the bartender.

3. Keep an eye out for new arrivals when they come into the living room after coat removal. Introduce each guest to as many others as you can, get a first drink served, and move on to whoever else needs help (a refilled drink, an introduction, a new person to add to their group). Usually there's one wallflower—a girl you know is really a doll, but *shy.* Try to move her into groups where she will be compatible.

4. Check the bar occasionally to be sure supplies of liquor and glasses are ample, also napkins and food platters. If a canapé tray is half-empty, refill it . . . don't wait until the last morsel is gone or guests will think there isn't M.I.K. (more in kitchen)!

5. If your radio is on a music channel, be sure the station hasn't suddenly started a news broadcast. Don't forget to turn records on the turntable over after they've played once.

6. My rule for hostess drinking is that you allow yourself *one* drink . . . after that sip tonic. Making guests happy is your *primary* concern, not having the time of your life (do that at someone else's party!). Incidentally, good hostessing and return invitations go together; pamper guests at *your* house and they'll love inviting you to *theirs.* Neglect them, and don't be surprised if you're ignored when they entertain.

P.S. If no one seems to want to leave, that's a sure sign of a party's success. If you're ready for it, one way to start the exodus is to suggest going out for supper. Call your favorite restaurant in Chinatown or a casual nearby Mexican beanery to see if they have room for your group. Everyone goes Dutch.

For even more party specifics see Section III, Chapter 11,—The Cocktail Party—of Helen Gurley Brown's *Single Girl's Cookbook* (Bernard Geis; $6.95).

Mixing Drinks for Men

With that special man in your life, there comes a moment when you want to have him over to your place for a cozy dinner à deux. No other place or occasion is quite so conducive to romance, to getting better acquainted, to a proposal, a proposition, or to whatever else you have in mind. As you sit together savoring your best casserole and gazing at each other in the soft candlelight, life suddenly seems gay, inviting, full of promises for the future. . . .

But, unless you know for sure he's a teetotaler, you'd better serve him a drink first! To a drinking male who's as dependent on a martini before dinner as he is on coffee in the morning, nothing can be so shocking, so productive of that sudden sinking feeling in the pit of the stomach, as to be asked brightly: "Would you like a drink? I've got Coke, Seven Up and cranberry juice."

If he's any kind of man, he will struggle bravely and politely through your meal. But don't be surprised if, just at the moment you thought you two would be sitting, fingers intertwined, telling each other your innermost hopes and dreams, he says: "I've got an idea! Why don't we drop down to Joe's for a fast snort or two?"

So do give him a drink—and make it yourself; don't ask him to play bartender just because that seems like a man's job. He may be a connoisseur in front of the bar and an ignoramus behind it. . . . Why show him up or put him on the spot? Besides, you wouldn't want to miss that look of blissful surprise that will come doubtlessly over his face when you hand him a large, handsome, impeccably prepared drink. (It is really quite simple to do, as I intend to prove.)

There are three general rules which you should use in preparing a drink for a man:

1. *Put in plenty of good liquor (Stick to the well-known brands.)*
2. *Use enough ice. (There's nothing sadder than a drink in which all the ice has melted.)*
3. *Use a glass big enough to hold the above. The double old-fashioned glass is a good size.*

Rule No. 1 is the most important. Most urban men make a fetish of the Big Drink and will pack themselves ten deep in front of any bar that offers a two-ounce shot.

One more rule. If you don't know what his favorite drink is, *do not* confront him with an Opal Cocktail or a Brandy and Crème-de-Menthe Float. (He may have come prepared for adventure, but not *that* kind of adventure.) Offer him his choice of the ordinary, standard potations—the odds are 50 to 1 that one of these is exactly what he wants.

Here is a list of the drinks most likely to succeed, together with directions on how to prepare them successfully.

THE HIGHBALL. This is usually whiskey poured over ice and diluted with either water or club soda. If your date is a recent graduate from the Pepsi generation, you might allow him ginger ale or Sprite as a mixer, but beware the man who demands something really oddball such as cream soda. Any tendency to mix good whiskey with obscene substances is a sure sign of moral turpitude, degeneracy and defective heredity.

If you don't know what kind of whiskey he likes, either offer him a choice of Scotch or bourbon or, if you have only one bottle, a good blended whiskey. (Never have just Scotch or just bourbon, since the devotees of one often can't stand the other.)

To make a highball worthy of the "21" Club or the Top of the Mark, drop three ice cubes into a largish (eight ounces or bigger) highball glass, old-fashioned glass or tumbler, then pour two ounces of whiskey over the ice. This is where girls often go wrong. You're so stingy with liquor! Next you can add an average amount—about two more ounces—of mixer or, probably a better idea, you can give him a small pitcher of water or bottle of mixer and let him pour his own. Should he ask for whiskey "on the rocks," use an old-fashioned glass, put in ice, pour in the whiskey, and serve. He may want a little water in this, so give him some on the side.

THE GIN AND TONIC is a highball which used to be considered a hot-weather drink but is now consumed, by some enthusiasts, all year around. Pour two ounces of gin over ice, add two or three ounces of quinine water, and garnish by dropping in a small wedge of lime, . . . this makes all the difference in what he thinks of you as a provider. Lemon will do in an emergency.

THE MARTINI. More fuss is made each year over this simple drink of gin and dry vermouth than over the Disarmament Conference at Geneva. There are two main types of fussers: the Dry, who complains about too much vermouth in his gin even when the vermouth was added with an eyedropper or atomizer; and the Moderate, who complains alternately that (a) there is too much vermouth, and (b) there is not enough. You can recognize the Dry Fusser by the wild alarm he manifests when you reach for the vermouth. One way to appease him is to pour a tiny amount of vermouth into a shot glass, hold it out to him and ask gravely, "Is that too much vermouth, do you think?" The Moderate Fusser is apt to give you very precise and intricate instructions. ("About 5½ gin to 1 vermouth, with a splash of vodka for extra lightness, and let the liquor sit on the ice for twenty seconds before adding the vermouth.")

It's not easy to lay down hard and fast rules on such a goofy subject, but you would not be too far wrong if you decided a "regular" martini was about 4 to 1, a "dry" martini 7 or 8 to 1; and an "extra dry" martini 11 to 1.

All martini lovers like their martinis very large and very cold. Use five- to six-ounce cocktail or wineglasses, prechilled in the freezing compartment of your refrigerator. And try to arrange dinner so that it is ready to be served about halfway through the second martini. If you allow the drinking to proceed into a third and fourth round, the atmosphere may become too alcoholic.

Martinis, Manhattans and other cocktails containing only clear liquids are made by stirring the ingredients with ice in a cocktail shaker or an electric blender.

To make *two* dry martinis, put six or more cubes of ice into your mixing glass, add six ounces of gin and three-quarters of an ounce of dry vermouth. Stir briskly about a dozen times with a long-handled spoon, then strain at once into chilled glasses. Garnish by dropping in either a green olive or a twist of lemon. (The easy way to obtain the latter is to run a potato peeler lengthwise across a lemon, bearing down rather hard. This will give you a thin, narrow strip of peel which should be rubbed around the rim of the glass, then dropped into the martini. It is not necessary to twist a "twist" made with a peeler.) For martinis on the rocks, use prechilled old-fashioned glasses and mix each drink in its own glass. If you make the martini with vodka instead of gin, the proportions should be 10 or 11 of vodka to 1 of vermouth for a really dry martini.

THE MANHATTAN is stirred like a martini. For two drinks, put four ounces of whiskey, one and one half ounces of sweet vermouth and a dash of angostura bitters into the ice-filled mixing glass. Stir about twelve times. Strain into chilled glasses. Drop a maraschino cherry into each glass.

THE WHISKEY SOUR is a favorite with men who want a whiskey drink but find the Manhattan too sweet. It must be shaken with cracked ice, but before putting the ice in the shaker, have your ingredients ready: four ounces of whiskey, the juice of one lemon, and a slightly heaping teaspoonful of sugar. Now fill your shaker two-thirds full of cracked ice. If necessary, you can make cracked ice a cube at a time by holding it in the palm of your hand and giving it a good whack with the wrong end of a table knife. Drain all the water off the ice before you start mixing. Then add the whiskey, lemon juice and sugar, shake *very* briskly about eight or nine times, and strain immediately into chilled glasses. If the mixing is not done rapidly enough, there will be too much water in the drink. There's an easier method of making sours, using an electric blender: Put into the blender one cracked or crushed ice cube for each drink you're making, add the other ingredients, and blend until the ice is completely melted. This will give you a perfect and supercold sour. Garnish it with a maraschino cherry and a thin slice of orange.

THE OLD FASHIONED. In an old-fashioned glass, put one-half teaspoon sugar, two dashes Angostura bitters and a teaspoon or two of water—enough to melt the sugar. Mix this well together, then add one large ice cube and two ounces of whiskey. Garnish with a slice of orange, a slice of lemon and a cherry.

The above are all before-dinner drinks. But if it's a luncheon or a morning-after breakfast you're having, he might well want a BLOODY MARY:

2 ounces of vodka
3 ounces of tomato juice
Juice ½ lemon
Pinch of salt, pepper, celery salt
Teaspoon Worcestershire
Dash Tabasco (optional)

Shake these ingredients well with ice (or use the electric-blender method), strain into a large glass and add two ice cubes to keep the drink very cold.

But, you may object, *all those drinks you talk about are the ordinary, humdrum ones. I want to serve him something different, amusing, outrageous!*

Buy a good brand of vodka and plunk it into the freezer the day before your dinner. Drink it "Russian style" in small, chilled glasses, making appropriate toasts each time and downing each glass at one swallow. While you're at it, forget dinner and make up some caviar sandwiches.

Serve him a *French 75*. (The name is from the celebrated French cannon of World War I and is an indication of the drink's alcoholic potency.) Into a twelve-ounce glass put the juice of one lemon and two teaspoons sugar. Stir, then add two ounces of gin and one ice cube. Fill the glass with very cold champagne, stir gently. Garnish with a slice of lemon, a slice of orange and a cherry.

Make one *Zombie* for the two of you and serve it with two straws. Zombie:

4 ounces light Puerto Rican rum
2 ounces dark Jamaican rum
1 ounce 151-proof rum
1 ounce pineapple juice
1 ounce passion fruit juice
Juice 1 lime
Juice ½ orange
2 teaspoons sugar

Put everything but the 151-proof rum in the electric blender with a cupful of crushed ice and blend for twenty to thirty seconds. Pour into a huge glass, decorate with cherries and chunks of pineapple, and float the 151-proof rum on top. Sip with straws. Do not make more than one.

Though he will probably think it quite marvelous and sexy of you to be such an accomplished bartender, be careful not to show much expertise about wines. For some unfathomable reason, most men consider the choosing, pouring and judging of wine to be an exclusively masculine prerogative. If you explain to him that although it might be rushing the vintage a little, you are opening a bottle of your *Lafite '61* in his honor, you'll probably give him a fit of the screaming meemies. So don't. Display a half-gallon of inexpensive wine on the sideboard and tell him you don't know one wine from the other. He may bring wine. (He ought to bring *something*.) Admire it greatly.

The Cosmo Girl's All-Purpose Bar

EQUIPMENT: With only a few dollars' worth of equipment you can be practically a "professional" bartender. Here's what you need:

1. Shot glass or measuring glass marked off in ounces and half-ounces.
2. Ice bucket (an inexpensive plastic one will do).
3. Long-handled metal bar spoon.
4. Stainless steel and glass cocktail shaker made with overlapping halves. Use the glass half for drinks that need to be *stirred*.
5. Six double old-fashioned glasses (for mixed drinks and those on the rocks).
6. Six medium-sized all-purpose wineglasses. You can serve martinis in these.
7. Bar strainer (to trap ice when pouring drinks out of your shaker).
8. Useful but not essential: Electric blender, ice crusher.

LIQUOR: If your piggy bank is undernourished, you can satisfy most common requests with a good bottle of blended whiskey (such as Seagram's 7 or Four Roses) and a bottle of vodka or gin, plus sweet or dry vermouth. You might want to try the popular new prepared cocktail mixes. A well-stocked bar, though, should contain: bourbon, Scotch, vodka, gin, rum. Plus, for after dinner, a good Cognac (Martell or Courvoisier) and some liqueurs (Grand Marnier, Galliano, or Kahlua).

MIXERS: Club soda, ginger ale, Sprite or quinine water.

STAPLES: Superfine sugar, Rose's sweetened lime juice, Angostura bitters, Worcestershire sauce, Tabasco, small green olives, cocktail onions, maraschino cherries, tomato juice, fresh lemons, limes, oranges.

The Perfect Little Dinner Party

All by yourself now . . . you are going to give a perfect dinner party!
FOOD
Cooking is possibly civilization's happiest art . . . instant creativity. Write a symphony and you may have to wait a *lifetime* for someone to recognize your greatness; *cook* well and almost immediate fame is assured. (All cooks love basking in the sensual pleasure of guests who

are eating *their* offerings.) I realized a long time ago, it's all very well for a girl to be rich, witty, and beautiful (!) but it *still* can't hurt to cook well!

How?

Take lessons. Work your way through Julia Child's *Mastering the Art of French Cooking*, Volume I (Knopf; $12.50) and then brave a postgraduate whirl with Volume II (also $12.50). Find a superb and patient cook willing to let you watch her work.

Be inspired by *Gourmet* magazine.

Master a few spectacular dishes . . . or concentrate on good one-dish meals. Learn chicken curry and *osso buco* from *Michael Field's Cooking School* (Barrows and Co.; $8.50) and *boeuf Bourguignon* as taught by Craig Claiborne in the *New York Times Menu Cook Book* (Harper & Row; $9.95).

Read cookbooks. If you need menu inspiration or thoughts about what can be cooked in advance, go to the experts:

1. *Never in the Kitchen When Company Arrives*. Morse, Theresa A. Doubleday, $3.50.

2. *Menus for Entertaining*. Elkon, Juliette, and Ross, Elaine. Hastings House, $6.95.

3. *The Perfect Hostess Cook Book*. Knopf, Mildred O. Knopf, $4.95.

4. *A World of Menus and Recipes*. Crum, Gertrude Bosworth. Bobbs-Merrill, $10.00.

5. *Menus for Entertaining*. Beard, James. Dell, $0.95 pap.

6. *The Joy of Cooking*. Rombauer, Irma S., and Becker, Marion R. Bobbs-Merrill, $6.95.

7. *Cooking with Helen McCully Beside You*. McCully, Helen. Random House, $7.95.

8. *The French Menu Cookbook*. Richard Olney. Simon and Schuster, $8.95.

Now for other essentials: (1) Explore your town for the best breads and pastry. (2) Find out who carries exotic imports (stuffed grape leaves, couscous, *nasi goreng*). (3) Woo a reliable butcher. (4) Find a good cheese store. (5) Learn something about wine . . . or buy from a wine dealer who is patient and enthusiastic with neophytes. Read wine-shop catalogs to learn about vintage and what is ready to drink when.

Know your limitations. Don't plan a meal with last-minute operations. And—if you can't cook at *all*, it's still possible to entertain beautifully by ordering supper sent in from a favorite restaurant or food-to-take-out place. Whether you're cooking or not, only a compulsive purist has to do *everything* from the ground up. If prepared strudel dough is better than yours (or you'd never even attempt it yourself), by all means use ready-made.

TABLE TALK

Let your fancy *go* in creating the beautiful table. Here are some thoughts: buy deep-dark cotton paisley in the yardage department and make a tablecloth to the floor for your round table; fringe or hem giant lap-napkins to match. Tailor a cloth in mattress ticking with gay pompom tape around the skirt and napkins.

As for food, if you want to serve more than the "finger foods" appropriate for cocktail parties, then you'll choose either a buffet table or sit-down dinner. I don't recommend the latter for more than six guests (eight if you're brave and clever). If you are serving *dinner*, say so on the invitation. If you're expecting ten to fifty people for a full cocktail hour-and-a-half starting at 7:00 P.M., followed by supper around 8:30, then you'll choose the buffet. It's always easier to let guests serve themselves *what* they want in portions *they* can eat. Then they take the food wherever there's room to sit down.

THE TABLE

Your first job is to set the table properly—do it early in the afternoon of the party. Here's what should be on it:

1. A pretty cloth or none—if the table surface is attractive.

2. Centerpiece of flowers and candles, *just* candles, a piece of sculpture, mobile, shells . . . anything that sets the mood *you* want.

3. Napkins . . . very large since they'll partially serve as lap trays for the plates.

4. Glasses (are you serving wine, beer, water?).

5. Forks. (Try to avoid any main course that requires a knife for eating. Only a juggler can manage plate, fork, napkin, glass, *and* knife seated on the floor or at a TV table. If you serve stew, simply make sure the meat is cut into small cubes and cooked fork-tender.)

6. Serving fork and spoon for all food platters.

7. Medium-to-large-size pepper mill and saltcellar. If table is very big, put a set at either end.

Note: Don't place all large serving dishes together. If the veal-stew casserole is to go at the left of the table, put salad bowl and vegetable platters on the opposite side. Balance is what you're after.

Here's what you'll place nearby on a serving cart, tea cart, or any mobile table: coffee and cups with sugar bowl, creamer, teaspoons, dessert plates and forks. Serving carts of metal, wood, plastic are available at all prices from mini to maxi budget. They help! Cover an inexpensive one with decoupage paper or a cloth to the floor; use it to wheel dirty plates to the kitchen all in one trip, to wheel clean coffee cups *out*. Serve dessert from your cart; have after-dinner liqueurs and glasses on it to wheel from guest to guest. This useful piece of equipment is *nearly* as much help as a maid.

As for dinner itself, the most important thing you have to do is make sure all cold food arrives at the table cold (don't put salad out half an hour before the stew) and the hot food hot (best reheat food to coincide with time you want guests to eat it). For buffet at 9:00 P.M., start oven at 8:15, reheat foods about 8:30 P.M. Or reheat on top of stove at 8:30. Start vegetables at same time if they are frozen. Make sure the total cooking time for vegetables is not more than half an hour, so everything comes out at 9:00 P.M. I find a timer most useful. When the bell goes off, I do too . . . off to the kitchen.

If you're having a sit-down dinner, then all above rules apply except:

1. Table is *formally* prepared with place settings that include service plate, or place mat, napkin, knife (or knives, if serving bread and butter), fork (or forks if you're having salad and dessert that require forks), tablespoon for soup (or if it's needed for dessert), teaspoon. Thoughtful hostesses serve *both* water and wine (or beer) with the meal, so you will need two glasses. The water glass is usually larger than the wineglass.

2. The menu can be expanded for sit-down dinners since all extra utensils required are easy to use while sitting at a table.

3. You may serve food from casseroles on the nearby serving cart *or* from family-style dishes placed on the table and passed from guest to guest.

4. Always clear the table of used plates and utensils before serving dessert and coffee.

5. It's better to serve liqueurs away from the table so guests can linger and sip in more comfortable chairs.

If you haven't enough of *anything* (glasses, dishes, silver), rent or borrow from a friend.

Stud the dining area with short, fat candles in colored glass holders—ruby red or royal blue or any color that suits your fancy.

For your centerpiece, wire together a mass of feathers, grasses, grains, and dried wild flowers. Or put one tiny clay pot containing a single rose at each place. Why not have masses of green vegetables as a centerpiece, or a "still life" in yellow—lemons, grapefruit, yellow squash, straw flowers. Huge bunches of parsley piled into a copper casserole are attractive.

Dishes needn't match, especially serving pieces, as long as everything "seems to go." Pewter, pottery, and wicker look smashing together. Whenever you see a lovely little pitcher or an irresistible blue and white plate or a fine Wedgwood platter (just one tiny chip), buy it. A beautiful small dish is a perfect ashtray. A pewter porringer complements after-dinner mints. I serve cookies on a Clark's Teaberry-gum glass pedestal, pumpkin soup from a hollowed-out pumpkin, cabbage slaw in a carved hollow of cabbage. Line baskets with a gay napkin for bread, rolls, crackers.

Frankly, place cards are stuffy and pretentious for a small dinner. I plan where I want people to sit, tell my husband who is going to sit on either side of him, and then each of us seats half the group. If you're having more than fourteen people at a sit-down dinner, make a little diagram for yourself so you'll remember who's where and handle it quickly when the time comes, or handwrite guests' names on standard blank place cards purchasable at any large department or stationery store. You can also make your own . . . any colorful paper or white cards on which you've written guests' names in Magic Marker.

I prefer *not* seating married couples or lovers together. I love intrigue and, too, I think it's thoughtful to let couples meet and chat with new people, also a courtesy to other *guests* who want to *meet* new people! Size up the situation and leave together those who are desperately in love or *really* going into a nervous frazzle if they're parted.

Disasters and Dilemmas

Here are some typical situations you will confront sooner or later, and what to do about them.

1. *A dinner guest is an hour late.* Serve without him. When he arrives, he can start with the first course and catch up as you proceed.

2. *The boss's wife announces she is allergic to flour.* She should have told you sooner . . . but she didn't. Be calm . . . tell her what is safe for her to eat. (Don't lie . . . it could be serious.) If it looks as though she may starve, open a can of tuna or offer to scramble some eggs.

3. *Only one guest brought a gift . . . will the others be embarrassed if you open it?* Yes. Better to open the gift quietly in another room and thank the giver later . . . *again* when you say good-night.

4. *The chicken is overcooked.* Don't apologize. Just serve it. Smile. Open another bottle of wine if you have one . . . maybe everyone will get too high to notice. Don't call attention to flaws or exaggerate them . . . never say, "It was so much better at Linda's house" or "Gee, last time I made this, it was so juicy." Do better next time. If something is inedible, truly inedible, call a delicatessen or Chinese restaurant to deliver in a hurry.

5. *You've spent three days cooking a gastronomic feast and don't want everyone to get too sloshed to taste.* Before dinner serve sherry, kir (white wine with a dash of *crème de cassis*), Lillet, Dubonnet, champagne . . . but if someone insists on hard liquor, don't be stubborn. A confirmed Scotch drinker must have his Scotch. And let the martini people mix their own—martini drinkers are perfectionists and each has his own concept of the perfect cocktail.

6. *One or two of the guests really admires something you've cooked.* Be flattered and offer to send the recipe. Be sure you have the right spelling of name and correct address; after dinner jot down which recipe is requested. In a few days dash off ingredients and instructions on a

three-by-five card and mail with a tiny note.

7. *A wickedly rich chocolate mousse is your dessert masterpiece and now two guests suddenly tell you they are dieting!* Since nearly everyone *is* dieting these days, or so it seems, it's not a bad idea to have *two* desserts on hand . . . a melon or grapefruit chilling in the refrigerator, fresh grapes in season, or homemade applesauce sans sugar for the weight-watchers, the sinfully rich goody for the rest of you.

8. *As you are about to serve fresh brewed espresso, one guest announces she is allergic to coffee and only drinks tea.* More and more dinner guests *are* requesting either tea or Sanka. Easy enough to keep a small box of a really good tea (darjeeling, Earl Grey, Formosa oolong) on hand, as well as a small jar of freeze-dried Sanka.

THINGS THAT ARE TACKY

Unlit candles.

Messy bathroom or kitchen floor.

Apologies . . . if the soufflé collapses or the cake cements, pretend that's the way it's supposed to be . . . or don't serve it.

Force-feeding your guests (have pity on those who are nursing an ailing liver, gout, or simply trying to diet . . . let them nibble if they *will*.)

Not enough liquor . . . economize on paper napkins if you must, but not the spirits.

Hysteria over spills or breaks. Pretend you *don't* feel like committing suicide over punch spilled on your grandmother's heirloom tablecloth, or the two broken Baccarat glasses.

Compulsive washing-up while party is on. Dishes can wait.

Not enough, or too small, ashtrays.

Disappearing into the bedroom with some fabulous man . . . *not* at *your* party, please.

Serving the same menu at every party or dinner.

Never entertaining . . . are you a hermit or a parasite? Try.

The Sponger

Watch out for parasites in disguise. Your love is a married man who says it isn't safe for the two of you to be seen dining in public. Is this really true or is he a cheapskate? Parsimony should not be encouraged! Just because you love to cook you should not tolerate habitual freeloading. Gently lead him to a discreet neighborhood restaurant.

Entertaining Away from Home

If cooking is your *least* developed talent, you may decide to save your entertaining budget for one special feast. Consider taking a dozen friends *out* to dinner . . . perhaps to a Chinese New Year's banquet, or to a Greek feast in a neighborhood restaurant. Both cuisines can be *relatively* inexpensive, especially if you work out the menu with the owner in advance. Tell him you'll provide the wine yourself, if you like, and that you can only afford to spend $5 ($7.50, $10?) per person, including gratuities. Pay by check before the party or sign with your credit card.

Since liquor is so expensive in a restaurant, you might invite guests for drinks and appetizers at your place, then walk or drive to the restaurant for dinner and wine. Back to your apartment for coffee, dessert and liqueurs.

Never plan a menu that you haven't tasted *yourself*. You don't want to discover that this chef's Moo Shu Pork is inedible while your guests are *eating* it. Once the restaurant owner has suggested a menu, you might have a run-through dinner. If any dish seems less than great, substitute. Never give a party in a restaurant where you haven't already eaten several times.

Perhaps you'll want to provide your own table decorations and place cards. Deliver them and the wine to restaurant earlier in the day, along with instructions.

The Unexpected Breakfast Guest

In my favorite fantasy, Sleeping Beauty's eyes flutter open, spidery lashes still miraculously intact, the fall tousled but secure, cheeks blush-pink. And there is Prince Charming bringing buttery hot *croissants*, strawberries and cream with a pot of strong black coffee—all in the prettiest matching breakfast china from Tiffany's.

Ah . . . fantasy. But then, *life* is not quite so beautifully organized. And do you *really* want an unexpected guest pawing through your kitchen, sorting through the stale crusts and aging cheese . . . bestirring flour weevils, a piece of salami so old it can walk by itself! Ideally, your kitchen reflects a paragon of domestic virtue. Realistically, unexpected overnight guests may catch you in a slovenly lull.

Hostess etiquette says that *you* wake up first, quietly—pull yourself and the bedroom together a bit. Less than attractive bits of underpinnings and detachable bangs and braids he might not have noticed the previous night should be tucked away discreetly.

Your "natural" beauty is lightly restored. Brush teeth and hair, shower, and scent yourself, then slip into your most flattering semidress. To the kitchen . . . where, hopefully, your shelves and minifreezer are stocked with the makings of a lover's breakfast.

Here are two suggested menus for such a breakfast:

MENU ONE

Broiled grapefruit (cut in half, sectioned, put under broiler for about ten minutes until slightly browned).

Spread canned corned-beef hash flat across a glass pie plate, break eggs into spoon-made hollows, sprinkle with grated parmesan cheese, and bake in a preheated 350-degree oven for about twenty minutes or until eggs are set. Serve with homemade bread or coffee cake (both heated), with good jam or preserves.

Brew fresh hot coffee in a scrupulously clean pot. If you don't have milk or cream on hand because you *never* use them yourself, don't get caught without powdered "creamer."

To serve: use a wicker bed tray or your mobile hostess cart. Put a large print cotton napkin on the tray to serve as a cloth (or a giant bandanna hankie); use its mate as the napkin. By all means have a tiny holder with a flower—real, paper, straw, tin—or a sprig of watercress or parsley if no flowers are handy. Use your best china. Dishes needn't match, but should blend. A charming note: use kooky or precious heirloom serving pieces—sugar in a pewter jigger or tiny glass shoe.

MENU TWO

Two cups of orange juice and one banana combined for a minute or two in your blender. Serve in wine goblets. My husband's favorite pancake . . . a giant one baked in the oven for twenty minutes while you prepare the rest of the meal. Here's the recipe: Combine ½ cup milk, ½ cup flour, pinch of nutmeg, two eggs lightly beaten and pinch of salt, beat gently with a fork for a minute or two . . . batter should be slightly lumpy. Meanwhile melt ⅛ lb. (4 tbs.) butter in 12-inch ovenproof skillet. When very hot, pour in batter and put immediately into *preheated* 425-degree oven. Set timer for fifteen minutes, then check pancake. When puffed and slightly brown, remove for a moment, sprinkle two tablespoons of powdered sugar over top, one teaspoon lemon juice . . . return to oven for a few more minutes. (If not puffed at fifteen minutes, wait five more minutes and then proceed with sugar and lemon.)

Serve with maple syrup, hot applesauce, and preserved lingonberries. Champagne is an excellent drink with it, followed by coffee.

Follow serving instructions given for menu one.

If your lover has slept *through* all this, he wakens now. You are gentle-voiced while serving the meal. He may decide to stay through lunch. That should be *his* treat.

Houseguests

Question: I love my mother, but when she comes all the way from Seattle she likes to get her money's worth and stays for weeks. *I want to carry on my life, but I want her to have a good time, too. What to do?*

Answer: Beloved mothers visiting for a week or ten days deserve your best and concentrated efforts. Do whatever you can arrange without slighting your job—lunch at posh French restaurants, a super new movie, the best seats you can afford to a play, historical sight-seeing, local museums, and the kind of shopping that amuses *her.* Hopefully, she has friends and relatives she also wants to see. If not, she's all yours . . . literally, if she isn't the independent type. Your man ought to join in at least part of the time—but don't overreact if he seems to disappear. If adored-one had to move out to make room for Mom and he's living out of a suitcase at a friend's pad, no *wonder* he's grumpy. Mothers who come for more than ten days should *not* expect or get continuous special entertainment. Talk it over frankly. You may be knocking yourself out to give more than she wants or expects. Mothers, usually, need rest . . . and they just want to visit with *you.* Don't hustle her out every night. She really may prefer to sit home gossiping with you while she pins your neglected hems.

Question: My roommate was positively rude to my mother the last time she visited. I don't object to her *practically live-in boyfriend, but she makes* my *guests, even my mother, feel uncomfortable when we put them up on the sofa. What to do?*

Answer: That's one of the roommate pitfalls. Set up guest rules in advance when you set up housekeeping, or do it *now* and stick to them. If the *two* of you want to run a youth hostel . . . great. But no roommate should be expected to welcome houseguests—overnight or weekend, family or libidinal—*except by mutual agreement.* If necessary rent a nearby hotel room for guests. *You* pay. Your most beloved school chum can use the sofa *overnight* while she finds a better roost, but that's it. If you don't like evicting a lover (yours or hers) at 2:00 A.M., better evict the roommate permanently.

Question: How do you coexist with a houseguest when you have only one room? Is privacy hopeless?

Answer: Your guest knows beforehand, of course, that sleeping at your house is only slightly more luxurious than camping, yes? But you can still do miracles to make her feel comfortable and welcome. Clear out a drawer or two so she needn't live out of a suitcase . . . make space in the bathroom to give her a somewhat permanent makeup station. Give her a set of towels, her own towel rack, a lovely scented guest soap, a foot of hanger space in the closet. Be sure there is plenty of food in the house. Tell her to help herself *anytime* she's hungry or thirsty.

If her bed is also your sofa or a rollaway cot, show Miss Visitor where to stash bedding in the daytime. She makes and unmakes her own bed. A screen, if you have one, gives some privacy, lets her read late without disturbing you. Other thoughtful touches: fresh flowers, a plate of fruit, ashtray on her nightstand, a good reading light, a few paperbacks to interest her, stamped postcards, a good map of your town, your favorite restaurant guide. I live in New York, so I always arm my guests with New York in Flashmaps, *The Underground Gourmet*, Kate Simon's *New York Places and Pleasures*, and a subway and bus map. You can do the same for your city, or if no books exist, type out your own guide. I buy dime-store slipper socks and hand them out to overnight guests, along with a fancy bar of soap, miniature perfumes or after-shave cologne samples.

And if you are eating at home, try to cook some things you know she especially likes—avoid any *dislikes*. Fuss over your guest . . . use real silver, cloth napkins, the good crystal and china if you have any. Put flowers on the table. Have some wine. Make her happy!

Feeding Foreign Visitors Without Panic

When I travel or live in another country, I am eager and curious about the food. I feel I am not only savoring the flavor of the dish but of the country and the people themselves. My recollection of places are bound up with people, sights, sounds, scents and tastes and I would no sooner forego one than another.

I like to try strange food. I do not mean that I enjoy everything I try, but I know whether I like it or not.

In Rome I like to spend my first morning at the Museum Villa Giulia, because I'm greedy and feel that in one stroke I have captured both Italy and ancient Greece. When my earthier appetite takes over, I head for a favorite restaurant or a friend's house where I may have my favorite dish, a *rissotto caldo* which resembles a thin pancake of rice over which wafers of fresh truffles have been grated and to which Parmesan cheese may be added. I am willing to accept reasonable substitutes, but if I were offered a hot dog with mustard in a limp roll I should feel anything but honored!

Yet, hospitable as we Americans are reputed to be, we fall into an equivalent error. We struggle to duplicate dishes from a visitor's homeland instead of giving him the surprise and pleasure of something unfamiliar. Before struggling to perfect a dessert soufflé Grand Marnier to serve to a Frenchman, heed G. B. Shaw who said, "In heaven an angel is nobody in particular."

If you are equipped to entertain at all, it shouldn't be any *more* difficult to have foreigners. It can be more challenging and fun than having the bridge-playing couple who live next door. If they'd be compatible, have both. But I offer a piece of advice from Picasso. Actually, I don't think Picasso ever cooked—his words of wisdom have to do with exercise in art—but they seem applicable to entertaining. He warned a pupil to work not just within but below his means—if the painter felt he could handle nine elements to handle only six. "In that way," Picasso said, "the ones you do handle, you handle with more ease, more mastery and you create a feeling of strength in reserve."

If you think you can cope with eight, have six. If you plan to extend yourself and serve one course more than usual, don't! If you make it *easy* for yourself, you'll make it *pleasant* for your guests.

Don't sell our own American cooking short—it's great! Visitors want to know more about our customs, food and life style. Give them the pleasure of associating a new dish with our land.

Typical American dishes vary from North to South and from East to West. It is surprising, for example, what a difference the cut of meat can make. The English, French and Italian version of a steak is usually the individual tournedos—equal to our filet mignon. So the choice of a juicy, broiled porterhouse steak or a sirloin big enough for six is far from banal. A double French lamb chop—commonplace here and no surprise to a Frenchman—is a delicacy to the Englishman. The English cut pork chops the way we do, but their lamb chops with the bone in the center are less tender. Ham is universal but our Virginia ham and North Carolina country cured hams are unique. If I were hesitant to have one as a main course, I'd slip a bit on a beaten biscuit to serve with cocktails or at tea.

A traditional Thanksgiving dinner is a delight to foreigners. Everything we might serve would be intriguing. If oysters were the first course, ours are juicier and have a quite different flavor. A corn bread and pecan stuffing for the turkey is typically American, as are baked yams or a sweet potato soufflé. String beans, creamed onions and cauliflower with browned bread crumbs might not surprise foreign visitors but a pumpkin or cranberry pie definitely would. Cranberries in any form are rare. If a dinner produces three surprises, bingo!

Corn, where it is grown at all abroad, is usually a coarse type, chiefly fed to cattle. So to most foreigners our fresh corn on the cob is something that they literally write home about. I like best to serve it boiled the minimum amount of time, just until the milk sets, with melted butter, salt and a pepper mill. It deserves one's undivided attention and I serve it as a separate course—usually the first. Sometimes I vary the routine by smearing the raw, cleaned ears with butter, salt and pepper, wrapping them in silver foil and grilling them over hot coals. This is a less messy variation of the system whereby unshucked corn is soaked in salt water and then grilled. In either case, the result is a haunting, richly nutty flavor. When visitors become hooked on our corn, I sometimes present it in other guises; off the cob but plain; mixed with baby lima beans as succotash; corn pudding with ham steak; corn fritters with almost *anything* or to replace potato pancakes with pot roast; as a homemade relish to go with cold meat; cream of corn soup; corn chowder; Indian pudding for dessert; and crisp, deep-yellow corn sticks; batter cakes made of Southern, yellow cornmeal and New England johnnycakes made of white water-ground cornmeal.

Maple, as in maple syrup for pancakes, is rarely known outside America. The trees are native to North Temperate regions and the chief source of the sugar in our country with the best sugaring off in Vermont. I serve the syrup on hot cakes and vanilla ice cream, and sometimes make a maple soufflé or a layer cake with maple icing.

New England clam chowder and all fish chowders spell America, so do soft shell crabs; also shad and shad roe which if broiled and dressed with bubbling hot brown butter with a squeeze of lemon are beyond compare. And from our Pacific Northwest: Dungenese crabs that have been boiled and are served cracked in the shell with a mustard mayonnaise.

Almost any typically native dish from New Orleans is uniquely ours because nowhere else will one find the combination of French, Spanish and Indian cooking. This is often, and mistakenly, thought of as French cooking but some of the herbs still used were originally known only to local tribes of Indians, and what could be more American than that?

We are a dessert-conscious country and although many of our recipes originated elsewhere, time and custom have made them uniquely ours. Ice cream is made here in greater volume for popular consumption than anywhere else, and for variety and quality ours would be hard to beat. The trick of letting a guest choose his own flavor of ice cream and concoct his own sundae is known to every den mother, but it goes over big with visitors. Oddly enough the more elegant the party, the greater the surprise; and the general effort is much less than one would suppose. I try to subtly push vanilla ice cream with a blueberry

149

sauce made from fresh berries lightly sugared, barely stewed and thickened with a sprinkling of cornstarch. Even sticking just to ice cream, the choices are infinite. But the No. 1 American dessert is apple pie; warm and running with spicy juices confined within two crusts. And that's what makes our pies *ours*, while just across the sea the pies lose their upper crust and become elaborate, glazed tarts. If you add a scoop of vanilla to a slice of apple pie you get something with a French name, but a local accent. Adding a piece of cheese to the pie is also typically American. Blueberries have an affinity for our soil and climate. I like to include blueberries in pies, cobblers, pancakes or muffins. Don't overlook peach or strawberry shortcake made with individual old-fashioned tea biscuits.

And now a few random notes and warnings: Serve Boston baked beans (but as an extra dish in case some guests find them unpalatable) at a buffet supper; English muffins are a local product and I have English friends who carry them home and keep them in their American freezers for a special treat!

Dinner is not always the best form of entertaining. Luncheons can be delightful, but beware of serving (even to ladies) our main-course salads: i.e., fresh fruit and cottage cheese, sunset (chicken, tongue and cole-slaw), Caesar or chef. Europeans view it doubtfully. Don't overlook afternoon tea: It's easy and your relaxed charm and warmth and the ambience of your home means more than the height of any soufflé. Penthouses and terraces are a novelty; the simplest meal served out-of-doors takes on glamour, especially for Northern Europeans whose climate seldom permits it. Our ubiquitous backyard grill is an ice breaker. A thick hamburger licked by a charcoal flame should be a must for every visitor.

Don't serve too many surprises at any meal; one dish that is standard is reassuring to fall back on and serve as a counterpoint to adventurous nibbling.

Don't try too hard! It's probably better to have sand in the lettuce than a grating edge of hysteria in the voice.

Greet your foreign visitors with warmth and enthusiasm. Why shouldn't you? . . . You know they're going to have a marvelous meal and they'll probably be saying, "If only we could get food like this in my country."

The Care and Handling of Cleaning Women

At last—an apartment that's all yours! And you're determined, starting now, that it will always look as fresh as the day you cleaned up the plastery mess left by the painters. In a rush of enthusiasm, you purchase enough labor-saving devices to put the population of Rhode Island on a two-day workweek. Best of all is your multipurpose all-in-one wonder vacuum with more attachments than you have pantyhose. Equipped with a two-speed motor, three-position handle, and rug-dial, this overachiever will scrub, clean, wax, buff, and polish your floors as well as beat, shake, shampoo, sweep, and comb your rugs. If you ever sort out the pads, nozzles, brushes, and crevice tools, you'll probably find the one that scratches your back and squeezes oranges. Congratulations, you're a lady of leisure. Right? Faster than an automatic cord-rewind comes the answer—wrong! No matter how much you think you need a labor-saving device, it needs you *more*. The ugly truth, as dreary as a bathtub ring, is this: your wonderful vacuum is only a heap of metal and plastic without a human to push and shove it around. And there's still laundry to do. And ironing. And the windowsills to wipe and the stove to sponge. Help! You need help!!!

HOW TO FIND A CLEANING LADY

THE HIT-AND-MISS METHOD. You ask everyone you know about her cleaning lady: Supposing she could come to you, is she thorough, reliable? How much does she charge? Maid-possessing friends will be delighted to talk to you; you'll hear all about major atrocities (ammonia spilled on the Oriental rug) and interminable minor kvetches (seven-layered paste-wax on the kitchen floor). Some stories are priceless, some you'd pay not to hear again. (Can there really be that many oversized maids and that many fragile cane-bottomed chairs collapsing together into splintery chaos?) But you listen, nod, commiserate, and soon discover you're spending more time worrying about "the servant problem" than Marie Antoinette *ever* did.

It's worth a try, if friends can't (or won't) provide any good leads, and you live in an apartment building, to ask the landlord, doormen, and elevator operators about neighbors you might talk with who have cleaning help. (This can be a super way to meet the somebody smashing in 11G).

THE PROFESSIONAL WAY. Most cities have employment agencies which provide occasional (when you think you need it) or regular (every Tuesday morning) household help. Look in the Yellow Pages under "Maid Service." (The entry "House Cleaning" usually refers to "heavy work," the big jobs you need do only occasionally, like scrubbing woodwork and shampooing rugs.) The maids provided by these services have been checked for references, meaning they probably won't *steal* anything, but they may or may not (like maids *whatever* their origin) know how to clean. Feel free to ask the service to send you the same maid again if you like her, or to request somebody else if you're not satisfied.

The big disadvantage of hiring a maid through an agency is that you pay more. The rate for competent cleaning ladies in most cities today is two dollars an hour, plus carfare and lunch. If your maid comes through an agency, you will pay at least $3.25 hourly to make up the service's costs and profits.

Maid services are especially helpful if you want household help on an irregular or very occasional basis. (Most cleaning ladies will come to you regularly only if you need them at *least* once a week.) Try a *service* for once-a-month cleaning or before and after a big party. To supply a helper, agencies require at least two full days' notice during the year and up to two weeks before a holiday.

MEETING YOUR MAID

Through one method or another, you've hired a cleaning lady for one half day (four hours) once a week . . . enough, generally, for most working-girl apartments. The night before she reports (this may be your first meeting) you have some work to do—*not* with a mop and pail (resist the temptation to polish and scrub the apartment so that the maid will know how *clean* you are). The work you do is with a pencil and pad. Check through each room and prepare a list of:

(1) Work you want done each week (i.e., kitchen mopped, rugs vacuumed, linens laundered).

(2) Things you want done every so often (it's *bad* for wood floors to be waxed weekly).

(3) Things you *never* want done (fooling with those precious crystal wineglasses).

At your first meeting, find out what your maid will *not* do. Some of these chores fall under the category of "heavy work" (you may have to hire a housecleaning service to wash down walls or do them yourself); others are a matter of choice (dishwashing and ironing). Some maids won't mind plopping your things into a nearby laundromat at the start of their half-day and picking them up before leaving; others will do laundry only if machines are no farther away than the basement. Whether or not she'll do hand laundry (panties, stockings) is also a negotiable point.

Be certain your helper knows where supplies are kept and that she's familiar with your cleaning equipment. Tell her if you prefer lemon oil to paste wax on the round oak table. If she insists that Brand X (your brand) is inferior to Brand Y, buy her brand. Assume, at least in the beginning, that she knows how to do the best job. Decide, too, whether she leaves you a note when the detergent runs low or you leave her additional money to keep the house stocked. Be sure she has enough *rags* to work with. One girl I know was tearing up her own T-shirts to supply these.

HOW TO BE AN EMPLOYER AND NOT A BOSS

Now, you've met and *like* the new maid . . . here are some ways to keep her happy:

FOOD. Some housekeepers bring a sandwich from home and help themselves to coffee; however *most* expect to put something together from your fridge. Ask which method she prefers, and, if she wants to eat in, keep her favorite food. (*My* cleaning lady likes hot dogs and chocolate cupcakes.) Do your part *responsibly!* It's no fun to be hungry and find only mayonnaise and a bran muffin in the icebox.

HOLIDAYS AND VACATIONS. If your regular day with the maid falls on a national holiday, you should give her that day free and with *pay* (just like on *your* job). She is also entitled to two weeks' vacation with pay; if she comes to you once a week, that means she has one morning off with pay every six months. (She'll probably prefer to take a continuous two-week vacation, which requires your cooperation, along with that of her other employers.) On the other hand, you can't expect the maid to stay idle and unpaid during *your* vacation times; regular housecleaning may be suspended while you're away (and not messing up), and she can concentrate on odd jobs like relining cabinets or cleaning closets.

THE LAW AND SOCIAL SECURITY. By law, if you're paying your maid at least fifty dollars in cash wages every three months, you should be reporting this to the Internal Revenue Service and sending them money to be credited to your maid's social-security account. The employer deducts 4.8 percent from the employee's wages, adds a matching 4.8 percent, and sends the total 9.6 percent to the IRS every three months. (The Internal Revenue Service will send you proper forms and charts.) Many employers of household help pay the entire 9.6 percent themselves. If your maid is paid by an agency, they are responsible for making the proper deductions and contributions from her check.

Many individual employers neglect to arrange for their maid's social security. Failure to comply with this law doesn't mean the FBI will be on your trail; it *does* mean your maid will be without retirement benefits. Be fair; be certain she knows her rights. If she doesn't have a social-security number, tell her to contact the nearest social-security office.

GIFTS. A Christmas gift to your maid is *essential*. One week's salary is *most* appreciated. If she's been especially helpful and nice, a personal gift is lovely in *addition* to cash. It also is thoughtful to remember her birthday. I favor an extra at Thanksgiving as well.

THE TELEPHONE. If you want the phone answered, tell your helper whether there's a special way you'd like that done ("Miss Jones's residence" or just "Hello") and ask if she feels comfortable taking messages. Naturally, the maid should have your office phone number in case disaster (the dishwasher overflows) strikes. If you live in an apartment building, she should know how to contact the superintendent and/or handyman in case of trouble.

KEEPING OUT OF THE WAY. Unless you work at home, you'll be out when the maid's in. It's quite the better way. The sweetest girls become *monsters* when household help is around! ("She *can't* have done a decent job in the bathroom in only fifteen minutes!") If you are there together, use discipline to let the maid do her thing while you do yours.

ATTITUDE

Some girls still think proper treatment for a maid is the way their mothers treated "the help" back in 1950. Forget it! Also forget that business of familiarity encouraging her to take advantage of you. Being her friend will probably get you lots farther with your housekeeper than being her icky, finicky, stuck-up employer.

LITTLE THINGS THAT COUNT. "Please" and "Thank you" notes will probably be your *most* important form of communication. *Don't* neglect the thank yous (my maid is the sensitive type and needs at least one *phone call* a week, telling how I adored the way she polished the silver, aired the rug, etc.). Your complaints should be polite, not crabby. Make them on paper, the telephone, or in person, depending on how *you* can best, and most graciously, convey the message.

Do not fuss over trivia (like how she's arranging throw pillows) as long as big things are right. Don't be too timid, either. Your maid may be so perfect you've started lying barefacedly about her availability to keep her yours alone, but for several weeks now she's forgotten to turn off the lights when leaving. This habit is driving you wild, but you're too timid to mention it. You write diplomatic notes and rip them up; what if she quits? Probably she *won't*. If she's as responsible as you've come to believe, she won't be offended nor should she be at a request.

BEARING UP UNDER (MINOR) DISASTERS. The maid doesn't mind doing dishes. *You'd* rather cut up a chicken. Sounds like a perfect relationship. Maybe. The first dish she breaks is an accident. The second time—it could happen to anyone. The *fifth* time, you suspect she's warming up for the Olympic discus throw. You lose—you should have switched her back to pillow-fluffing after trauma four.

The *occasional* mishap (even your favorite vase heartbreakingly shattered) should be tolerated if you and your maid have a basically sound, ongoing relationship. But what about other not-so-happy situations—where you suspect the maid is nipping in for *one* hour instead of the paid-for four. Or her disposition is so sour that it curdles yours! If coats of old wax have raised your kitchen floor one full inch, if the books and pictures are never dusted, you may have to face it: your maid is *no* help at all. And that brings us to:

THE FIRING LINE

Your first impulse is to tape a note to the door: "Permanent Plague.

Keep Out Forever," and hope that ends a miserable relationship.

It won't. Neither will a phone call. Firing must be done person to person, or how will you get your key back? Alas, for most girls, telling a maid it's all over is tougher than delivering the same news to a man gone wrong. Here's how many have mustered the necessary fortitude:

(1) Remind yourself firmly that you've hired a maid to make your life *easier*, not more difficult.

(2) Remember how hard you are working *yourself* to pay her salary.

(3) Know exactly *why* you've had it with her, and be prepared to rattle off *specific* complaints. This will supply moral strength in case the maid tries to fight (or cajole) you into taking her back.

(Note: One week's severance pay is due your fired maid if she's been working for you between six months and a year; after a year, it's two weeks'.)

We hope, of course, that your maid is a perfect doll and not at all firable. A *good* cleaning lady is a simply wonderful boon to your life, as *unexpendable* as (and no more costly than) the weekly trip to the hairdresser's that makes your horrible hair behave. So don't let the Puritan Ethic ("I really *ought* to do it myself") rob you of the graciousness and ease of having help. After pegging away all day at the office, you *deserve* lots of your own sweet (uncluttered-with-chores) time at home. Enjoy!

20. BEING A GUEST

It's lovely to be sought out as a weekend guest *unless* the two days turn out to be a *nightmare*, replete with spiders, mosquitoes, children, and dogs. *Don't* let it happen to you!

Among the solid American institutions in which I, as a city girl, had begun to lose faith was the coveted weekend-in-the-country. I don't mean at some tumbledown with my beloved, or at the lake with my family, but as a single-girl houseguest. Now, as eligible, charming, sexy, vivacious, fascinating career girls, you and I are *prizes* . . . valuable beyond price as weekend guests. All couples with weekend hide-aways need people like us to *share* them, because: (1) they'd go bonkers with only each other to fall back on for company, and (2) if their place is something *special* (an architect's dream in glass and stone on the beach), the proud owners (like greedy bullfrogs snapping up an endless supply of tasty flies) need a steady supply of sophisticated, with-it, *new* admirers. Of course, there are still a few naïve couples around who figure they're doing us a favor by getting us out of our drab little city lives (hah!) and into the life-giving country air—but we all know where the favor *really* lies. So *beware!* I can't count the times when, eager for the sun and fun of a sporting two days with friends, I'd arrive weary and rain-soaked, only to find hidden horror in every weekend hour . . . *stuck*, a whimpering, helpless victim, until Sunday evening. And then, quite recently, I discovered a simple way to visit friends at their beach houses and mountain cabins—without tears, or bruises that frequently come from being a captive playmate to your host's three prepubescent children.

My secret? Advance information from the host and hostess. Just a few questions to be asked and answered before the visit, but each one loaded with clues as to what (and whom) to expect from the weekend. I recommend the system. If you like the host's answers, you accept his invitation; it will probably be a visit to remember. If they prove unsatisfactory, send your sincerest regrets and save yourself for the friends who truly *deserve* a lovely girl like you. Remember, you're available as a guest only to the hostess who is fully prepared to offer the accommodations, activities, and ambience that make you *feel* your best and *look* your best. Of course, when that call with a weekend invitation *comes*, you'll couch your questions in such a subtle way that your host-to-be won't realize he's being tested, weighed, rated on your is-this-weekend-going-to-be-worthy-of-me? scale.

QUESTION 1: WILL I BE PUTTING SOMEONE OUT OF HIS BEDROOM? This is a tactful way of finding out whether you'll have a room to yourself or a couch-in-the-living-room setup. At the risk of sounding bourgeois, I do insist on a clean, comfortable bed located in a bedroom (not alcove), with a mattress at least three feet above the floor. The higher the bed, the more protected I feel from wagging tails and tongues of household pets and crawling wildlife. (I once awoke at a beach cabin unable to move . . . pinioned to my camper cot by my host's English sheepdog, who had draped himself lovingly over my chest.) Under no circumstances will I share a bed with a stranger, although I don't mind sharing a bedroom if positively necessary (provided it's a large double room and my roommate's not a mouthbreather.)

QUESTION 2: DOES IT GET COLD AT NIGHT . . . SHOULD I BRING SOME WARM CLOTHES? Although prospective houseguests rarely consider such matters as room temperatures when accepting invitations to country houses, comfortable indoor temperatures are a *sine qua non*. A blazing fire alone cannot always eradicate soul-chilling clamminess. Last Decoration Day, in a beach house on Shelter Island, I spent two days and an entire night rolled into flannel pajamas, sweaters, slacks, tennis socks, and sneakers. Even my Saint Laurent head scarf couldn't restore the "look" I had wanted to achieve that weekend. Stuffed into layers of wool and stretch nylon, I could only stand upright or lean apprehensively at best. All ablutions were out of the question, of course. *All.*

QUESTION 3: WILL MEALS BE CASUAL OR DO YOU PREFER MORE FORMAL DRESS? This is your way of finding out whether you'll be able to get a hot breakfast or merely croissant-and-coffee, a poolside alfresco lunch or sand-stuffed hot dogs at the beach, and whether a satisfying dinner is possible even *with* your diet. Should you care about these things on an informal holiday? Yes, for you must never underestimate the power of the inner woman! Neglected, she can leave you looking flat, haggard, and irritable. Besides, it's the fresh orange juice and crunchy bacon that make your eyes flash and your cheeks glow in the country air. Should your hostess apologize for the absence of Cook that particular weekend, you might volunteer to mix Bloody Marys while she scrambles eggs and heats *brioches*. (It should never be the other way around). *You* set the flowers out while she serves luncheon. Meals should be ample and appetizing. A hungry houseguest is not a happy one.

Just a few weeks ago, my friend Joe invited me to visit one of our old college chums at his place in Bucks County, Pennsylvania. Chum and his wife were new parents and wanted to share their joy with us. Without advance information I agreed to go along. We purposely slept late the next morning to avoid the necessity of our hosts serving us breakfast. By 11 A.M. we were both ravenous. It soon became apparent, however, that our hosts did not go in for Saturday luncheon *either*. At 3 P.M., with bellies growling and anger rising, Joe and I stole into the kitchen to scrounge for a morsel of food. Surprise, surprise—nothing in the fridge but four tiny jars of baby gruel. Although our hostess called out to us later to watch the baby take his pablum, poor Joe couldn't even look. He was afraid he'd snatch the dish, baby, and all, and smash them over the head of the new papa!

Dictum: Find out well in advance, if you can, not only *when* meals will be served but also *what* will be served. You can pretend you need to know whether it's fish or meat as a guide to selecting the appropriate wines, beers, and ales you'd like to contribute to the weekend. You are a *"connaisseuse."*

QUESTION 4: WHO ELSE WILL BE THERE? Details on other guests—houseguests and cocktail guests—can clue you as to what clothes, books, and magazines to bring with you and what questions to frame for some chic repartee. Names, professions, and marital histories tell a lot. If the guest list shouldn't suit you, you might rely on your usual Morse code of "oh"s and ah"s and "huh"s to get your message across (i.e., you had hoped for somewhat *more* stimulating company).

QUESTION 5: IS THERE SOMEONE WHO MIGHT GIVE DIDI AND ME A RIDE? Since your host and hostess usually see to it that you and your toy poodle are transported to and from the country in style and comfort, a bachelor-on-wheels is often commissioned to be your weekend chauffeur. That's wonderful! Particularly if he drives an air-conditioned Cadillac. Or a two-seated Alfa Romeo. But if the vehicle has more than two seats, you might ask about other passengers. As sole passenger, you are reasonably sure of comfort and the privacy of several hours alone with your driver. If the second passenger is an attractive man, the ride may still be worth sharing. You'll be alone with *two* men! But if the *extra* passenger is female, the transportation is complicated. Pack some goodies for the trip—a thermos of coffee, fruit, cookies—and play superthoughtful hostess in the car. That way you'll seem to be in charge . . . and so generous and unselfish in your thinking. You are!

QUESTION 6: ARE YOU STILL PLANNING TO INVITE THAT MAN YOU'VE BEEN TELLING ME ABOUT? It doesn't matter whether your "date" will be a fellow houseguest or someone brought in just for dinner, your hosts should—if they want *you* as a guest—cater to *your* tastes in men. At least *one* eligible man ought to be lined up for the weekend. Of course, the superhost will have a *spare* male on call, just in case an emergency prevents number one from arriving. Contingencies should be covered, for this is *your* weekend. Try to check out the possibilities before you accept the invitation. (What fun to get a line on that special man who will be waiting to meet *you!*)

Of course, if the host is your man-of-the-moment, your truest love, you needn't ask the above question. Nor any of the others, my dear. You're in for a heavenly (hazardless) weekend!

Guide For Party Girls

Some girls *always* have a perfectly fabulous time at parties. Socially gifted creatures just born to mix and mingle. Hostesses clap hands when these girls arrive, full of sunshine and friendliness and I'm-so-glad-to-be-here that everybody wants to meet *them*. Then there are the rest of us, so filled with anxiety we can barely push the doorbell. Here is a guide to coping with party agonies that has worked well for others and could do the same for Shy Little You.

WHEN YOU DON'T FEEL LIKE GOING IN THE FIRST PLACE

The party is at eight.

It is now six.

You feel rotten. Also old, haggard, ugly, drab. Your hair just lies there like a commercial for a new dulling agent. Your eyes have apparently lost weight and are so small they can barely be seen. Your wardrobe has been stolen by elves and cunningly replaced with tacky replicas which neither fit nor flatter.

In other words, you are *doomed*.

The experiences of many girls have shown that this kind of pre-party slump is actually a very good sign. It is the low before the high. The lull in which you gather speed and strength before storming the halls of pleasure in full party gear, flags flying and victory assured. How many times have you heard a girl say, "I was going to stay home and wash my hair, but I forced myself to go—and *that's* the night I met Dan."

In other words, you are *not* doomed.

Force yourself to do the personal things that you know can make you feel better and look better.

Some very personal things:

Have a massage. If it perks you up and makes you feel like a lean, supple tigress, it's worth the money.

Strip bare and climb into bed for a flat-out catnap. Set the alarm or ask a chum to call you if you're afraid of sleeping through. All busy, successful people know the benefits of a quick snooze. Skin, hair, eyes all seem to glow afterward. Best of all, you feel *rested*.

Soak in a hot tub or gasp in an ice shower to stir you back into shape.

By this time, the elves will have sneaked back in and returned your original wardrobe. You must choose between a New Zingy or an Old Surefire. If you're still feeling fragile, think back on the last time you had a scandalously marvelous evening. What were you wearing? Wear it tonight. This choice combines the mysticism of a good luck charm with the practical fact that it probably looks great on you.

All this pampering takes time. Console yourself with the old better-late-and-*great*-than-never-maxim.

As you arrive at the party, send out sexy waves. Think erotic thoughts. (Oh, go ahead!) Cuddle an inner-eye memory of a private moment. Murmur a few sly words to yourself, which can be anything from "Here you go, you sexy bitch" to something unprintable. In this way, you will communicate musky messages that men may not quite decipher but to which they will intuitively respond.

WHEN YOU GET THERE AND FIND YOU HARDLY KNOW ANYONE

That sound you hear is your heart sinking.

Instant drought afflicts your mouth, inside and out. Saliva evaporates while your lips are glued shut as your slithery lip gloss turns thick and icky.

This is known as feeling uneasy in a demanding social situation and is as natural as sunrise. Many wish to die in this situation. None have. The floor will not open and dump you into the alligator pit. If your hostess is as bad at her job as most are, prepare to make the move yourself.

If you are with a man, steer toward the drinks.

If you are alone, steer toward the drinks.

Amble slowly through the crowd. Make eyeball contact wherever you can, smiling a greeting as if to say, "Maybe we know each other and maybe we don't but it's nice to see you anyhow." In passing, greet women as well as men.

If it's a *big* party, ask, "Which way to the bar?"

Or, "Has anyone seen the hostess?"

A drink gives you something to do, something to sip, a prop to hold.

BAD MOVE: Sitting down. This immobilizes you faster than a broken leg. Stay on your feet.

GOOD MOVE: If you see another isolated couple or solo man or girl looking around uncertainly, play the heroine by saying, "We seem to be in the same boat—not knowing anyone here." *Et voila!* Your own little group within the group has started to form.

BAD MOVE: If you see a tight knot of guests all jabbering away in animated discussion, you can lurk on the perimeter for a few minutes, but don't try to bust in. You may get such a cold shoulder as to cause double bronchitis.

GOOD MOVE: If left standing alone, keep your head up. No slumping. Create a makework chore for yourself. Help yourself to some dip. Pass the canapes. Find a cigarette. Walk into the bedroom to tousle your hair and then return. Make a phone call even if it's a fake one. Anything so your muscles won't atrophy.

Then, if no man has waylaid you . . . and your hostess is still not doing her job of introducing . . . and you haven't yet achieved the party confidence to sashay up to the man with the great shoulders—start talking to another girl. Preferably a married one who will then introduce you to her husband, who will then talk to you until all of a sudden you are relaxed and talking to people and can more easily circulate among the rest of the guests.

BAD MOVE: Seeing a divine man and brazenly rushing up like a runaway fire truck. This strikes fear in the heart of the most heartless man. He will disappear at the first opportunity.

GOOD MOVE: Seeing a divine man, pick up that huge Mexican bowl of yum-yums, and pass them around until you get to him. Then, as you purringly offer him sustenance, you can say, "We haven't met, have we?"

WHEN YOU SEE A MAN YOU WOULD LIKE TO MEET

If you know your hostess well, level with her and ask her who he is, and will she introduce you?

If you think your hostess may shriek something cute like, "Jeannie here is dying to meet you!" then simply say you think you know him but you're not sure, and who is he?

Knowing his name, smile hello at him across the crowded room, and—when the constant movement of a party draws you nearby—greet him by name and say how great it is to see him.

Or, gradually work your way to his side, and do the cliché things. Ask for a cigarette. Ask what time it is. Admire his tie, suit, sideburns, whatever.

BAD MOVE: Nix on fancy openers or arch meet-cutes. Do not say things like, "What do you think of Pan-Asianism?" (Unless he happens to be president of the Pan-Asiatic League.)

Nobody loves a smart-alec.

GOOD MOVE: Smile.

Meet his eyes with yours.

Think: "I'd like to know you better." It will show. Promise.

If you can't think of anything else to say, say, "Hi." Period. Smile again.

WHEN EVERYONE MELTS AWAY FROM YOU

"Pardon me for a minute," he says and leaves and doesn't come back.

Nightmare! You feel ugly and stupid and rejected; you decide to get your coat and go home. Don't! (Terribly demoralizing to leave on a downer.)

GOOD MOVE: Realize that nobody noticed that the rat took off and didn't return. Why couldn't he just be getting you a fresh drink? Remember, many men have *got* to frisk *every* girl at a party. He probably left somebody for *you*. He isn't really dumping you as much as compulsively moving on.

Now go back and reread the section on "when you get to a party," as these good suggestions apply to the girl who has to start mixing all over again.

WHEN YOU HAVE TROUBLE TELLING THE MARRIED MEN FROM THE SINGLE MEN

NEVER ASK: "You married?"

This congeals the most hot-blooded man.

Apart from the obvious wedding band or telltale suntan gap on the ring finger, a surefire approach is to steer the conversation to credit cards or what day in the week June 17th is.

Why?

He will open his wallet to show you his credit card pullouts and his calendar. There will doubtless be pictures of kin. You will say, mildly, "Oh, what adorable children." Or, "What a gorgeous girl."

He will then explain who they are . . . hopefully, his sister and twin nephews.

At a huge, mob scene party, a shortcut is to give the maybe-married a sudden, exuberant hug. If he has a wife, she will materialize through the crowd in about three seconds. This sort of thing saves time.

BAD MOVE: Allowing a maybe-married man to monopolize you. If he is married, he will rejoin wifey at party's end while you, poor lamb, will find all the other men are taken or gone.

GOOD MOVE: If a man seems cagey, he probably is married. But if he's being overtly attentive, don't dump him. Draw him into a large group, saying, "I want you all to meet this fascinating man." It makes you look good, sought after, and enlarges your area of activity.

WHAT TO DO WHEN YOU ARE STUCK

If twenty minutes with the house drunk or house bore is all you can bear or you're scared the sweet couple sheltering you is getting restive, then you must get on to another group.

GOOD MOVE: Try incorporating some of the people standing nearby into your gathering. Lean over to them and say, "We're trying to decide who is the better actor, Steve McQueen or Clint Eastwood. Whom do you vote for?" Or take the sweet couple over to meet anyone else you happen to know at the party. Just say, "Come on, I want you to meet so-and-so," and march them off. They'll like that.

BAD MOVE: Introducing the drunk to *anyone*.

Other desperation possibilities: Excuse yourself to go to the ladies' room, the buffet table, or to make a phone call again.

IF FOOD IS A PROBLEM

Anxiety makes lots of girls itchy about food at a party.

You may turn into a nervous, compulsive eater, cramming food into your mouth.

You may suffer from the kind of party nerves which cause you to knock over glasses, tip over the cranberry sauce, and allow the curry to slide off your plate onto the floor.

If food is your problem, deal with it affirmatively. Eat before you go to the party. While it may be a shame to deny yourself the culinary experience so adroitly conceived by your hostess, the real issue is priorities. Do you go to parties to meet men—or to eat?

Should a good male provider insist on fixing you a plate of goodies, then dig in and enjoy. And be glad you didn't fix one for yourself two seconds before.

WHEN YOU SEE YOUR "EX"

Ex-husband or ex-beau, if the wound still hurts, don't aggravate it. If the parting was friendly, *you* be friendly . . . but aloof. Do not go over to him. Unfair though it may be, unless you married a millionaire scientist the second time, the implication is always, when you scoot over to see him, that the *girl* got dumped.

Smile a friendly greeting. If he wants to talk to you, let *him* make the move. Unless the man you're with knows who the Ex is, don't even *consider* explaining. There are two good reasons for this: If your former man is outrageously handsome and overtly divine, then you look like the pathetic loser, and that makes your new man feel inferior.

On the other hand, should your Ex look like a stand-in for Neanderthal Ned, you look even more pathetic and your new man may wonder what you see in *him* if *that's* an example of your taste.

Finally—and this is hard—couldn't you try, just once, to *forget about yourself?* Forget how self-conscious and shy and socially inhibited you are. Don't plan on a party being a disaster for *you*. Mix, force yourself to talk to everyone. You might even have a good time.

163

Guide to the Cocktail Party

The cocktail party, for all the unkind things said about it, is very much part of a girl's life these days. And for the single girl, looking for a free meal, an escort, a prospective husband or an expanded social circle, the rules of etiquette governing her party strategy are not so elementary as how many martinis to consume or what dress to wear.

She must know her ABCs thoroughly—Attitude, Behavior, Consideration for the Future—studying them beforehand and practicing them on the spot if she hopes to make the grade and reap any rewards. There are definite rules for the girl gadabout to observe when going to a cocktail party, and other dicta when hostessing one in her own living room.

Here are twelve cocktail party tips sure to produce a higher date rating:

(1) ATTEND every single party to which you are asked. There is truth in the adage: You never know whom you will meet. If the truth is too bitter to stand for long, leave.

(2) GO EARLY. Be one of the first arrivals. The hostess won't be so busy; you'll be introduced to everyone. With a few newfound friends to fall back on, you can mingle more easily. You won't have that petrified feeling that occurs when you walk into a room full of strangers and are told, "Make yourself at home."

(3) WEAR SOMETHING DIFFERENT. Don't be just another female sporting basic black with pearls. A bright red dress is a good attention getter. So are a bare back, a cleavage front and anything that shows off a good figure. I spent a wonderful year on the cocktail circuit when I wore Parisian stockings with *seams down the front.* It did become boring to hear people say, "Haven't you got your stockings on backward?" But I was noticed to the extent of two dinner dates that might otherwise never have happened.

(4) SPEAK UP. That remote pose, cigarette in hand, ogling the room over a drink, is fine for someone who has Brigitte Bardot's bosom or Liz Taylor's eyes, but it won't get Miss Average anywhere but her own company. If a man looks interesting, go over and talk to him. But make sure your talk is good. A few planned opening ploys help. An anecdote about the time you paddled a dugout canoe in the South Pacific is an example. So is a delightful bit of gossip (nonmalicious, please). But don't use words like *cute* or *divine* or *sweetie.* Don't prattle about children, your psychiatrist or how good you are on your job (men aren't afraid of successful women—only those who *talk* about their success). And stifle that impulse to ask, "What do you do?". You'll find out by letting him tell you.

(5) TALK TO OLDER PEOPLE. They'll think you're such a well brought up young lady and you never know whom you can meet through them.

My friend Alice went to a cocktail party where everyone was the age of her parents. She found herself with a debonair Wall-Streeter of sixty-plus who turned out to be charming. When the investment broker said, "What a nice girl you are" over their second shared Scotch, she confided, "What I want is a man who looks and acts just like you!" The gentleman countered, "I have a bachelor son—a doctor." The next week Alice met Don, and six months later they were married.

(6) MAKE FRIENDS WITH ANOTHER GIRL—preferably attractive and married. Almost every husband has a bachelor friend. Usually the happily married woman will be glad to serve as decoy and see what she can snag for you. Besides, married girls think single women lead "fascinating" lives and like to hear the work and play details. One good turn deserves another.

(7) CARRY PENCIL AND PAPER in your handbag in case a man asks for your number and doesn't have the props with him.

(8) GO ALONE even if you're timid. Asking a platonic friend to escort you will confuse things. You can't go around explaining "I came with John, but he's really looking for a girl and I'm hunting men." Be alone. Then other guests will try to see that you don't stay that way. Take your chances and hope you'll have interesting consequences to reap.

(9) NEVER BE A PARTY REMNANT. If no one asks you out to dinner, leave early. Don't remain with a hangdog look that begs "Please take me home. I'm all alone." Say you have a date—and accompany the lie with your most winning smile.

(10) CALL YOUR HOSTESS PROMPTLY the next day to thank her. Telephoning is nicer and less formal than writing—and you can find out all you want to know about the other guests. If you liked one man, tell her. She may pass on the information and flattery may get you everywhere—at *least* an invitation for a drink.

(11) MAKE OVERTURES. Call any woman you've met and liked at the party within a week and make a luncheon date. Do not call a man for two weeks and then never with a ruse such as, "I just happen to have two tickets for the theater next Tuesday." Instead you might say, "I'm having a few people over for drinks a week from Sunday." If he can come, ask others. If he can't, forget the whole idea until the next time you need it.

(12) STAY HOME BETWEEN 6 AND 7:30 P.M. the next night. That's when people usually call if they've been struck with your endearing young charms.

All a girl needs to go to a party is a freshly set hairdo, repartee and the ability to arrive at home base if she doesn't score a hit. Although giving a party means thought, effort, time and expense, it's definitely worth it. The single woman must entertain if she is to maintain her place in the social sun. She can show off, as a hostess, easiest and best at a cocktail party.

I enjoy my own parties most. The people seem nicer (all personally selected); the menu consists of my favorite dishes; the day is always extremely convenient.

As for the technique of entertaining, it's the big things that count—the people and the atmosphere. Learn all the tricks (preplanning so as not to be harried, best china and silver—never paper plates—rented glasses, scads of pretty posies, twice as many people as chairs). But the real effort should go toward having a stellar crowd of guests in the room and a feeling of genuine hospitality in the air.

Here are twelve cocktail party-entertaining tips in addition to those in our "Hostess" chapter.

(1) DON'T ASK "OBLIGATIONS." If someone has entertained you and you think he'll add to the fun, that's fine. Otherwise X should mark his spot on your list. Parties composed of "pay backs" are disastrous. Your guest list should be made up of people you want to have.

(2) NEVER, NEVER JOIN FORCES WITH ANOTHER GIRL. You'll save money at your own expense. Her friends may not be your type and will reflect badly on you.

(3) BE SURE TO INVITE SEVERAL GIRLS WHO ARE PRETTIER THAN YOU. Otherwise it looks as if you fear competition. Besides, good-looking girls often know good-looking men and homely girls do not.

(4) DON'T SPARE THE STAGS. Extra men give an event a four-star rating. Your married girlfriends will love to flirt with the wary bachelors. Don't waste time worrying about your time-to-time beaux dating *your* friends. They may as well pair off with your friends as your enemies.

(5) DO NOT ASK A BEAU TO HANDLE THE BAR FOR YOU unless you're *sure* he'd love it! He may siphon out whiskey but be so annoyed that he'll flee out of your life after the party. This request scares men almost as much as being taken home to meet Mom and Dad. Ask your best friend's husband, your brother or an ex-boyfriend who knows you're not after his scalp. Or pay a bartender.

(6) MAKE UP YOUR GUEST LIST OUT OF CONSIDERATION FOR OTHERS—not calculation for yourself. There should be someone for every guest to meet. Sexes and ages don't matter. A girl bound for Paris would love to meet a worldly Parisienne—or Parisien; a resident in surgery would like to meet an internist with a booming practice and the chance for referrals.

(7) ASK PEOPLE YOU KNOW WELL. Have three quarters tried and true friends and one quarter people you know slightly and want to know better. You'll feel at home and so will the invitees. Nothing is worse than those parties where everyone whispers, "I don't know the hostess—I can't imagine why she asked me."

(8) GIVE THE PARTY IN HONOR OF A FRIEND. This is an excellent technique. Ask a friend whom she would like to have invited. You do a favor and at the same time meet new people at your own party.

(9) GIVE THE PARTY FOR A SPECIFIC REASON—a birthday, a new job, a holi-

day. A young record producer asks people in for drinks each time she cuts a new disc. A raison d'etre for the party starts it off as a success.

(10) CONCENTRATE ON FOOD AS WELL AS DRINKS. Too much liquor can make for a bad party. Real hospitality requires more than potato chips and olives. Make the effort and concoct hors d'oeuvres. Spread your table with a cold vegetable dip, a bowl of celery and olives, caviar-stuffed eggs, a cheese board, cold ham and hot biscuits (made from frozen ones). People will think of you as a real hostess.

Even better, serve supper. It can be simple—buttered fettucini and tossed green salad . . . cold salmon with green sauce, cucumbers and hot French bread spread with chives . . . a potato, cabbage and sausage casserole (this recipe is in *The James Beard Cookbook*). For more super ideas see the previous chapter on "Being a Hostess."

(11) IF YOU MUST ECONOMIZE, DO IT IN STYLE. For instance, you might give a Danish Mary party (Bloody Marys made with aquavit instead of vodka). Or offer your thirsty guests gimlets (lime juice and vodka or gin), bull shots (bouillon and vodka) or stingers (brandy and white crème de menthe). All of these will cost much less than hospitality based on good Scotch, rye and bourbon. Never give a bring-your-own-bottle party. That's for college kids or those who still act as if they were . . . unless the purpose of the party is a wine-tasting and each guest contributes two bottles of her favorite wine.

(12) MAKE NO PLANS OF YOUR OWN FOR AFTER THE PARTY. The considerate hostess does not boot everyone out so she can go to dinner with one of the guests.

Whether you are guest or hostess, you may not find the gentleman that dreams are made of right away. You may turn up a bachelor who wants to keep his status quo, a thirty-year-old boy who craves his mamma, an elderly rake, a man of your own age who's interested mainly in sex, or a "neuter" who wants to prove his masculinity by stepping out with a female when he'd rather be home with Bruce. Don't turn up your nose at any of these; they can take you to the theater, ball games, dinner—and other parties.

Life on the cocktail party circuit is not *always* beautiful. Some parties will produce nothing but boors and bores. At others, despite your efforts, you'll fizzle and another girl will get all the play. But remember, the basic law of society circa the Seventies—you meet more people by going to and giving cocktail parties than by staying home and talking to yourself.

21. TWO FOR THE ROAD

Travel with a man, strictly *platonic*, is a quaint, old-fashioned notion. But I suppose it survives. Certainly you may find yourself and a male boss or co-worker jetting across the country together and checking into the same hotel or adjoining suite. Cross your fingers the good man has never heard of Women's Lib because the only *sane* way to travel is with a man in chivalrous attendance, tucking the blanket around your feet, organizing the luggage, retrieving your lost makeup case, sending back the undercooked eggs, and making sure you have time for a little nap before dinner. Of course you *may* also wing away on a European jaunt with a "just-good-friend," both eager to collect hearts and adventure along the way but with no libido panting for each other. *Usually*, when a Cosmo girl travels with a man he is a lover or possible candidate or maybe even her roommate. And there are certain rules of peripatetic pussyfooting to consider.

Question: "Should I go away for a weekend with a man I have not yet slept with?"

Answer: "Not yet" suggests you have been thinking about it . . . if sexual intimacy seems implicit in this invitation and you feel ready, and eager . . . accept. Otherwise, stay home. It can be tense and embarrassing to spend the last half of a long weekend with a man after you have thrown him out of your room in the Black Bass Inn.

Question: "I get so nervous when I check into a hotel out of town with my lover. We're both married to other people and I can't believe we can get away with this much longer. What to do to ease my anxiety?"

Answer: Take two single rooms . . . not adjoining, under two different names, preferably your own. It is easier to explain what you are doing in a single under your own name than in a double under a fictitious one. If caught, lie well. The extra $10 or $20 this costs will be more effective than $20 worth of tranquilizers.

Question: "When I travel with a man, who pays for what?"

Answer: The rule is flexible. When a man invites you for a weekend at Stowe or a week in Cuernavaca, he usually pays all travel and hotel expenses and you take care of personal incidentals. When you and a lover decide together to spend a vacation with two weeks in Jamaica, or a walk across Iran to India, you most likely go Dutch, or share expenses on a formula based on your comparative incomes. Unless your love is a Rothschild or a Rockefeller . . . then he *ought* to pay for everything and let you save your funds for bartering in the marketplace, buying presents for you, him and friends! Traveling with a man is like *living* with a man (see Part Three, Chapter 11): You may go as his guest, share expenses, or pay for *him*. Work the financial plan out *before* you go. Be detailed and specific to avoid unpleasant misunderstandings later.

Question: "Who brings what? And should we stuff everything into my big suitcase?"

Answer: One enormous suitcase is like the mummy's curse: it will kill you . . . too heavy to carry, too big to push. And if you decide to separate in Marrakesh, you'll be able to slip away with less fuss and bother each carrying his own valise. That way you can bring whatever you need and you're *safer* with two tubes of toothpaste, two razors, two spray cans of deodorant . . . nobody can blame anybody for leaving a crucial tube of shampoo at the hotel in Toulouse.

The Artful Check-In

We've come a long way, baby . . . but not as far as you may think. Most American hotel managements are as puritanical as ever. Fraud, deception and chicanery are encouraged under the guise of morality.

In most European hotels, an unwed couple (as well as a wed one) surrender their passports at the check-in desk or fill out a police form with *true* names and information. Then they are escorted to a double room without a murmur. Just hand your passport to your beloved and let him take over.

In America, no identity card is required, but candor is discouraged. At the St. Regis in New York, an unwed couple requesting a double under their true identities will be told they must take two rooms. A two-bedroom *suite* with adjoining bath is permissible. Many large hotel chains will not assign a double room to Mr. and Miss even in their overseas inns. What to do? A suite is marvelous if you can afford it; otherwise lie and check in as Mr. and Mrs. Alas, hypocrisy *breeds* fiction and then fiction becomes your only recourse!

In the Caribbean you simply register as Mr. and Mrs.—no passport or I.D. is required. If you go the Hilton or Loew's route overseas where passport *is* required, reserve as Mr. and Mrs. If anyone questions the mismatched surnames on your passports, give them a withering scowl and explain: "That is my professional name." Or . . . "I guess Women's Lib hasn't reached the Old World yet." Or blush demurely and explain

169

that you were married aboard the S.S. *France* en route to Europe for your honeymoon—no time to adjust the passport. Be firm and convincing . . . steamroller the smallest objection.

Regarding who *comes* to someone's room, hypocrisy also breeds cheating. Few posh hotels and fewer motels keep *track* of visitors to your room, so a man can register for a single and sneak his inamorata (you?) right past the desk clerk. This is fraud, however, and down-putting to the girl. Not recommended. If you've just met in a study group at the A.M.A. convention, that is something else.

COUNTRY	PASSPORT OR I.D. REQUIRED	UNWED COHABITATION
1. Canada	no	varies/best bet, register Mr., Mrs.
2. Denmark	yes	yes
3. England	no	varies/ register Mr., Mrs.
4. Finland	yes	yes
5. France	yes	yes
6. Germany	yes	yes
7. Greece	yes	yes
8. Israel	yes	yes
9. Italy	yes	yes
10. Jamaica	no	yes (except for major hotel chains)
11. Mexico	no	no
12. Morocco	yes	yes
13. Netherlands	yes	yes
14. Norway	yes	varies/ register Mr., Mrs.
15. Portugal	yes	yes
16. Spain	yes	yes
17. Sweden	yes	varies/ register Mr., Mrs.
18. Switzerland	yes	yes
19. U.A.R.	yes	no
20. U.S.A.	no	no
21. U.S.S.R.	yes	yes (except with Soviet nationals)
22. Yugoslavia	yes	yes

EIGHT RULES FOR DEALING WITH SERVICE PERSONNEL
(in a hotel, restaurant, on a plane, train, boat, etc.)
1. Smile.
2. Use their name, if you know it . . . never Mac, chief, boy.
3. Say please.
4. Ask—don't command.
5. Tip well.
6. Say thank-you.
7. Smile again.
8. Contain your exasperation in cases of misunderstanding. Avoid sarcasm.

THINGS THAT ARE TACKY

Stealing . . . anything! Towels, ashtrays, hangers, that cunning little pepper mill. Steal away with the desk clerk or the waiter if you will, but NOT the accessories.

Shabby taped-together luggage. Canvas and vinyl fabrics are inexpensive . . . start saving for a smashing new collection of totables.

Ordering the stewardess about . . . no wonder she prefers playing geisha to men.

Blind America-Firstism. Yes, patriotism. No, chauvinistic arrogance. Avoid lines like: "How much is that in *real* money?" (when the merchant quotes you a price in pesetas).

Litter.

Smuggling . . . is it worth the anxiety and your guilty conscience?

Wrinkles. Pack cleverly . . . don't drag along that impossible cotton ruffly thing when you look so smashing in knits and jerseys; take washable synthetics. Steam out wrinkles in the shower when you can.

New shoes. What are you, my dear . . . a hopeless masochist? Nothing will do for serious sight-seeing but well-broken-in shoes.

Airplane Kind of Love

Airplane love *is* almost storybook stuff, as many a career girl has found out. It *does* happen. It wasn't just the little old man with the homemade bomb that skyrocketed *Airport* to the top of the best-seller lists. And it wasn't just the plane running out of gas that made *The High and the Mighty* so exciting. Suspense is splendid, but so is *sex*.

High-flying has high potential for even a quiet-living girl—provided she's ready at flight time with charm, her *best* face and figure, and adventure on her mind. You're up in the clouds, suspended in space, alone with destiny and a mixed bag of that marvelous specimen: *Homo sapiens*, male version. He can't get away from you; *you* can't get away from him; it's cozy! If you play the airplane love game right, you can stay up on Cloud Nine for *weeks* after a flight. Some hints:

Try to avoid sitting next to Marty mama's boy on your flight. If that's impossible, just be patient and plan to collect another man before you leave the plane.

Sally Bowes spends fifty secretarial weeks a year taking dictation and typing letters in an office high up in Chicago's Prudential Building; when she comes down to earth for the remaining two she wants a holiday she can remember with pleasant vibes. A pretty girl, just twenty-four (with streaked blond hair and legs made for looking at), Sally is very practical.

"Most of my friends save for fifty weeks, splurge for two. I don't see it that way. I *do* save for my vacation—last year I went to London and this year I'll go to Rome—but I never count on spending much once I reach my destination. It may sound funny, but if I splurge on myself before I leave, I save in the long run because I always find someone to splurge on me when I arrive.

"And I don't just mean *when* I *arrive*. I usually meet someone *before* I arrive. Not that my new-found friend always lasts the full two weeks—sometimes he's there on business for a day or two, or after a while someone more interesting comes along. But there's nothing better than arriving at that airport halfway around the world, already just the right degree "attached" to a man. Think of the trouble you save in changing money and getting through customs and taking taxis with your own guide. Even if he's American and not too experienced in foreign travel, he's a *man* (and a blessing). It's gratifying when other men from the plane turn around to watch you, too—they're interested, especially when you look *interested* in the man you're with. Once, on a trip, the other men practically lined up as we walked out. It was almost like going down the aisle!

"What's my plan of procedure?" Sally pauses and looks around the Marina City apartment she shares with a girl friend who's a TV production assistant. The furnishings are sparse but each piece is good; leafy plants fill the gaps. "I have ground rules," she says. "First, not much luggage, and *never* those hard-looking cases—instead, something rich like leather. And no magazines or books in my hands. You don't want to *look* as though you're prowling, but you also don't want to give the impression you've been dying to read that particular book, either. If you miss out on a 'connection,' the stewardess will always give you a magazine.

"You must look *expensive*. Get a tan before you go, even if you only get it with tinfoil on the roof. And travel in something non-businesslike—silk jersey in a smashing pattern, not necessarily bright but beautifully cut!"

Sally stops again, reflects, "Of course, it doesn't have to be pure *silk* jersey. I had a great time in London last year in Banlon! Anyway, never show up in a three-piece tweed with an orchid on your shoulder! Girls who wear jersey look as though they know *how* to travel, where they're going—and like maybe someone sleek is waiting for them in Rome. You're also more apt to attract a man in first class.

"To 'catch' the man in first class you've got to be at the airport a bit early," says Sally, running her hand through her streaked hair. "Not *too* early—about half an hour before flight time. That gives him a chance to *see* you, though not really enough time to make contact. Then you'd be amazed how many first-class passengers come back to tourist, ostensibly to stretch their legs once you're aloft. And when you're stretching *your* legs, if you see someone who interests you sitting on the aisle, you can always miss grasping the back of his seat and touch his shoulder instead. You can say, 'Excuse me, I'm *sooooo* sorry.' If you've picked the right man, he'll take it from there."

(Sally advises that you *invest* in first-class yourself when you can. Most businessmen on expense accounts are in that section.)

Liz Karlin is twenty-seven, with the poise of forty and the enthusiasm of a twelve-year-old. Her short dark curls dance, her blue eyes dazzle, and although she isn't pretty, she's got *something*. When Liz gets near an airport, she says she comes alive.

"I really do *love* airports. There's always something going on—planes, people, fabulous places to go to. I get chills just hearing them announced on the speaker. I've got just one problem when I travel—at least I *thought* it was a problem. I always take along everything I own—books, tennis rackets, clothes, and candy bars!

"The first time I flew I was worried about this. Some girls are so *organized*—everything they need is in one duffel bag. Me, I clambered aboard my first flight—a Western shuttle from Los Angeles to San Francisco—like a refugee. But I'll tell you something—if that flight had been longer, I'd have had enough dates to keep me busy for a year.

"First, a man asked if he could help with my gear when I was getting on; I let him, but he wasn't the greatest, so after we were on board I thanked him and sort of barred his sitting next to me. Then I started organizing—what to put up on the rack with the pillows and blankets and what to put under my seat. Somebody else came along to help with *that!* Now I've got the checking situation down to a science. If you take long enough arranging your stuff, you can spy on all the good men! You have to get up on the seat to stash your coat away, of course, and the aerial view is *magnificent*. And if someone interesting comes down the aisle, you can ask *him* to help. Of course, you've got to get out *in* the aisle to see how much space you have under your seat, right? And how to wedge everything in. Last time, on an American flight, my cosmetic case slipped as we took off and whacked the guy behind me on the shin. *Oooh*, was I apologetic, and *oooh*, was Acapulco a blast, even

173

if you could always tell my date by the bruises on his leg.

"Getting back to candy bars, I swear they work if nothing else does. The best are chocolate covered peanuts or M&Ms. What you do is offer the man next to you some candy. If he accepts, you're on your way. If he refuses, you've got two choices: either accidentally spill some in his lap (that's risky because he may jump up—like one cute guy next to me who jumped up and hit his head and wouldn't speak to me for the rest of the trip) or, better, start counting the candy pieces slowly, separating the big peanuts from the small or the red M&Ms from the rest of the pack. He may think you're crazy, but after a while the prospectus he's studying gives way to fascination and he'll begin to study *you*. Last summer I flew to Martha's Vineyard on one of those private executive planes and I took along a bag of carrots. Well, I sat next to *the* Nicholas deB. Katzenbach and, since I couldn't think of anything governmental to say, I offered him a carrot. It didn't work though—his wife was waiting for him at the airport. But it's not everyone who offers carrots to Nicholas deB. Katzenbach!"

Not all girls are bold and sassy. Even a shy girl can find airplane love if she knows where to sit, or how to make the most of prearranged seating arrangements.

Helene Stern is twenty-eight, teaches math in elementary school, and lives at home. Her life, she says, used to be a gray haze, and so were her holidays, until she met a sympathetic stewardess.

"I'd always thought certain girls have all the luck," Helene says. "They get on the plane alone, have a seat by the window alone, but next thing you know, they're sitting between two men, chatting away, having drinks and a great time! And *you*, you started out the same way but you're still alone, just dropping off to sleep when you hear them all laughing. It's like some kind of conspiracy. Well, on my last flight there was a really nice young stewardess who took one look at me—she could see I'm no Sophia Loren—and she *put* me in Seat D, the one in the middle, with a guy on either side. There *I* was, laughing and having a good time for a change. Now I stay awake, *don't* bury myself in a book, and if there's a choice of seats, I take the one in the middle."

"Every winter I go to Puerto Rico," real-estate agent Barbara Brown says, "but I seemed to end up sitting at the far end of the pool, watching the bikinis at the outdoor bar. This time *I* wanted to have a good time, but how should I go about it? When I got on the plane, the answer dawned. As my girl friend and I walked down the aisle to the rear seats, to avoid the noise and, presumably, because it's safer, I realized we were passing all the men! By avoiding what we thought were pitfalls, we were avoiding the men as well, and how many would we have a chance at once we landed?

"So I turned to my friend and, bold as could be, told her we'd look for seats up front. She thought I was out of my mind, but before we even sat *down*, we'd scored! We couldn't find two seats together so we both took aisle seats, each beside a man, and in view of several others. It was fabulous! We *both* met men. One of mine lasted through the whole vacation."

If you don't meet someone on the plane, you have another chance getting off. Marcia Cauley did it—and if she can, anybody can!

"I was struggling up the aisle at the end of the trip with my book, handbag, coat, *and* overnight case, coming back from Chicago where I'd been visiting my aunt. When you're carrying things and everybody's climbing out of seats, the aisle gets crowded and seems *so* long and narrow. Invariably, I whack someone before my trek to the door is over.

"Last time I hit a man with my handbag. Oh, it was by mistake, of course!" Marcia's eyes lit up defensively, but her smile is more Mata Hari than mouse. "I apologized profusely. He just smiled and said he wasn't carrying anything, so could he help me.

"Based on the 'good-scare training' most girls are raised on, I'd ordinarily imagine the man running away with my case, but I decided to be *trusting!* He ended up carrying my cosmetic case *and* my suitcase, flagged a cab, and gave me a lift to town. We didn't have a date, but last week he phoned me—and do you know what he said? That I was the girl who intentionally bumped men with her luggage so she could start a conversation." Marcia looks uncertain. "Do you suppose girls really *do* do it on purpose?" She smiles. "Anyway, we're going out this Friday."

A nervous girl can have a smooth flight, too.

"I'm so nervous about flying," says Jani Waters, a secretary at a large Detroit law firm, "that if M. Pompidou sat next to me in first class on Air France I wouldn't know!" Space nerves or no, Jani attracts men.

"I recently sat next to a man with Paul Newman-blue eyes—I remember because they almost hypnotized me. We were on the way to Paris and we talked for *seven* hours! Well, I started out being nervous but got so fascinated I even forgot we were on a plane. I might not have been his kind of girl on the ground (he was awfully intelligent—four languages and all that), but I had all that time to sink into him. He took me out my first night in Paris and I'll never forget it."

Flying at night has certain advantages, even if you're a day person!

Maggie Jerrold has long, strawberry-blond hair and green eyes like GO lights. A serious researcher, she's often asleep by ten P.M., but when it comes to flights, Maggie flies by night.

"There's something about a night flight that really is *sensual*," Maggie says. "I flew TWA's night flight to Madrid in June. I figured I could sleep on the plane and be ready for sightseeing the next morning without losing any time, especially since I had only four days in Madrid.

"Well, I had noticed a handsome European (skinny suit, sideburns, soft briefcase) looking at me as we boarded, but when I didn't see him in tourist I figured that was that. I settled down to read for a while, and before too long the stewardess turned out the overhead lights. It was so quiet that when a shadow stopped next to me I jumped—not exactly the chic thing to do! The shadow belonged to my Continental, who asked me to join him for a drink.

"There wasn't anyone in the last row, so we went back there and the stewardess brought us bourbon after bourbon (he charmed *her*, too!). I learned he was Spanish, lived in New Orleans, was going to Madrid on business, and then to visit friends at a bullfighter's ranch near Seville.

"We talked and talked. It was all so *intimate*—lights out, shoulders touching.

"By the time we got to Madrid we'd made a dinner date for that evening, and he told me what to see during the day." Maggie blushes slightly. "It turned out we were staying at the same hotel. If we hadn't been, I'd have moved to his. He was just too good to lose.

"I've seen him in New York since I've been back, and we have fun, but the magic I knew in Spain—that *beautiful* magic—has sort of gone. I've thought of going back to Madrid, but I think I'll go somewhere else next year. I'd be afraid to break the spell. But I *am* sold on night flying—it's that intimate thing!"

What do the targets themselves have to say about the tactics of the high-flying female? Let's hear from two of them:

Jay Kenny is a fair-haired (though slightly balding) boy wonder in banking, solid but spiced with humor. On summer weekends he flies to New York from Pittsburgh then on to Southampton for the weekend. The Sunday-afternoon flight back to Pittsburgh is even better than the flight out, according to Jay:

"I meet more people. I usually fly first class because there are only two seats across—and, besides, the complimentary drinks help make up the difference in price. Well, this one time we were about to take off and, I thought, great, it's not crowded. Nobody sitting next to me, a couple of extra seats around. Then in came this pretty blonde—features like a young Marlene Dietrich—and plunked herself down beside me. Well, I went on reading my *U.S. News & World Report*, when she started telling me how she had almost been late, had made the plane at the last minute, and on like that—very chatty.

"Then she said she was a model. 'What kind of model?' I asked. 'Photographic,' she said, pulling out her portfolio. 'Do you want to see my pictures?' 'Sure,' I said.

"Well, out came these eleven-by-fourteen-inch prints—I mean really *big*—and, suddenly, there's this terrific shot of her in a bikini sitting on a log—in color! *Unbee-lee-vable!* I really hoped nobody was noticing the art exhibit, but everybody on the plane seemed to be looking, and the stewardess was coming with another drink. I *needed* it.

"The girl, I suppose, was about twenty-four, and had a beautiful figure, and now that I had seen her in the skin, so to speak, I thought the friendly thing to do was to offer her a ride to town when we got to Pittsburgh. Well, when we got to her hotel I helped her out with her bag and said, 'I've got to get going.' I got this great big warm goodbye, and then she asked if I wanted to come in for a drink. I'd planned to catch up on some work at the office but I said O.K. So I went back to get *my* bag and pay the driver. I said, 'Guess I'll be getting out here, too." And he said, 'She seems like a lovely girl.' I couldn't think of anything to say, so I said, 'I just met her!'

With that, the driver got out of his cab, came around to me, and said, 'I'd like to shake your hand.' He even carried my bag for me. Today, I don't know my airplane pal's name—she got married. But I've never forgotten *her*. It's like she's the girl in the song, 'Laura'—the one who stays in your brain."

American bachelor Bob Harris is filled with a lawyer's persuasive words, and uses them to praise night flights.

"Last time I was on one out of Dulles Airport to Panama City, there was this wild dress on this magnificent girl—a South American beauty with shiny black hair and olive skin. Rich, too. Her name was Maracel.

"She was amazing. I didn't have to make a move. Not that I'm shy, but she didn't even give me time to make an advance. She just followed me on the plane and sat down next to me. The man who had been assigned the seat came in and showed Maracel his ticket, but she said we were old friends and we hadn't seen each other in a *long* time and *would* he mind taking *her* seat up front because she was *so* excited about finding me on the plane.

"Well, what could the poor guy do? By the time Maracel finished her explanation we were old friends." Bob whistles softly. "Night flying can be pretty lonely, but Maracel made it a groove." He whistles again.

"And when we got to Panama City she had a chauffered car waiting for her and we went out a special exit at the airport. I saw her later—took her to dinner and dancing at the Panama Hilton. The longer the flight the better your chances, but a night flight's best of all."

Conclusion: Don't overlook any opportunity for flirtation on high. You won't if you're tuned into airplane love both inflight *and* on the ground.

Remember that your departure *time* is almost as important as your destination. Weekday flights are not for you, unless you enjoy the nursery atmosphere of couples traveling with young children on family plan. *You're* going to take off on a weekend—do you *know* how many tycoons fly on Sunday nights in order to get a Monday-morning head start on business trips?

The earlier you are at the airport, the more time you'll have to discreetly survey and select the most promising seatmate material. After you've picked your target, maneuver a place in line *behind* him at the check-in counter. Unless the airline agent hates girls, you'll probably be assigned the seat right next to your bull's-eye, or at least within shooting distance across the aisle.

Once aloft, don't (how could you?) ignore the crew. The stewards are every bit as suave and attractive as that ship's steward it took you six months to get over last year—but they're *sharper*, because they've learned to work *fast*. Even that craggy captain isn't too busy to notice which pretty thing is sitting *where* on the plane. When he comes back from the cockpit to pay a courtesy call on his passengers, ask him a question about the weather ahead or the estimated landing time. He might not have time for more than a quick reply *then*, but if he likes your smile, voice, or perfume, he may turn up to recheck your terrain after touchdown.

Now, just suppose—all strategy notwithstanding—you've spent the whole flight in unromantic darkness because the grandmother next to you couldn't enjoy her "naptime" unless the overhead reading light was *off* and you kept *quiet*. This is not the moment to blame the fates and sulk—you've still got the baggage claim ahead of you. Purposely stride up to the wrong counter, stand next to a breathtaking prospect, and look helplessly for your luggage in vain. Complain rather sweetly that it *must* be there someplace. Unless the man's got a personality problem, he'll help you search for your suitcase.

If you're lucky enough to be in Europe just off an international flight, you can approach almost any Italian-suited thing and ask him: 1. Where to go through customs, and if they'll confiscate your cigarettes because you've got more than one carton; 2. Where to find a taxi, and how much you should tip the driver to get you to *wherever you're staying* (yes, yes, he'll get the message); 3. How to say "dry martini" in Portuguese.

No matter where you land—Kansas City or Oshkosh—there's still something you can do if the plane hasn't yielded anything worthwhile: Go back to the beginning of this section, substitute the word limousine for the word "plane," and start over. The trip from the airport to the hotel has the same rules and, if you play it right, can set you up with a man to keep you company until you wave him goodbye when you embark on the second half of your round trip to an airplane kind of love.

How To Behave On A Boat

If, in the middle of dinner, your date suddenly asks you whether you own a pair of rope-soled shoes, don't look at him as though you think he must buy his shoes through a mail-order catalog. He is probably about to invite you for a cruise on his boat. Such an invitation is both a compliment and a challenge, and means that he thinks you are (a) a good sport who will be helpful to have aboard or (b) so decorative he doesn't care if you help out or not.

There's only one problem: The cruise is for Sunday next and the only boat you were ever on was a rowboat at Girl Scout camp—which capsized. How do you prepare for the excursion?

QUESTIONS TO ASK

Whether or not you decide to confess to him your ignorance of boating (which is what yachting people call yachting), there are certain questions which anyone, neophyte or old salt, is entitled to ask about a prospective cruise.

"What kind of a boat do you have?"

The main thing you want to know is whether he has a sailboat or a powerboat. On a sailboat, you will have to help sail the thing, which can be strenuous at times, or keep out of the way of those who are sailing it, which can be even *more* strenuous. On a powerboat, you can expect to spend a great portion of your time sitting on deck with a drink in your hand and looking pretty.

"How long will we be out?"

Knowing how long he *expects* to be out may be of help to you in planning your day, but the cruise may take longer than anticipated. Don't plan anything *else* for that evening.

"Is there a destination, or will we just be cruising around?"

If he's going to stop for lunch or drinks at some island resort or swanky yacht club, you may want to take along something dressy to change into.

"How long have you been boating?"

This is *the* most important question. Some boat owners are new to boating and have only the vaguest idea of what they're doing. That will make *two* of you. Ask, "How long does it take to learn piloting and navigation?" If he looks blank or says, "Who needs *that*? Anybody can steer a boat!" you may want to quickly remember a previous engagement for the day of the cruise.

WHAT TO WEAR

He expects you to know what to wear, just as he expects you to know how to steer a straight course the first time he hands you the wheel, and, of course, how to cook in a small galley. So remember, it is often cold on the water and it is always wet. He might enjoy seeing you in a bikini, but it would only annoy him to see you turn blue because you don't have a jacket. You *always* need a jacket or sweatshirt on a boat. The weather can change at any time.

As for assembling your outfit, just start at the bottom and go on from there. Remember when he asked if you had rope-soled shoes? I hope you do. Leather soles scratch the teak deck or make black marks.

Actually, any soft-soled shoes will do—nonskid rubber, rope, cork. The powerboat owner may not mind thongs with composition soles, but in sandals, you could stub your toe on a cleat or cut it on something sharp. In bare feet, there is even more likelihood of your hurting yourself, and it is considered unthoughtful to sit there bleeding all over the deck.

If you already own an old, beat-up pair of sneakers with holes in them and some faded jeans, you're in. The saltier and goofier your clothes, the better. White pants are all right; stretch jeans or shorts are fine. The kind of thing to avoid is any material printed with anchors (You're trying too hard) or brass buttons (They might scratch the teak on the boat).

Although some powerboats are completely enclosed except for the decking, the same general rules of attire are usually observed. If you sit on the powerboat deck or bridge, the air is just as cold and salty as if you were on a sailboat. (However, on a yacht-sized cruiser with lush appointments, when your only exposure to the elements is going aboard and getting off, you can dress more formally.)

If the invitation is for drinks when the boat (either sail or power) is at anchor, or if it is a gala occasion calling for regular cocktail clothes, he will probably tell you; otherwise, the informal dress I have described is a must.

SEAWEED VS HAIR

Even if you have the most Sassoon of cuts, after it has been whipped around by a fierce ocean breeze and pelted with droplets of seawater, it will be unmanageable, to say the least. Wear a wide hairband, a full scarf or straw hat that ties down. Parkas and some sweatshirts have hoods, which do help, and hoods don't blow away. Take a hairpiece.

THE THREE S's

Whatever else you take, don't forget these: seasick pills, sunglasses (The big wrap-around goggles keep out the most sun) and suntan lotion. Two hours of sun on the open sea is equivalent to four hours of it on shore. And don't assume you *won't* get seasick. Take some pills. (Ask your doctor which kind to get. Bonine and Marezine are two well-known brands.) Take a pill before you go out. After you get sick is too late.

BE NICE TO HIS BOAT

Now that you know what to wear and what to take with you, let's talk about "her." A boat is referred to as a female and she is a rival, in a way. First of all, she is probably his most cherished piece of personal property, and he has undoubledly lavished a lot of money and care on her.

So even if his beloved looks to you like the oldest, clunkiest boat in the harbor, find something nice to comment on. Say she has a nice paint job, an interesting name, a good galley (kitchen), is *well found* (well equipped), is comfortable, has a roomy cockpit, or, once you are out on the water, that she is *sea-kindly* (rides the waves nicely), or *points* beautifully. If you can't think of anything else to say, tell him his boat has *character*.

STINKPOTTER OR RAGBAGGER

It is unlikely that your date will call his boat a yacht, as that sounds pretentious; and boating people, remember, make a fetish of being plain, unsophisticated and unpretentious . . . while boating. They may go home and put their emeralds on later.

There is some disagreement concerning the definition of the word *yacht*, but "a privately owned pleasure vessel" is a generally accepted one. Some say a yacht should be over 20 feet long, that it should be ocean-going and have sleeping quarters; others insist that *any* sailboat is a yacht; and still others claim that a powerboat is not a yacht unless it is over 50 feet.

There is a good-natured rivalry between powerboat owners (stink-potters) and sailboat owners (rag men or ragbaggers.) Sailboat people like sailing because it is an action sport and does not burn up a lot of fuel or create fumes (which give the powerboats their nickname.)

Powerboat owners prefer the comfort of the cruiser, its speed, the protection it gives from the weather, and the fact that *not* so many preparations are needed before taking off for a cruise.

Powerboats cost more to run and some cannot take a heavy sea. A sailboat can take the sea better, but unless it has an auxiliary motor, you could be becalmed and sit out on the ocean for hours. There is a rolling motion in a powerboat; the movement of a sailboat is up and down.

Finally, powerboats outnumber sailboats by more than two to one.

THE SKIPPER IS BOSS

If the man who looked at you so adoringly over cocktails snaps at you like a stevedore boss once aboard his boat, remember that his first responsibility is the safety of his vessel and passengers. Do what he says first, ask questions later.

ANATOMY OF A BOAT

Once aboard, you will notice that space is at a premium, which is the reason for keeping a boat Bristol fashion (a place for everything, and everything in its place). The deck is known as *topside*. The lower part of the boat is *below* or *belowdecks*. The cabin in any vessel is known as the *house*. *Aft* is the back (the *stern*); *forward* is the front (the *bow*); *port* is your left as you face the bow; *starboard* is your right.

The *compass* tells you where you are going, and the *wheel* or *tiller* steers the boat. Those little round things are *portholes* or *ports*—not windows and that rope or chrome fence around the boat is a *lifeline*. The *forecastle* (slurringly pronounced fok-sil) is the forwardmost section of the belowdecks and the kitchen is the *galley*.

In a sailboat, the ropes are called *sheets* and they control the sails (hence the expression, "knowing the ropes"). The *ha'yard* hoists or lowers, the sails, and the *winch* is a crank that pulls the sails. If he has power winches (the equivalent of three men pulling), he can sail the boat alone.

On a powerboat, the *propeller blades* are toward the stern and they rotate to propel the boat through the water. The engine can be put in either forward or reverse, and the latter also makes the boat stop (by reversing the gear), as boats have no brakes.

If the boat carries a *dinghy* or *lifeboat*, it is definitely a yacht, and if he owns it, he can afford to keep you and the boat in luxury. Be *extra* nice to him.

THE HEAD

One of the main reasons for going below is to visit the *head*, the nautical term for toilet.

Don't throw *anything* down the head—not even a match. It will cost at least thirty-five dollars for mechanics to dismantle it. Be considerate and read or ask instructions first—there are no plumbers at sea. You will notice that the head door is latched *back* . . . and open. You have to unlatch it before you can close it. That is done so the door won't bang when you are in rough water.

BE HELPFUL

If this is a maiden voyage (for *you*, not the boat), the first thing you should do once aboard is to announce that you're ready to help any-time he needs you. Then sit down out of the way—don't hover at his elbow. When he does ask you to do something, make sure you know exactly what he means. *Heave* means to pull (on a rope). *Secure* means to tie something down. (Make him show you the proper knot while the boat is at anchor; don't try to learn it while the boat is running under full sail.)

WHY DIDN'T YOU TELL ME IT WAS GOING TO RAIN?

If the weather changes, it isn't his fault. Be a good sport. Smile. Tell him what a great sailor he is, and how romantic it is to be out with him. Because it is. It is magical and hypnotic . . . watching the trans-lucent blue, the salt spray. Once you are under way, he'll relax and no-tice you, and maybe even put the boat on automatic pilot.

DON'T JUST WALK OFF—STAND THERE AND DO SOMETHING

When you come into port, even if you are soaked to the skin and ex-hausted, don't *ever* just walk off. Help get things "shipshape." Equip-ment must be stowed, the sails stuffed into bags, the hatch closed, the decks washed off. When all this is done, smile sweetly and thank him for the marvelous day. He will probably ask you out again and before you know it, you'll be a sailor, too.

SOME BOATING TIPS

Whenever you see anything uncoiled, coil it up right away.

Ordinary soap will temporarily seal a gas leak.

Don't jump from the boat to the dock unless you want a broken ankle for a souvenir.

If you want to get to know a skipper, sign up for a class in piloting and navigation.

If you want to get to know the skipper better, suggest he put the boat on automatic pilot.

GLOSSARY FOR NAUTICAL NOVICES

Aft: Facing stern.

Avast: Stop. As in "Avast heaving!"

Bow: Forward.

Bunker Berth: A bed on a boat.

By the Board: Something that fell overboard, such as a hat that should have been tied down.

Canvas: Sails.

Companion Ladder or Companionway: How to get below when you've had it.

Dead Ahead: Any point that the boat is approaching directly.

Deck: The planked floor of the vessel. What you don't bleed on, or scratch.

Dinghy: A small, open boat.

Dogwatches: Two-hour watches between 4 and 8 P.M. If he puts you at the helm or wheel while he sits with a drink, he's treating you like a dog.

Galley: That funny little kitchen.

Gear: Your stuff.

Halyards: Ropes or tackles used for hoisting or lowering sails.

Hatch: Opening in deck.

Head: What costs thirty-five dollars to dismantle if you throw anything down it.

High Heels: Nautical translation unprintable.

Leeward: Away from the wind.

Log: Something you make entries in, or what the skipper may sleep like if you let him drink too many navy grogs.

Marry: Joining ropes together. If you master the art, he may think of another kind of marrying.

Mooring: Place where the boat is permanently anchored.

Port: Left as you face the bow.

Porthole or Port: Round window.

Ragbagger: A sailing kind of sailor.

Stinkpot: Powerboat.

Stow: What do you do with your gear.

Swab: What you do with the deck—wash it—while he drinks navy grogs.

Trick: Period of duty at the wheel. If you find yourself sitting there while he snoozes, you've been tricked.

White Pleated Skirt: What you don't wear to go boating.

Windward: Toward the wind.

Meeting Men While Traveling

There you are (can't you just *see* yourself!) zipping around Rome after dark in a sporty Ferrari, a well-tailored masculine shoulder next to yours . . . and *there* you are marveling at the Taj Mahal by moonlight while a male voice tells you how a shah built it in memory of his wife . . . and—flash—hey look, it's *you* again, sipping champagne at Montmartre in the small hours of a Paris dawn, clinking glasses with an escort you've known for three delightful hours.

When a girl travels abroad all by herself, these scenes can actually happen. She's not likely to find a *husband* en route. Finding a husband *can* happen, and occasionally does, but no girl in her right mind should count on it. She *can* count on a series of pleasant flirtations, though, providing she uses foresight.

Along with brushing up on your tennis, practicing a few helpful foreign phrases like, "Are all the men of your country so handsome?" and making sure you have packed some sexy clothes, remember the following:

Don't flit about too much. Even if you're not taking off for Florence first thing in the morning, perhaps he *is.* So for a man-meeting destination, choose the sort of place where people seem to settle for a while. You don't want anything too far off the beaten path, of course, but there are lots of places that strike a happy medium between a remote wilderness and the top tourist haunts you want to avoid because feminine competition is keen.

Pick a good place and stay for at least a week. If you're young with a good figure, there is nothing like a beach resort in summer or a ski spot in winter. Meeting people is the primary aim in these places. You're there to make new friends and so is everyone else. If you're not so young but still appreciate male companionship, look for a place with a casino; gambling affords opportunities for gamboling. Or try a mountain resort or a spa. Many a romance has started over a bridge table, while taking the waters or comparing the merits of mud baths.

Go where your type is In. If your hips are considered too wide in the United States, they'll be pluperfect in Turkey; Turks like their women Rubens style. If tweed suits you, consider Scotland or Ireland. Blondes go over big in Mexico or any Latin country; brunettes rate in Scandinavia.

Do be practical. If you are seeking more than a passing fancy (i.e., you don't want to have to move halfway around the world if you two should marry) go where you will meet people from your home area. For example, Easterners abound in the Caribbean; Westerners head for the west coast of Mexico and southward into South America.

Do consider the seasons. In summer, the world is overrun by women in search of mates. You'll have much more chance of attention in winter, where there is less competition from compatriots.

Go where the men are. Males congregate in ski resorts, on golf links and tennis courts. Resort areas near mining and archaeological expeditions are a good bet; after hours men prefer a live girl to a mummy. A little research beforehand pays off in dates.

Don't turn up your nose at fellow Americans. That nice Antonio can be very good company for an evening in Rome, but his home is Rome and yours is New York. Whereas that accountant Bill Jones may not have a charming accent, but he does live two miles across town. Don't give up Antonio. Just make sure that Bill has your telephone number—and that you have his.

FIFTEEN SUREFIRE WAYS TO MEET MEN ABROAD

Back home it is standard procedure for you to chase your quarry until he catches you. It doesn't work this way abroad. Once you manage to meet him, he'll do the pursuing with pleasure. To the foreign man, you are the new girl in town who won't be around long enough to be a threat to his freedom. He feels secure in this knowledge. On the other hand, the American man abroad is easily available, too; he's lonely and needs you just as much as you need him.

So the basic problem becomes the initial encounter. Here are a few methods that may not result in a permanent twosome but should at least bring about dinner for two in a local restaurant.

(1) PLAY HELPLESS. The damsel-in-distress strategy works much better outside the United States. Standard devices: Be unable to understand the currency, cope with change, read the street signs, get on the right bus, follow directions from the slip of paper in your hand, or read your map. On ships you can be confused by a life preserver, on buses by where to get off, and on planes by how to hook a seat belt. All these dilemmas make it necessary for you to ask help from a man. (When

choosing your prospect, pick one who is not wearing a wedding ring. Most Europeans do wear wedding rings, often on the right hand; so in nine cases out of ten you are pretty safe with the man minus the band.)

(2) MAKE FRIENDS WITH THE HOTEL EMPLOYEES. Get acquainted with the concierge or hall porter. He's the best friend you can have. Explain that you are alone; maybe he'll introduce you to fellow guests.

Another important contact is the maitre d'hôtel. Once a friend of mine was dining alone at her hotel. She talked a bit with the maitre d', asking him several tourist questions. When a stalwart blond Viking came in and sat down alone, the maitre d' noticed my friend giving the man the eye. Soon the helpful maitre d' reappeared at her table. "Miss, the gentleman at the corner table is a Mr. Olaf Olson," he explained politely. "He is from a good family and is a successful businessman. His wife died over a year ago. He has asked that you join him for dinner. Would you? You have my assurance that it is perfectly all right." She had a very pleasant evening. Never underestimate the authority of a headwaiter.

(3) GO DOWN TO BREAKFAST. It is a temptation to start the day in the solitary elegance of your room. Don't. Sip a cup of coffee in privacy if you must, and then head for the dining room. Go early. Men don't sleep late; they rarely have a tray in bed; and some of your best possibilities for the evening will be businessmen who have early appointments. As you eat, survey the scene, and smile at anyone who looks promising. At 9:30 A.M., this cannot be construed as an overture, but should you meet the gentleman at cocktail time, he might return the smile, along with an invitation. As we've pointed out, men get lonely, too.

(4) TALK IN HOTEL ELEVATORS. The lone man riding with you may have a wife, but you can take a chance in this nice impersonal atmosphere and make small talk. I once ventured, "I hear the *France* is going to leave two days late because of the strike." The man turned out to be similarly becalmed in Paris. Two hours later we were dining together.

(5) SIT IN THE HOTEL LOBBY. From this vantage point, you can spy out just what possibilities are available. If you feel awkward, utilize props like the European edition of the *Herald Tribune*, a murder mystery, or the always useful cup of coffee. Don't relax at random; do the lobby sitting when there is something—or someone—to be seen, for instance, when the crowd from an ocean liner checks in, at the cocktail hour, or just after dinner.

(6) GO PLACES. Your hotel may be your home away from home, but you don't go abroad to feel at home. Get out and go places. Take a tour; your seatmate may turn out to be a fascinating man. Sporting events, such as a bullfight or rugby game, can be most productive. You can't be suspected of trying to pick up someone if you just turn to your neighbor and say, "I don't understand what's happening; perhaps you

can explain." Through your hotel you can gain admission to local sporting clubs abroad. It helps if you can really play tennis; if you can't, play a watching game.

Festivals are excellent for meeting men. Whether it's a music festival in Spoleto, a wine-tasting in Burgundy, or the running of the bulls in Pamplona, walk in and you become a part. The same thing holds true for local dances given by societies. You'll find these advertised in the papers. You'll probably be the belle of the ball and you'll certainly be the only lady tourist to think of it.

(7) CHANGE YOUR MONEY AT AMERICAN EXPRESS, NOT AT THE HOTEL. The walk to the office will benefit your waistline—and you never know who will be in line with you. Don't go directly to the money-changing desk; read your mail until someone interesting appears.

(8) GET FRIENDLY WITH A MARRIED COUPLE. This is a four-star way for a single woman to meet an eligible man abroad just as it is at home. Couples are usually delighted by a change of face, and they'll man-hunt for you. But don't sponge. Pay your own way.

(9) TAKE THE LOCAL TRAINS. The compartment holds six people in first class, eight in second, and one of them might be a male headed in your direction. Even if he isn't a handsome stranger, he might know one.

(10) MAKE THE MOST OF YOUR LANGUAGE DIFFICULTIES. A man with a smattering of English will be delighted to come to your rescue. If you can say, "Please," "Thank you," and, "How do you get to the hotel?" in his language, he is bound to tell you, "You have a wonderful accent. Where did you learn to speak so well?" This technique brings top results in the Latin countries.

(11) PICK A CAFÉ AND MAKE IT YOURS. If you sit in the same spot and have coffee every day at the same time, you will be noticed by fellow habitués, usually male. Outdoor cafés like the ones on the Via Veneto in Rome, Piazza San Marco in Venice, and Boulevard St. Germain in Paris are prime spots for man-watching and -catching. In Latin countries, if a woman sits alone, it signifies a willingness to be approached.

(12) LOOK UP EVERYONE. If Aunt Mollie, who is really a mess by anyone's standards, told you to look up her dressmaker's cousin in Paris, do it. She may send you to a friend in Bayonne who knows a man in Lisbon.

(13) ATTEND CONVENTIONS. One of the newest travel gimmicks is the holding of medical, psychiatric, legal, advertising, chemical and public-relations conventions in major European cities during the summer season. If you are vacationing during July and August and are going to Paris, Rome, London or Vienna anyway, why not adjust your schedule and stay in the same hotel where men of a friendly and congenial profession are convening? It's easy enough to find out when and where from the professional societies at home.

(14) SPEAK UP. One of the best things about traveling abroad is that

you don't have to wait to be asked. You can make the first move. If you see an attractive man, do something, don't just stand there—or some other woman will act first. Why not learn one interesting fact about each country and bring it into a chance conversation with a national? For instance:

Scotland—"I just can't wait to eat scones."

Holland—"Please tell me how to pronounce Scheveningen?"
(It's Skay-vah-nin-gun, and if you learn, you're considered a linguist. During World War II, many a German was spotted, despite a flawless Dutch accent, by the way he mispronounced this tricky word.)

France—"Why is the average Frenchman such an individualist?"

Italy—"Do you really pinch strange girls on the street?"

Turkey—"Does anyone at all still wear a fez?"

Germany—"How is it that German men are able to get so much done—and still have time for women?"

Argentina—"Can you explain your political system to me?"

(15) USE THE HOTEL BAR. Lots of men who hate to swim, skate, fish or shoot ducks love to get their exercise from lifting a glass to their lips. Here are three general rules to follow: (a) You can go alone into your hotel bar, but I find it better to sit at a table. A girl on a barstool is a clear come-on signal to any man in the room and he'll be annoyed if you don't respond amorously later. (b) It is a good idea to introduce yourself to the bartender as a recent arrival. Then if someone bothers you, you can signal the bartender for help against a pest. You can also enlist the bartender's help if someone interests you. (c) If you are uncomfortable about going into a bar alone, but feel you should, don't. You'll be so obviously tense that no one will dare to try to strike up an acquaintance.

Almost all the methods I've listed involve some form of the pickup—a technique that is sure to pick up your trip overseas if applied with judgment, discretion and predetermined limits. With a sixth sense of what's right and what's wrong, you can safely meet some interesting people, enjoy delightful aperitifs, a good dinner, an evening at the opera and dates back in the United States. Nonsense pickups can result in trouble. You can lose your money, become involved with unsavory characters, and end up in the wrong hotel room.

Abroad, however, you can do things that you might never do at home. A woman must make social overtures or she will spend her time alone. She must respond when overtures are made to her. The pickup that you would reject at home with a shrug can be extremely pleasant abroad.

VIVE LA DIFFERENCE

Meeting men on foreign soil is only half the battle. The other half is understanding what makes them tick—and there's the challenge. The differences of language, psychology, customs and courting impose boundaries on what *should* be a simple matter of woman meets man, and vice versa.

You won't solve the mystery of mankind on a brief trip abroad, but you may be able to improve your dating rating if you have a little fore-knowledge of the men you will meet here. Here are some thumbnail sketches that should help you while you are sparring for an opening:

THE GERMAN. Brush up on your Freud, Jung and Adler. The way to a Teuton's heart is through his psyche. His opening maneuvers are through your mind. Instead of concentrating on moonlight and roses, like the Frenchman, or love at first sight, like the Spaniard, he focuses on the inner meaning of love. "What does love really mean?" he will ask soulfully as his hand moves up your arm. "Where do you feel our relationship is headed?" he wonders as he stares into your eyes. If you meet his soulful and psychological standards, he will proceed to the physical plane.

Never judge a man by his clothes in Germany; you may pass up a rich Ruhr industrialist or a nonworking baron. Inverse snobbery is at work here. Germans regard shabby lederhosen and sloppy knapsacks as status symbols—even if you don't.

THE ITALIAN. By his own admission, the Italian is a little like a *pavone* (peacock). Handsome and temperamental, he defiantly expects to be admired. He delights in expressing his emotions by tears, tantrums or tearing his wavy, pomaded hair. He often prefers to talk about love rather than make love, but this volubility, rather than action, is really one of his charms for the tourist. Many tourists don't really want an affair; they just want to be flattered. (*Caution:* Married men feel especially free to flirt in Italy. Their religion, Catholicism, makes divorce unlikely. The wife doesn't care about her spouse's extramarital affairs as long as she holds on to her wedding ring. The only person who can really lose out is the other woman.)

THE FRENCHMAN. Gallantry seems to lie in a Frenchman's attitude, not his actions. You can wait all day for him to open a car door, produce a *jeton* for a telephone call or peel his own fresh peach. These are services that he expects *you* to do for *him*. But when the subject is sex, he's delighted to take charge. He will go to enormous lengths just to provide such props as moonlight, candlelight, Degas etchings, Debussy preludes and a delightful pied-à-terre overlooking the Quai Voltaire. He is egotistical, sure of his manhood and quite confident that he is the world's sexiest creature. Because of this confidence, he likes his women to be witty, talented and accomplished.

THE SOUTH AMERICAN AND SPANIARD. He prefers women who are fragile, feminine and responsive to the arts of music, ballet and, naturally, love. Customs of other countries appall him. He is shocked, for instance, by the Englishman who prefers dinner at his club to a date with a blonde. His aim is to conquer. Making you feel like a woman makes him feel like a man. Compliments, oglings, and lengthy propositions are his *taza de té*. His is the happiness of pursuit. The more he chases you, the happier he is, so the game is to prolong resistance as long as possible. However, keep this in mind: Those same romantic speeches, the lovelorn poems, the "I-die-if-I-don't-win-you" attitude that he practices with you at cocktail time, he will be using five hours later with someone else.

THE IRISHMAN. If you are hunting for a husband from old Erin, do your looking in Boston, not Dublin. The marriage rate is appallingly low in Ireland, and takes a lot of luck and hard work to land a man. Irish men are mother-dominated; they look for a girl just like the girl who married dear old dad. A girl can start going steady with one man at seventeen—and find she's still doing it at forty. The slang for *courtship* is *lines*, and the lines are long.

Despite all the talk about blarney, the modern Irishman rarely makes complimentary speeches. When he does, he might go as far as, "You're not looking bad tonight." He dances well, golfs, swims, plays tennis, is lively, amusing, good fun, but hardly rates the term *sexy*. As one Irish girl put it to me, "You're more than safe ninety-nine times out of a hundred—that's why so many Irish girls leave home!"

THE ENGLISHMAN. The over-thirty man is often still a bachelor who has remained deeply attached to the Queen, his mother, his nanny, his club and his collection of cricket bats.

The English male of any age has good manners. Always the perfect gentleman, he will make his pitch casually. For instance, "How about it, my deah?" over a cup of tea or a glass of warm beer. If rejected, he takes it with a stiff upper lip; there will be no scene. But the average Englishman is more on the make than the Continentals. (One friend insists that "Every Englishman has the soul of a Profumo.")

Once away from the rigors of weather and the British caste system, the Englishman expands into the gayer, sophisticated human being that makes him a favorite with American women.

OTHERS: BRAZILIANS like their women beautiful, but it helps if you have both a face *and* a fortune. The DUTCH prize cleanliness and cooking; sport a shiny skin, talk about food and you'll go over big in Amsterdam. The ISRAELIS are independent, virile, attractive and the bonds of matrimony are not too tight. They are a hardy breed, too, for they have been trained in warfare since the age of sixteen.

In addition to classification according to nation, there are certain universal types that know no boundaries, to wit:

190

THE REMITTANCE MAN. This type is not limited to Somerset Maugham novels or remote islands of the Pacific. You can find him anywhere surroundings are picturesque and living is cheap. In fact, there is a new breed that abounds in Majorca, Ibiza, the lesser Caribbean islands, and other offbeat spots—the American university graduates living on a pittance supplied by a businessman dad to keep sonny out of the family business and the family's hair. Sonny supplements the remittance from home by doing occasional piloting, skin diving, or selling multicolored cork ashtrays. Rarely does he need new clothes; his uniform consists of shorts, cotton shirt and sandals. For women, he usually depends on local talent.

Doing the palm-tree circuit one winter, I arrived at Cozumel, Yucatan, and the first night there I felt I had walked into a Maugham short story. A nice-looking man, ex-Harvard, ex-playboy, invited me to have a drink. He seemed eligible and I accepted. I couldn't have been more wrong. The ex-patriot had not one but *two* female roommates in his thatched hut. They were dark-skinned sisters, Nola and Lorna, who had come with him to Cozumel because life had become too hectic back home on Grand Cayman. It was a perfect design-for-living setup, with only two problems: The man had a wife and three children back in Connecticut, and the two sisters didn't speak to each other.

These remittance types can prove very useful for learning spearfishing while you're on an island, but don't expect to reform them and lure them back to a rose-covered Iowa cottage.

THE GIGOLO. This type comes in two varieties: amateur and professional. The former is content with an evening on the town; the latter seeks a new way of life. Both expect you to foot the bills. Any lady in search of a gigolo can find one in any of the flashier hotel bars. From then on, proceed at your own risk, but know what you are doing. And watch your purse.

THE QUOTA SEEKERS. Many foreign men are eager to marry American girls—not for their charm or money, but because of the quota system of United States Immigration Laws, which limits admissions from some countries. It's up to the girl to decide whether her suitor is motivated by true love or by his desire to enter the United States outside the quota as a spouse of a citizen.

THE UNWANTED MALE. In any country in the world, you will meet the man in whom you have no interest. Whether he is a missionary who wants to reform you or a crook after your good American dollars, a virile youth who aims to seduce you or just an uninvited pest, the problem is to get rid of him. The solution is slightly more difficult on foreign soil than in the United States, because foreign men find it quite hard to believe that you don't find them irresistible. However, there are some time-tested techniques:

Wear a wedding ring. A simple gold band from the dime store lends you authority when you say demurely, "My husband doesn't like me to go out with other men."

Use the "I'm-too-busy" approach. Tell the unwanted gentleman that you're taking a tour and you've already paid for it. This works particularly well in large cities. Just as no New Yorker wants to visit the Statue of Liberty, no Parisian wants to spend hours tramping through the Palace of Versailles.

Tell white lies. You can always suffer from tourist stomach, be too tired, have a job assignment you must do.

But be sure you really *don't* want that male. Don't let middle-class conventionality ruin what might be an exciting adventure. A fan of the French theater, I had spent several evenings watching the Jean-Louis Barrault repertory troupe. At *Amphitryon* and *The Cherry Orchard,* I was particularly intrigued with the performance and personality of the blond leading man.

After this intensive exposure to the Barrault company, I was going through the Galeries Lafayette one afternoon, when I saw a blond gentleman whose face was familiar enough to be someone from back home. I nodded a polite greeting.

To my surprise the gentleman burst into words. French words. *"Comment ça va?"* he hailed.

Startled, I looked closely at him and realized it was the repertory company star. Only this time he wasn't Jupiter, just charm personified. I had become so well acquainted with him from the audience during the past week that I thought I knew him. I was embarrased.

He was undaunted. "Have you eaten yet?" he asked. "Perhaps you would care to join me."

To my amazement I heard myself saying, "Oh, I'm so sorry, but I can't."

The moment that I realized what I had said (a direct quotation from my maiden aunt) I could have thrown myself into the Seine.

The stage star, unaccustomed to such rebuffs, was already heading in the direction of Men's Underwear. Some months later he married his leading lady. I've always wondered what might have happened if we had broken French bread together.

22. MONEY, OF COURSE

Nothing is much more depressing than poverty . . . especially your own. The poor little match girl is a *drag*, but than so is Miss Rich Bitch flinging her money around. Truly, solvency is downright sexy and knowing the rules of contemporary Money Games is a boost to your poise and confidence. How you handle money is revealing. Are you a parasite? A sloth? Or, hopefully, a sorceress? No matter how little money you earn, you *can* pay your way. And even when you've plunged and gone too far, common sense, imagination, and a little *class* will help camouflage your personal recession.

How to Open a Charge Account

Nothing—not even star sapphires—will make you feel quite so rich as walking around with three dollars in your Gucci handbag (bought at a half-price sale) and thousands of dollars of potential credit . . . symbolized by a hefty handful of celluloid credit cards. Respect the intoxicating danger of credit and enjoy the thrill. It's a joy to buy when the mood strikes even if you don't get paid till next Thursday. And it's elegant to take a man to lunch and pay without fumbling for change or counting wrinkled dollar bills and worrying that one more martini is going to wipe out bus fare home. (Keep a list of them on file with the correct account numbers . . . notify store immediately if the cards are lost or stolen.)

Alas, some befuddled creatures were born to abuse charge plates. They live in a dream world where the magic words "Charge it" mean you *never* have to pay. To keep a good credit rating, pay bills *promptly* or at least make a token payment if the grand total is clearly beyond your bank account for the next few weeks.

Revolving charge accounts are particularly dangerous. All you are obligated to pay is $10 (or in some cases 20 percent to 25 percent) of the bill and a "tiny" interest charge is added to the balance each month. If you bother to read the fine print, you will realize you are paying 18 to 23 percent interest a year for the privilege of extended credit. *Always read the fine print.* And also try to avoid these.

If you are new in town, or want to open your first charge account, credit references are necessary. Don't panic. If you have ever paid a telephone or electricity bill or even rent, that's credit. And unpaid utility bills in one town can follow you to the next like a little black cloud of doom. And that black mark on your credit rating is tough to live down ... even when it's the store's mistake. So straighten out mysterious overcharges and errors at once. If you can't pay a bill due to a serious fiscal emergency, call the credit manager and explain, instead of simply ignoring it . . . give him some idea of when you hope to pay. That call may persuade him to avoid filing a complaint immediately.

Your Investment Portfolio

Once you hit the upper brackets you can hire a full-time money doctor to handle your investments. But perhaps even now you have a few dollars to stash away, or maybe a few thousand from an unexpected bonus or inheritance. The stock market? Well, the market was a joyride for a few years and then the boom was over. Now you need caution and a well-known investment firm, one with patience for the small investor, to take on your mini-account. Or you may decide to trust your hoard to a mutual fund or a savings account.

Why not take a course in investing? Or start an investment club, co-ed, of course. You'll learn about money and make new friends, too, lining up speakers, interviewing brokers, attending stockholders meetings.

Before accepting anyone's advice, it is wisest to read up on the market and its mechanisms. Learn the market jargon: The New York Stock Exchange, 11 Wall Street, New York, N.Y. 10005, will send free literature. If you're in New York, do take a jaunt around the Exchange on a free guided tour.

Excellent sources of information include: *The Money Game,* by "Adam Smith"; Ira Cobleigh's *Happiness Is a Stock that Doubles in One Year,* Random House; Morton Schulman's *Anyone Can Make a Million,* John Kenneth Galbraith's fascinating study of 1929, *The Great Crash.* Classics in stock-market literature include Gerald M. Loeb's *The Battle for Investment Survival* and Benjamin Graham's *The Intelligent Investor.* In paperback try *How to Buy Stock* by Louis Engel.

How to Pay for a Man

One of the most delicious dividends of being a successful career woman is the joyful "duty" of taking a man to lunch . . . buying drinks for him or even dinner. As a publicist, editor, researcher, buyer, department chief, account executive, lawyer, photographer's agent . . . you have a chance to eat lunch with men you'd *never* see after dark (he's married or you are, or he's jet-set social and you're upwardly mobile but not *that* mobile). *Six* men could be eager to hear the details of the new campaign you've thought up . . . or just an evasive author or salesman may drift by not quite noticing you until he's stopped with a question or comment and the suggestion you two discuss it over lunch.

Lunch is on you. How do you pay? The man who is often taken to lunch by women won't squirm or duck as you study the check, quickly go over the addition (let's hope you're not a cretin at math), compute the tip, deposit the cash on the table or surrender your credit card.

Unfortunately, even with the Women's Lib banners flying, some otherwise sophisticated men are still uncomfortable when the woman pays . . . *maddening*, but there it is. As a militant feminist you might think, "Tough luck, let him squirm. He has to learn." As a secure and considerate enchantress, pamper his ego and banish his ill ease. There is one superbly silky way to handle the situation. Take him to a restaurant or club where your firm has a charge account. Instruct the maitre d'hôtel or manager to *allot* the tips and send the bill to your office. Sign the check at the front desk as you leave or, if they know you, you won't even need to sign. No flash of green is even seen . . . no sign of a check disturbs the mood.

Even if your firm has no charge accounts, make a similar arrangement at any restaurant where you are known . . . or at any somewhat sophisticated place. Arrive a few minutes ahead. Explain to the manager or maitre d'hôtel that you want to sign in advance . . . that he should add the proper tips without presenting the bill. I once took the New York *Times* food critic, Craig Claiborne, to lunch at a front-rank French restaurant. To avoid a fuss over who might pay, I presented Madame La Proprietresse with an envelope of bills . . . more than enough for lunch, I was sure, asked her to distribute the tips and return the balance. As we left, Madame whispered that my funds were just a little bit short but "Don't worry . . . it was nothing." I hadn't figured on a $14 *dollar* bottle of wine. I made up the difference later. Well, anyway . . . you see it *can* be done with cash too. No reputable restaurant would ever abuse this liberty. And I assume you wouldn't try it in a fly-by-night tourist trap.

If you want to preserve male ego but don't have the time or patience to spin this elaborate cocoon of finesse, then just master these rules of thoughtfulness:

1. He asks for menus. Just because you're paying doesn't mean he abdicates the usual male prerogatives.

2. Let him suggest, especially if he knows the restaurant, and order. If the waiter asks you a direct question, answer the waiter.

3. You suggest wine . . . "Don't you think we ought to have half a bottle of wine with this?" but let him ask for the wine list and choose.

4. Let him ask for the check (at your request), and if he seems sheepish, remind him in a light way that it's your *company* that's paying. "Isn't it marvelous to spend two hours over lunch and let DDD&Q pay for everything" . . . or . . . "Capitalism can't be all bad when it lets the Internal Revenue Service buy us lunch." Or . . . "My company could afford to feed us like this every day now that we have three books on the best-seller list."

5. He may feel he just *can't* give in and make one last effort to pay. Say, "But I *must* pay . . . my office is being picketed by Women's Lib" . . . or . . . "Today fulfills my Women's Lib pledge." Not too heavy, of course. If he still insists, surrender.

6. No need to wrestle him at the checkroom . . . it's only 50 cents. Let him pay . . . but have the change ready just in case he slips off to the Men's Room.

7. If he is an office chum and you're splitting the check, let him pay and give him your share at the office, not on the street.

8. If several of you are splitting a check, it's silly to start toting each individual order—"I had the cottage cheese, Kathy had eggs Benedict, Ruth had franks and beans." Divide equally unless someone's share is really considerably less. Then say, "Jenny didn't have drinks, wine or dessert, so I charged her two dollars less."

9. If someone neglects to pay his share, it is perfectly proper to give a verbal nudge: "Your share of lunch yesterday came to $6.25 with the tip."

Extracurricular Entertainment

One of the smoothest possible ways to pay for a man's dinner out-of-town is to invite him to your hotel room and order from room service. Just sign the check. I'm assuming you *want* to be alone with him, though.

If he is usually penniless because he is an artist, a student, or an organic farmer, and is your guest for dinner in a restaurant, pretend your company is paying, even if it isn't. If he seems doubtful, insist. Make a big thing about how clever the two of you are to manage dinner at an employer's expense. If *he* happens to be your employer . . . for goodness' sake, why are *you* paying?

How to Be Blissful Though Broke

What a bore being broke . . . let's hope it's just a transitory torment. Your first job pays a pittance, or you are "fashionably unemployed" (no joke even if you're not alone in the unemployment office line).

Don't crawl into a cave. You want a social life, a chic fresh image, friends to cheer you until the crisis is over. Definitely you do *not* wish to be known as the town cheapskate. Remember:

1. You're "a little low" or "looking for a new job"—no need to apologize constantly for being broke.
2. Stop sighing over what might have been, or . . . if only.
3. More affluent friends *don't* want to hear how lucky they are

Pinch-Penny Shopping

I once wrote an article called "How the World's Richest Families Pinch Pennies." There was the staggeringly rich Chicago matron who bought her golf dress in Marshall Field's basement . . . an elderly dowager in Detroit whose chauffeur drove her to a discount store to buy damaged yarn for her knitting . . . a prominent New York heiress who stewed prunes overnight on the pilot light of her stove—to save about half-a-cent worth of gas. Economy isn't just practiced by *you*.

Luxuries that you need and frivolities that make you more beautiful and happy are sometimes more important than *staples*. For example, convenience foods may be a wild extravagance or they may *not*. Sometimes frozen orange juice is cheaper than fresh-squeezed, or fresh spinach costs twice as much as frozen. Usually fresh vegetables in season are cheaper *and* better. Read prices as well as amounts on labels as if you were about to sign a contract!

Protein does more for your body than carbohydrates; put your money into eggs, cottage cheese, meat, chicken, fish and lots of green vegetables (some diet experts say you need *nothing* but these two kinds of food, plus a little fat). We *know* you can banish bonbons, chips and dips, carbonated drinks, imported crackers, and starchy snacks from your life. *Everything* will profit—skin, figure, and budget. Protein needn't mean sirloin or chopped chuck . . . try frozen flounder fillets at about 60 cents a pound. Sipping iced water from a thin crystal goblet is more elegant than drinking ginger ale from a jelly glass.

Never let yourself fall apart in the name of economy or self-pity. Be frank with the hairdresser. Tell him money is a little tight. Ask if he will let you shampoo at home and come in for a set. Or trust your limp ringlets to apprentice hands at a community beauty school . . . free or at a big discount.

Never economize on *cleanliness*. But escape the clutches of a costly dry cleaner and spiff up a bundle of knits and woolens for pennies in an automatic dry-cleaning machine.

Shop off-season and haunt the sale rack. March is the time to buy ski clothes and winter coats. In late summer bathing suits and sports clothes are a steal. Check discount stores and the local five-and-dime for summer handbags, sandals, costume jewelry, cotton gloves, hankies, hair ribbons—even rich girls are refusing to succumb to luxury items at full price. Browse through thrift shops, too. I once found an unlined fox skin for $2 that is now my sexiest and warmest fur cossack hat. An old evening bag for a dollar or two is an absolute treasure. No one will know it wasn't your grandmother's.

Read the labels. Don't wash when it says "dry-clean only" . . . if it says "hand-washable," by all means follow instructions. *Don't* toss into the machine.

If tiny, you can buy in children's departments. Look there, too, for boots, shoes, bags at considerable savings.

Minis are now tunics. Pants cut down become gauchos. If you sew, that satin dress might become smarty pants. Don't just lengthen last year's wardrobe . . . go through the closet and rethink belts, sleeves, pockets, hems. A drapery cord becomes a perfect belt. Some odds and ends of silk are now a patchwork evening skirt. Adapt. Improvise! And do learn at least to put up a hem.

Everything you need has its season. The following table lists the best months to buy, according to store sales, special promotions, clearances.

Air conditioners: February, August

Appliances (small): January, February

Bedding: January, February, June, August

Books: January (or second-hand bookstores)

Building materials, lumber: June

Cars, new: September (before the new models come out)

Cars, used: February, November, December

China, glassware: January, February, September

Coats, women's: February, April, August, October, November, December

Curtains: February, August

Dresses: January, April, June

Drugs, cosmetics: January

Fabrics: April, July

Foundations, lingerie: January, April, June

Furs: January, July, August

Housewares, furniture: January, February, June, July, August, September, October

Linens, blankets: January, February, March, May, August, November

Luggage: May

Piece goods: June, September, November

Radios, stereos, refrigerators: January, February, July

Ranges: April, October, November

Rugs: January, February, July, August

Shoes: April, June (men's: January, July)

Silverware: February
Sportswear: January, February, July
Television sets: May, June
Toys: January, February, November

Mother Hubbard Entertaining

Do what you do with style and confidence and no one will suspect it's a brink-of-bankruptcy celebration! For a dinner party that costs only a few cents per person, brew a giant cauldron of chili; serve with home-baked bread (comes to about 20 cents a loaf). Get your date to supply a keg of beer. Or give a progressive dinner with several girl friends. Each prepares a different course and the party moves from one house to the next, devouring the feast. *You* do the soup course—a fabulous cold pumpkin soup with sour cream floating on orange slices . . . or how about *dessert*—a darkly wicked chocolate mousse or apple dumplings with topping that is half whipped cream, half sour cream, scented with fresh-grated nutmeg. Later . . . espresso coffee with anisette and curls of lemon peel. Shop the specials for that week. Use only seasonal produce. Don't attempt something you've never tried before. Fill pitchers or lovely old bowls with wild flowers—free from the fields—or homemade paper flowers . . . or great bunches of parsley tied with green velvet ribbon, or weeds. You'll be eating parsley on everything until it wilts, but it's good for you! Why not a bring-your-own-bottle wine tasting . . . you peel, slice, and sliver a giant bowl of fresh vegetables and do a piquant watercress dip for these. Offer chunks of French bread to clear the palate between bottles and, for a late supper, linguini with a zesty *pesto* sauce, mixed green salad, and coffee.

Gifts Without a Price Tag

The gift you make yourself is infinitely precious unless you happen to be one of those rare unfortunates with ten thumbs and no imagination. Then the priceless gift you can give is *time* (see Part Two, chapter 18 for more gifting ideas). Give more thoughtfully than ever now that you are broke. Some examples:

Homemade-anything-to-eat: Rose-hip jam, orange-sour cream cake loaf, pecan crescent cookies, pickled carrots, pineapple chutney, your own curry mix, sugared pecans, chicken liver *pâté* in a 69-cent earthenware crock.

Funny old side table, $2 from the Salvation Army, transformed by you with a *faux* marble or tortoise-shell finish.

Spicy pomander ball, clove-studded orange with a pretty ribbon to hang it by.

Papier-mâché cherub for the Christmas tree.

199

Tablecloth made of fifteen giant bandanna hankies sewn together; matching napkins.

Anything crocheted or knitted.

Anything in patchwork.

Sachet of dried flowers; or a dried flower arrangement, tied with velvet ribbon.

Your time as a baby-sitter, cupboard-paper liner, or chauffeur . . . library rearranger . . . or Christmas shopper for a busy friend.

Now, what can *you* add to our list? Write it down. And if you know you aren't going to be affluent by *next* Christmas make your "homemade" list in the spring or summer and start work no later than May. Don't be surprised if you look back on it as the most rewarding Christmas of your life.

Everything You Ought to Know about Tipping (even though you may not want to know!)

Tipping is an art. There is the standard tip you *always* give, the "thank-you tip" to the person who is extra nice, the bribery tip that says, "Look how nice I am . . . now take care of me." And there is the tip that says, "Isn't it fun to work for a princess like me?" and the "I-bet-you-didn't-know-how-much-I-appreciate-you tip." Then there are the monster Christmas tips that sting like blackmail.

Is tipping your Waterloo? Are you Lady Bountiful to friends and stingy as Scrooge to nameless outstretched palms? Overtipping is *supposed* to be bad manners, and it's true that Miss Rich Bitch brassily papering the room with green is often buying sneers and snickers rather than the love she dearly craves. But *adequate* tipping is simply required of a seventies girl. And gracious *overtipping* is *never* wrong. It's an *attractive* excess . . . to say thank-you in cash, with a smile and a compliment, and *mean* it.

"Overtipping" may also be an intelligent, rational compromise with the realities of life. You are outrageously generous to the cleaning lady because she is a gem and you can't replace her. Or you ask yourself: What would it cost me if I had to contract for this service? That's what my friend Carol does. Carol is a rich, traveling sales representative with an apartment on Park Avenue and two cats she adores. Whenever she is away overnight she tips one of the doormen to feed her cats. "I could probably get away with $1 a day, but I give him $2," Carol says. "It takes him all of four minutes . . . but I *love* my cats. I am a comfortably-fixed lady and it would cost me $2 a day *each* to put them in a kennel; so I still save $2 a day! I *don't* tip the man who sorts the mail . . . he is boring, fresh, and drives me up the wall."

Christmas cash may sound a bit crass, but there's really no substitute for negotiable greenery. Crinkly new bills in a gift envelope with a compliment and a thank-you soften the crass. Never give *naked* money . . . *always* a personal note. Most thoughtful of all: a gift *with* your cash or check. It can be something that costs pennies—fudge or fruit-cake you made yourself, or a little wooden Santa for the Christmas tree, or something special, hopefully not a cliché ordered wholesale by the dozens and handed out perfunctorily to everyone who passes, but something chosen especially for *that* person. Even more thoughtful . . . a gift for his children . . . a book for a new reader, an "Instant Replay" game for the football fan, Raggedy Ann towels for five youngsters under eight.

You are not Happy Rockefeller or Raquel Welch and no one expects you to tip as they do. You work hard for your salary, which is splintered and torn by taxes. (Of course, so does Raquel and so is *her* salary.) Know what is expected in tips and what is wise . . . to wring the biggest dividends from your tipping dollars.

And of course you will bravely halve the standard tip or leave nothing at all if you're seriously insulted, neglected, or harassed. You'll feel better by *explaining* the holdback . . . tell the manager or headwaiter or cabby . . . "You've gone a mile out of the way, dropped me off on the wrong side of the street, and insulted me for the last three blocks. . . . I'm saving your tip for the Salvation Army." If really mad, tell City Hall . . . the Better Business Bureau . . . the police . . . or the anti-discrimination council.

Ready now! (If you ever feel perhaps you're being a little chintzy when you tip, it's probably because you *are!*)

DELIVERY BOYS AND MESSENGERS: At least a quarter, perhaps more in storms and blizzards (especially if your company is paying). Your *regular laundry and cleaners' delivery man*, $5 at Christmas or 50 cents each time. The *United Parcel man*, a gift or cash at Christmas if he knocks himself out getting packages to you when you're almost never home. A quarter to the boy who carries your groceries to the car.

DOORMEN, SUPERINTENDENT, JANITORS, MAINTENANCE MEN, ELEVATOR OPERATORS IN THE APARTMENT HOUSE: For any special service beyond the call of duty, $1, $2, or $5, depending on the service and rent, (i.e., no tip for repairing the plumbing, but definitely something for putting up the bookcase). Most of the staff is tipped at Christmas, with the total depending on where you live—megalopolis or small town—and how luxuriously. Perhaps 2 to 2½ percent of your yearly rent to be divided prudently, more to your "pets" and champions. Example: If your rent is $120 a month ($1440 a year) . . . you might divide $40 between the doorman ($10), the superintendent ($20), and the janitor ($10). If your rent is $300 a month ($3600 a year) . . . you would divide about $75 between three doormen, two maintenance men, and the superintendent—with more to the ones who help you most, plus an extra little gift, perhaps something for their children.

THE DOORMAN WHO KNOWS YOUR BOYFRIEND IS LIVING THERE. Something extra if he's been sweet and comradely . . . just a standard Christmas tip if he's prissy or rude.

DOORMEN, NOT YOUR OWN. A quarter for getting you a cab. Fifty cents or more if he showed enthusiasm and ingenuity in a driving snow or rain.

TAXICABS. In big cities tip 20 cents on fares of $1 or less, 25 cents on each additional dollar, 20 percent on large fares, and a little extra for special help . . . like actually getting out of the cab to wrestle with a trunk or lugging it up stairs. Small-town tips are lower and often nothing is expected on a fixed-price trip . . . but anything is certainly appreciated. Tip nothing at all . . . or an insulting pittance . . . if mistreated or given a run-around.

PORTER, SKYCAP. The posted per-bag fee plus a little extra. Or 25 cents a bag . . . 50 cents if it's a medium-sized monster. If you pull up to the air terminal in a chauffeured limousine with Hermès luggage and a mink polo coat flung over your arm, tip like an heiress. Play Princess when traveling on an expense account . . . within reason, of course.

AIRPLANE AND AIRPORT PERSONNEL. No tips. Only the Skycap who carries your bag from the baggage claim to the street is rewarded.

TRAINS. Dining-car waiters, 15 percent. The head steward is tipped only if he does something special. Porters, 50 cents for a day trip, 50 cents to $1 per night in a berth, more in spiffier accommodations.

HOTELS. The *bellboy* or *doorman* who unloads luggage from the cab, 50 cents to $2, depending on how you travel, what you carry, and the elegance of the hotel. Same rules apply to the *bellboy* who carries bags to your room. More is needed if you're traveling with pets and wigs and trunks in Elizabeth Taylor style. *Bellmen* get a quarter or 50 cents for a telegram or a parcel delivered to your room, the page boy who summons you for a phone call rates a quarter ($1 if the call is from Warren Beatty). *Chambermaid*, $2 a week or 50 cents a day; 10 percent of the room tab in posh hotels. Leave the money in an envelope marked "chambermaid" when you check out. *Doorman:* 25 to 50 cents if he gets a cab, nothing if he just helps you into a waiting car. *Bell captain:* $1 or more for reservation or special services. *Telephone Switchboard:* No tip is expected, but if you're a phone fiend, why not. I once left a giant box of chocolates for the operators at the Beverly Wilshire Hotel after they had cheerfully serviced more than seventy-five calls in a four-day period. *Room-Service Waiters:* At least a quarter, or 50 cents in deluxe hotels, on a *tiny* check, otherwise 15 to 20 percent of the tab.

MOVING MEN. $5 to $10 for two men, $12 to $15 for four men . . . more for extra services, plus $5 to the elevator starter or janitor who helps . . . $10 if your life-style warrants.

PARKING LOTS. $3 to $5 to each man at your regular garage or lot at Christmas. In transient parking . . . a quarter for delivery of the car . . . 50 cents for a special service, like talking to your dog or tucking your precious Jag into a protected corner.

SERVICE-STATION ATTENDANT. Ordinarily not tipped, but if you find a real hero, bring a reward at Christmas.

CHAUFFEUR. 20 percent of car rental.

BARS. 15 to 20 percent, 15 to 25 cents per person *minimum* for one drink.

FRIENDS' SERVANTS. No tip is necessary on an overnight stay unless you need extra care and handling. On a weekend, $1 or $2 to each person who serves you—maid, waitress, chauffeur . . . more for pampering or help in super-emergencies, like fallen hems and stained chiffons. Give tips just before leaving, as inconspicuously as possible. Remember to smile and say thank-you.

CLEANING LADY. One or two weeks' salary at Christmas time plus a gift. Don't forget her birthday, and $10 extra is nice at Thanksgiving.

RESTAURANTS. In small towns, 10 percent of the check . . . more likely 15 percent. In big cities, 15 percent in ordinary restaurants, 20 to 25 percent on the snob circuit. In elegant restaurants and night clubs, leave 15 percent for the *waiter* . . . five percent (never less than a dollar) is handed to the *captain* (or so designated on the charge you sign). The *wine steward* gets 10 percent on the wine but never less than a dollar. Now and then the *maître d'hôtel* gets $2 or $3 or $5 . . . whenever he saves a special table as requested. The *maître d'* who makes you feel like Princess Yasmin deserves something special at Christmas or for a *"bon voyage"* when he takes his summer vacation. In chic New York gold cuff links from Tiffany's and a few shares of a hot stock are considered proper gifts for a favorite snob *maître d'*! A quarter goes to the *powder-room attendant,* (*so* tacky to sneak off without paying!), 25 or 50 cents to the *hatcheck girl,* a quarter to the *cigarette girl.* No tipping needed in *cafeterias.* In some smaller towns there is no tipping at a *counter.* In New York and other large cities, 15 percent or a minimum of a quarter for sandwich and beverage, a dime on a cup of coffee, is expected.

THE BUTCHER AND FISHMONGER. In New York the butcher is tipped for boning chicken breasts and the clerk in a fish store gets a dime or more for prettying up each fish. I don't approve, but there it is.

AT THE HAIRDRESSER'S. Tips vary from modest in small communities to sheer hysterical madness in the status-salons of Manhattan and Beverly Hills, running from 15 to 35 percent of the entire bill. Give the shampoo girl 20 percent of the shampoo cost, in snob salons at least $1; the manicurist 20 percent of *her* tab. The hairdresser gets 20 percent for whatever he did; again, $2 is minimum in a snob salon. The cloakroom attendant gets a quarter unless she did something special—ran out for your yogurt or tuna sandwich, then 50 cents. The owner-operator and his wife the manicurist are sometimes tipped, but in some communities tradition says no. When you don't know local custom, offer the tip and if it is refused, simply say, "Oh, of course . . . I see." No one is offended. In fashionable salons do not tip the resident genius-owner. (The *nonowner* genius is tipped extravagantly!) Mr. Kenneth, Marc Sinclaire, and Vidal Sassoon of New York are virtually *buried* in costly goodies every Christmas . . . cases of vintage champagne, ostrich wallets, and gold pillboxes from Cartier's . . . nothing is too excessive for the sorcerer in your life.

23. GENEROSITY IN ALL THINGS

I come from a long line of Generous Spenders, although some people might say Slobby Spenders.

All of my antecedents were lucky enough to be talented, and, with their various talents, they usually earned enough to live with taste and style. They amassed friends, plaques, books, just plain things, and lots of pride; their pride often made it seem necessary for them to continue in these habits long after their financial assets had drained away.

No one among my relatives ever saved a cent for a cloudy day, and when the clouds gathered, they gathered in bunches. But in the curious fashion of families—before analysis convinced us relatives are usually a bad influence—they helped each other, automatically, without guilt, recrimination, or question. They accepted the ebb and flow of fortunes; a fierce sense of loyalty and pride kept everyone in food and warm clothing during the most dire times. No matter how bad things were, somehow a small gift always materialized for every occasion—a handkerchief, a scarf, a homemade coffeecake. And when a visitor arrived, there was always something extra to eat. We had no patience with stinginess and no tolerance for it. Our family measure of stinginess may have been off base by average standards. To some extent we judged other people by their lavish remembrance of occasions and their servings of food. If there wasn't a good portion of food left on the serving dishes after the meal, the hostess was not quite generous! As a result I find it difficult to love anyone who doesn't feed me when I visit.

Was my family buying love? Was much of their generosity merely pride? (But then *is* pride something mere?) I think their pride was perhaps based on the ability to love and to give with genuine pleasure. They enjoyed entertaining and gift-giving because these were creative arts. Beauty and good taste were not formal obligations, but a way of life. The worst insult one could sustain was when the recipient of a gift

205

or a meal said: "But you really shouldn't have . . . " or "How can you afford . . . ?"

People who find great virtue in financial security and great morality in a savings account would, indeed, consider these relatives of mine Slobby Spenders. Generous people always run the risk of being called Slobby Spenders—just as careful spenders run the risk of being considered stingy. But it may be *why* rather than how a person spends his money that makes the difference between the two. For instance, if a person makes a lot of money and feels guilty and uncomfortable, he often compensates by overtipping waiters, porters, cab drivers. That is Slobby Spending. But the person *seems* generous.

Enough of my relatives. Let's discuss where *you* stand.

Suppose you're planning to rent an apartment. If you earn $100 a week and rent an apartment you hate for sixty dollars a month *just* to save money, that is stingy. (Nearly all living-index tables show that it is O.K. to spend a fourth of your income on rent.) With the same income it would also be stingy for you to decide to share an apartment with a roommate when you have never liked living with someone else. Unless you planned to spend all your waking hours out, you'd eventually make yourself *and* your roommate miserable. Conversely, if you're saving your money to go back to college full time, the sixty-dollar unshared apartment makes sense.

Now for the other extreme. With the same income, if you spend $150 on an apartment because it has a chic address, that is probably Slobby Spending. But if your personal environment is *important* to you and you see an apartment with a delightful view—or a terrace, and you love plants—*spend* that $150 and consider yourself generous. (Giving is a habit that starts with *an appreciation of your own pleasure*.)

Stinginess . . . Slobby Spending . . . Generosity. Starting with the least appealing and saving the best—generosity—for last, let's examine them.

STINGINESS is going to lunch with the girls and making an issue over pennies: "But you had a side of coleslaw . . ." or "You had cheese on your hamburger."

STINGINESS is seeing something you *know* your boy friend would really enjoy for his birthday and not buying it because he didn't spend that much on yours.

STINGINESS is asking people to come over for coffee and not having anything but. (Buy a small bottle of domestic brandy and some strawberries and real whipping cream for strawberry-dunking.)

STINGINESS is not having someone over because they haven't had you over and they can afford to more easily.

STINGINESS is not buying yourself a flower-printed bra because no one will see it, anyway.

STINGINESS is always saying, "I would like . . . but I can't afford." It is also not buying candy at the movies because it costs twenty-five cents more.

STINGINESS is saying to a hostess who hasn't much money, "Don't go to any trouble . . . I'll eat first," or "I'll bring my own meat." Don't impose your own mingy feelings on others; they wouldn't have asked you if they hadn't wanted to.

STINGINESS is not staying up to talk with him because you might be docked at the office for being late.

STINGINESS is when he asks you to go to a nice restaurant and you say, "But it's so expensive." Say "Thank you." And don't order something you hate just because it's the cheapest thing on the menu.

STINGINESS is a kind of morbid fear of pleasure—a becoming *accustomed* to discomfort. Stinginess is being afraid to be *too* alive or to enjoy the available delights.

Enough of stinginess! It is a miserable and totally unfeminine attribute that smacks of tight-pursed lips, serviceable white cotton underwear, and a good gray all-purpose winter coat. Stinginess is a censorship of pleasure.

Now for SLOBBY SPENDING:

SLOBBY SPENDING is earning $110 a week and spending $140. It will only make you miserable, inundated with bills, and pressured to a point where you can't enjoy anything you own.

SLOBBY SPENDING is investing twenty dollars in a gift for your boss because "He is used to nice things." Buying gifts for their cost rather than their content is always slobby. And in case you haven't heard, taste is not measured by money, even by expensive bosses.

SLOBBY SPENDING is having more clothes, shoes, hairpieces, furniture, silver cigarette boxes than you can take care of. The labor of upkeep suffocates pleasure.

SLOBBY SPENDING is buying the first new anything because no one else has it yet.

SLOBBY SPENDING is impressing your mother with a big practical gift (color TV?). Send her a smashing bit of costume jewelry you'd really like for yourself.

SLOBBY SPENDING is buying clothes for dogs.

SLOBBY SPENDING is never buying anything really beautiful or expensive that you will have the rest of your life but always collecting junk.

SLOBBY SPENDING is buying five of anything because it's on sale. Or anything that's on sale just because it *is*.

SLOBBY SPENDING is using your credit cards and charges for big purchases when you work freelance.

SLOBBY SPENDING is giving anything solid gold to a man you have known less than six months.

SLOBBY SPENDING is taking a cruise because you might Meet Someone. Take a cruise only if you really want to go where the ship is going.

SLOBBY SPENDING is buying skis, a motorbike, fun fur (when you're over twenty-five), and then asking your parents to pay for it.

SLOBBY SPENDING is having a mink coat and no medical insurance.

SLOBBY SPENDING is having your hair done but not ten dollars to buy your parents an anniversary present.

SLOBBY SPENDING is carting home underground publications, African artifacts, caftans, and handmade sandals so you can pretend to yourself that you are with the In revolution. It's more effective and less expensive to get out and meet people. And they won't *need* impressing with accessories if your *convictions* are in order.

SLOBBY SPENDING is using money instead of energy and time. (You rationalize that you can't possibly make your own hors d'oeuvres or put up a ham.)

SLOBBY SPENDING is buying sterling flatware on time—before you have met THE man.

SLOBBY SPENDING (if you're married) is not saving *any* of the household money for gifts for him, and so it turns out your husband gets the bills for his own presents.

SLOBBY SPENDING is serving pâté and filet mignon to people you want to impress. (Save it for your man and feed the others antipasto and fettuccine.) Similar slobbiness is taking a rich girl friend to the most expensive restaurant in town, and then taking the girl who really loves you to a coffee shop on her birthday.

SLOBBY SPENDING is paying ten dollars to be seen at a fashion luncheon, pledging only five to the charity involved, and telling yourself you contributed fifteen dollars to charity. *Go* to the luncheon, but admit it's for your own pleasure, and if you really *care*, go lick envelopes.

Now for the good thing, GENEROSITY. The thin red line between SLOBBY SPENDING and GENEROSITY is almost always: Is this thing bought (given, donated, served) with love (pleasure, conviction)? If so, it's probably GENEROSITY.

GENEROSITY is giving presents if it isn't a birthday.

GENEROSITY is *budgeting* for entertaining and gifts so you don't go into shock because those records you gave him or that little dinner for four cost fifty dollars. If you earn that one hundred dollars a week, try to put forty dollars a month aside for play—and presents. Keep your gifts around two dollars to five dollars. It can be done.

GENEROSITY is giving services when you can't give money. Spend an hour a week as a volunteer nurse's aide at a local hospital, supervise children at a day-care center, or read to elderly people at a home for the aged. Baby-sit for a couple you like. And don't meow about how you'd like to give them something . . . but. . . .

GENEROSITY is not getting yourself so strapped that you can't stop talking about being broke. It's having the grace not to make others uncomfortable.

GENEROSITY is learning not even to *wonder* about whether your gift to them cost more than their gift to you.

GENEROSITY is not commenting on the cost of things all the time. If you think someone is overdoing, *never* say "Why did you make such a fuss?" or "You're always so *fancy!*" or "Don't those fresh flowers cost a fortune?" That is just horrid. Generosity is being able to enjoy taking a little.

GENEROSITY is, if a girl friend is strapped, taking her to lunch and not saying a word about her finances.

GENEROSITY is not calling your parents collect and also not calling them just on holidays or when you have a problem. If they lived in town, you'd have them for dinner sometimes, wouldn't you?

GENEROSITY is telling your man, "I have free tickets for. . . ." They weren't. You know when you *have* to lie.

GENEROSITY is buying yourself some small but pretty new thing after you have been penny-pinching and acting ratty to everyone because you felt deprived. Martyrs are not lovable.

GENEROSITY is having your relatives over and asking some of your friends, too. Don't always make relatives feel as though they're an obligation.

GENEROSITY is when someone admires something like your felt-tip pen or ladybug stickpin and you give it to them—not because you can get another one easily, anyway, but because you enjoy their delight.

GENEROSITY is learning to give without feeling self-righteous—learning not to snarl at strangers, or salespeople, even when you've gone around all day wanting to sink your teeth into someone's ankle. It's learning that a salesclerk will not mind if you don't buy something if you say, "Thank you for your time" and that a simple "I love it, but I can't afford it" is better than a critical "That costs too much."

GENEROSITY is concerned more with an attitude toward living than with a precise expenditure of money. Keep your mind and your hand open—both to give and receive. Your purse will take care of itself.

24. THE ART OF APOLOGY

Apology, if used properly, can be a powerful means of communication. As such, it can be very hard to do; it seems much easier, sometimes, to try and forget the whole thing and hope the other person will, too. But suppose you make a mistake while drawing a picture: do you *leave* the messy line, hoping no one will notice, or do you go back and erase it? It all depends on what you want *your* picture to look like, just as it depends on how you want to *come through* to other people.

Done well, apology is a simple act of erasure. It clears the record, and in so doing can banish anger and hurt feelings. It seems agonizingly difficult *only* if, instead of apologizing for one isolated act or series of acts, you feel as though you are apologizing for your whole existence. Nobody wants or expects you to grovel and say, "I'm sorry I'm me, I'm a total washout." That sort of thing only makes other people think. "If she *says* she's such a washout, probably she *is*." Good apologizing is, above all, accurate. Know what you are apologizing *for* and stick to it—don't overload it. Learn to apologize and keep your dignity.

However, for a lot of people, the simple process of saying "I'm sorry. I was wrong," is simply loaded with irrelevant associations—"cathected," as the psychiatrists say. Take, for instance, Mary Jane, who has an exaggerated belief in the power of apology. "I'm sorry, I'm sorry, I'm sorry," she says incessantly, in a ticlike fashion, hardly even realizing she's saying it. Scolded her boss finally, after a long period of patience, "Mary Jane, *stop* apologizing. Sometimes I even think you're apologizing for existing." "I'm sorry," said Mary Jane, "I'll try to stop." What did the boss want to do then? Right—give her a pop in the chops. Mary Jane isn't *really* sorry about existing, or anything else—her motives are much darker. She wants everyone else to say, "Oh, Mary Jane, it's all *right. Don't be sorry, you're right and I'm wrong, you poor dear, how could I have wounded you so?"* This is what she'd *like* to accomplish, she thinks—but the fact is nobody likes to be made to feel guilty all the time, so the result is she infuriates everybody—which might be what she really wants to do underneath everything. Layers upon layers! Mary Jane is a little, self-effacing girl, a background person, a reflector of other people's ideas and dress and opinions—and unfortunately the only way she's found so far to get much reaction out of people around her is her constant abrasive apologizing.

The reason apologizing gets so loaded with meaning for some people is that the notion of being wrong and being punished for it is so basic, even though apology—as it *should* be used—is a very sophisticated concept. Some mothers make the mistake of constantly exacting apologies from their children when they do something wrong (which Mary Jane's mother might well have done). "Susie, apologize to Mrs. Jones for getting her rug wet. . . . Apologize to your brother for taking his toys. . . . Apologize to Mommy for not eating your lunch and wasting all that good food." If Susie apologizes, she is off the hook—a policy she may follow all her life. She will think that apologizing has the automatic effect of undoing a wrong, and it will be a hard blow to find that some awful thing she has done has *consequences*, something her mother never bothered to teach her. Imagine Susie twenty years later, already with a police record—she has become a sociopath. She ignores traffic laws, she overdraws at the bank, she runs up huge charge accounts that she can't pay. She's *terribly* sorry afterward, everybody—*so* sorry, and then she goes out and does the same thing again. It wasn't much of a step to minor shoplifting, and she couldn't believe it when she found herself apologizing to the boys at the local precinct—and they weren't listening. "But I've *said* I'm sorry!" cried Susie indignantly, as they booked her. "I'm *sorry!* I'm *sorry!* What more do you want?"

All girls with mothers like Susie's don't end up in jail, of course. Some women, also believers in Apology Power, are always trying to get *other* people to apologize—usually men. (This was once more fashionable than it is now, as in old movies: "Carl, I think you owe me an apology for . . . last night." "I'm terribly sorry, Alice. I lost my head.") The sound of a man apologizing apparently satisfies a profound need in a lot of women, but men seldom apologize.

This unfortunate pair of facts is one of the essentials in the war between the sexes (which is still going on, unisex or not). Listen to Alice sobbing on the phone to her girl friend several years later: "And can you imagine . . . he *admits* he was sleeping with her and he *knows* how miserable I am and *he won't even apologize!*" What's happened to Carl, who used to be so sorry all the time for his bestiality? He never meant it, that's what. He apologized to Alice—not *constantly* (never!) but occasionally, to make her feel powerful—because he knew few things had such a heady, aphrodisiac effect on her. Martinis, subdued lights, sexy music, and a good, well-placed apology. And now—"He never apologizes to me anymore, never! I'll bet he apologizes to *her* all the time!" And the fact is that if Carl *did* apologize to Alice, in the right way, there is no doubt she'd forgive and forget. What's the matter with the man—and all men, as a matter of fact? If they realized where a little smart apologizing could get them, they'd develop it into the high and subtle art it deserves to be.

But most men (and some women, although this does seem to be much more characteristic of men) regard apology as a face-losing act. They can't be sorry about anything. "Jim wouldn't apologize if he ran over you with a truck," says one girl of the man in her life. "The word 'sorry' isn't in his vocabulary—except when he tells me I'm a sorry sight." Jim won't give in to what he feels is a female trait, and in a way he's right. A lot of women really *enjoy* apologizing, just as they enjoy a good breast-beating session or a good, tearful, bleeding-heart confession. But the notion of being a tiny bit feminine terrifies Jim, poor Jim. Or could it be that he doesn't even apologize because he's so hostile he's *glad* he did all the mean things he did? This is unlikely, unless he's downright sick; more likely those mean words and deeds come out of fear, and apologizing for them would be giving up his defenses, giving up the very things that saved him. He must stick to his guns or lose his substance.

This, of course, is the crux of the matter. It is much less important to women to stick to their guns; they frequently slide and slither between varying points of view with an ease that men find appalling. They not only find it appalling—they are continually asking women *how* they can be so self-contradictory, so changeable, and *why* on earth they keep saying things that have to be apologized for afterward? Why don't they just shape up? (Or, why can't a woman be like a man?) But since they obviously can't, and since they see nothing wrong with changing their minds, women look upon apology as a necessity, something to make the world more pleasant and digestible, like good table manners. You just do it, that's all. While to men apologizing is tantamount to throwing down arms, running up the white flag, coming out with hands held high. And that, possibly, is why women are after them to do it all the time!

How To Apologize The Right Way

1. Make your apologies count. Ration them out like rare pearls. (They aren't *really* like table manners—you don't blow on your soup six days out of the week so everyone will be grateful when you don't on the seventh.)

2. Don't say you're sorry unless you mean it. All *that* does is make you angry inside like poor Mary Jane. And be specific. If at 8, in the restaurant, you discover that you forgot to bring the concert tickets, which *you* were supposed to bring, and John or Joe tells you (directly or indirectly) that you're an incompetent, unreliable nincompoop, *all* you

need to apologize about is forgetting the tickets—*not* for being a nincompoop; you aren't. And you *should* apologize for not remembering—no nonsense about how since he's the man he should have been responsible for the tickets. If you were to do it, you were the one who goofed. Say you're sorry sincerely and it's up to him to forgive you if he can find it in his heart to do so.

3. To make it easier for him to forgive you *anything*, try to remember the tickets next time. What drives men mad is women who apologize profusely and then do the same thing again the next day. Some women seem to think it's cute to be absentminded and empty-headed, but most men, unless they're terribly avuncular or badly in need of dominating a girl, find it a big bore. Dependability is more attractive in the long run these days.

4. If you're one of those girls who find it difficult to apologize because it feels like selling out to the devil, and yet you *know* how meaningful it could be if you did it, consider this. You and he are having a terrible argument; your whole relationship is at stake; each of you is trying to figure out what the other is getting at, each of you is trying to convey something without giving in. One burning issue is that he is furious because you were (he says) necking with his friend Harry at a party the previous night, besides being scandalously and oversexily dressed, and you're always doing that sort of thing and you are, in fact, an exhibitionist. You don't agree with any of this. You were as usual sexily but not oversexily dressed, and the only thing that could be construed as necking (and *then* only by the farthest stretch of the imagination) was that you brushed cigarette ashes off Harry's shoulder, which you, in fact, dropped there. But, says he, how could you have dropped ashes on his shoulder—what were you doing, straightening his hair? I was *gesturing!* you say. I was telling a story and I *gestured!* He: I told you so—you're an exhibitionist! What he's really saying is, you're mine and don't you dare be sexy to any other man; you're saying, I'm trying you out just a tiny bit to see if you still care. But he's really upset—he wants an apology, though he doesn't say so. You think this is absurd—there's nothing to apologize for, you'd die first. As always in such situations, it doesn't really matter who's right and who's wrong—what matters are your needs and his. He needs some concession from you (even though he might secretly think he's carried this all too far); you're willing to give one but not to admit you were at fault by apologizing. Should you? Can you? Well, at least you can say, "I'm sorry you're upset. I can see how you'd be terribly annoyed," or something similar. That tells him you're on his side, which is what he really wants to be reassured about. Harry and the ashes are really side issues.

5. If you really want to make inroads into his soul with The Perfect Apology, try this. You come on before there's a *demand* for apology. Same situation as above—but he *isn't admitting he's angry. You* know

it, because you caught a glimpse of his frosty smile as you were tidying up Harry's shoulders, but he doesn't know you know. Don't hope it will go away—nothing ever does. Apologize. You can afford to do it, because you have been accused of nothing. You can say something like, "I think I was behaving a little stupidly with Harry last night, and I'm sorry I did—I hope he didn't take it the wrong way, he's kind of conceited." This accomplishes several things. It opens the discussion, it shows you are conscious of your behavior, and it makes Harry a perfect target for both hostilities, which must go somewhere. Above all, it says, "I was wrong, I've changed my thinking," which is exactly what an apology should say, and no more.

25. COEXISTING WITH WOMEN'S LIB

Coexistence with our militant sisters takes intelligence and tact. You cannot stem the tide of Women's Revolution (should you indeed want to) with insult . . . naiveté—"It's all too much for my fragile brain" . . . or praise that damns—"Well, I certainly am for equal pay and childcare centers, but I wouldn't be caught dead without my bra. . . . What are all these Lesbians up to?"

The Women's Liberation movement is many-splendored, multi-splintered, and worthy of *sincere attention*. Even if you think the general idea is *totally* outrageous, you cannot defend your position in ignorance. And, like sex and politics . . . the Women's Lib debate is impossible to avoid.

If you don't know much . . . say, "I just don't know. . . . Tell me what you mean." And then listen . . . *really listen.* "Are you willing to be nothing but a sex object?" you may be asked.

"I love being a sex object," you might reply. "And my husband is a sex object too, and so is Robert Redford. . . . Gender is wonderful . . . but I hope and assume we are more than mere sex objects."

An ideal way to learn more about the movement is to join a consciousness-raising group, or form your own, and subscribe to some activist publications. Try *Up from Under* and *Liberation*, both available from 339 Lafayette Street, New York, N.Y. 10012. Read a few books: a must, *Sexual Politics* by Kate Millett. A selected reading list appears at the end of this chapter.

Meeting once a week, week after week, in consciousness-raising is a kind of group therapy—free. You discuss what it means to you to be a woman . . . what it means in our society . . . what is gender . . . what should it be? You share emotional experiences. Not only do you learn what your sisters are thinking, but you gain friends, identity, kinship, and possibly some surprising insights into your own head. If you don't dig it, just stop going.

Remember, ridicule is a fool's way of argument . . . especially when you may not know enough to ridicule.

When a simple discussion threatens to elevate into a terribly heated emotional bloodletting—neither side is listening, neither one is moved an inch—it is good manners to retreat. Silence is strategic. Your attacker will wind down slowly. And peace is restored, without insult, name-calling or making a fool of yourself . . . or her.

SOME RECOMMENDED BOOKS

1. Bird, Caroline. *Born Female: The High Cost of Keeping Women Down.* McKay, $5.95.
2. De Beauvoir, Simone. *The Second Sex.* Bantam, $1.25.
3. Firestone, Shulamith. *The Dialectic of Sex: The Case for Feminist Revolution.* Morrow, $6.95; Bantam, $1.25.
4. Friedan, Betty. *The Feminine Mystique,* Dell, $0.95.
5. Greer, Germaine. *The Female Eunuch.* McGraw Hill, $6.95.
6. Mead, Margaret. *Male and Female.* Dell, $0.95.
7. Mead, Margaret. *Sex and Temperament.* Dell, $0.95.
8. Millett, Kate. *Sexual Politics.* Doubleday, $7.95.
   (Paperback by Avon available August, 1971).
9. Morgan, Robin, ed. *Sisterhood is Powerful.* Vintage, $2.45.
10. Thompson, Mary Lou, ed. *Voices of the New Feminism.* Beacon, $5.95.

26. A QUICKIE ETIQUETTE QUIZ

Some etiquette rules have stayed the same . . . some have changed. Take this quiz and see how *au courant* you are.

1. A single girl signs business letters to Saks explaining why that minimink payment will be late: (a) Susie Stephens; (b) (Miss) Susie Stephens; (c) Ms. Susie Stephens.

2. A married girl signs letters to Sears asking them to come and repair her lawn mower: (a) Mrs. Crabgrass; (b) Mrs. Anthony Crabgrass; (c) Cleopatra Crabgrass.

3. After sitting on your *derrière* all day, you almost fall flat upon it when, on a crowded bus, a man offers you his seat. You would really prefer to stand. (a) You thank him but say you'd prefer to stand—no explanation; (b) explain why you'd prefer to stand; getting off soon; (c) thank him and sit down.

4. Everybody in your office calls the company president by his first name. It's all very informal. Should you: (a) show him you're informal, too, by using his first name? (b) avoid using any name at all? (c) ask him what you should do?

5. Never again, you've said, but you've done it—accepted a blind date. He suggests that new foreign film, *A Molester and a Pervert.* You say something like: (a) "All right, why not?" (Why give him trouble on his first date with you?) (b) "I'm more the romantic type; could we skip the movie?" (c) "If you don't mind, I'd much prefer to see Dr. Dolittle."

6. It's dirty-joke time. You (a) make it clear you're not that kind of girl; (b) laugh; (c) smile vaguely and drift away.

7. A couple you meet at a cocktail party urge—really urge—you to "drop in anytime." (a) You do just that because you know they really mean it; (b) phone first; (c) forget it, because people never mean what they say at cocktail parties, anyway.

8. You're divorced and the mother of two small children. Your ring is: (a) still on the third finger of your left hand; (b) on the right hand; (c) not worn.

9. You've stayed overnight at the home of your future mother-in-law. Which is most correct? (a) Write a thank-you note? (b) Telephone your thanks? (c) Send a gift?

10. Is there any social occasion when you rise for a man your own age—or even younger? (a) No. (b) Yes.

11. You're going to splurge on some good personal stationery. To be the most correct, should you choose: (a) white or ivory; (b) medium or light blues and grays, ecru, or pale green; (c) stationery with monogram or name and address in scarlet, charcoal, or some other strong color on lighter paper?

12. When introducing your stepchildren, refer to them as: (a) my husband's children; (b) my stepchildren; (c) Bobby and Susie.

13. You don't drink. You're not AA—you just *don't* drink. The office gang invites you to the Friday-after-work blast. You say: (a) "No thanks, I don't drink"; (b) "I'd love to"; (c) "I don't drink, so I'm afraid I'd just be a drag."

14. You must write a message of condolence, but your handwriting is terrible. Also, dozens of people will be sending beautifully penned notes in this case. Should you: (a) type yours; (b) skip it since your note probably won't be missed; (c) take pen in hand, even if you have to print kindergarten style; (d) send a beautiful printed condolence card and sign your name?

15. The waiter's pencil is poised. (a) You give your order to the captain before your escort; (b) wait until your friend orders so you'll know whether to choose Chateaubriand or a chili dog; (c) tell your escort so he can order.

16. You've observed eating, European style—you know—fork in left hand, tines down while meat is cut, then plop meat into your mouth with fork held the same way, same hand. In the United States, this is considered: (a) O.K., if you yourself are European; (b) quite acceptable for anyone, now; (c) incorrect—always change fork to right hand after cutting meat.

17. Suddenly you're receiving birth announcements from every girl you've known since you all wore boots only in bad weather! (a) You buy a gross of silver spoons; (b) send a card or note welcoming each baby into the world; (c) do nothing unless you really want to.

18. What! Elbows on the table? After being yelled at all those years? It's all right now—(a) among friends; (b) between courses; (c) at informal parties, only.

19. You meet friends at a party. It is O.K. to: (a) kiss them on the mouth; (b) on the cheek; (c) kiss men as well as women on mouth or cheek.

20. You're engaged—how wonderful! Your fiancé is called away on a business trip. It's all right for you to go out on a double date if: (a) the man is an old friend; (b) married friends ask you to accompany them and the wife's brother; (c) it's never all right.

Answers

1. (c) Ms. Susie Stephens

2. (c) *Sign*, Cleopatra Crabgrass—then, underneath your signature, type, print, or write clearly: (Mrs. Anthony Crabgrass).

3. (c) Sit! . . swoon! . . thank him! Kiss the hem of his cape even if he looks like Dracula—even if he *is* Dracula.

4. (c) Don't avoid the issue—meet it head on, looking up at him through your fringiest false eyelashes—ask his advice. What are presidents *for?*

5. (c) If he offers a specific alternative—you'd rather see Dr. Dolittle.

6. (b) or (c) If the joke is funny, laugh! You don't have to slap your thigh and roll on the floor in paroxysms of raucous ho hos . . . even a mini-ha ha will do. However, you have to play it by ear. If the joke is *not* funny and is *filthy* (if it starts a chain reaction of filthies), if you're with cretins—pretend to see a stranger across a crowded room and drift away.

7. (b) Phone first. They may *still* mean it—but make sure.

8. (c), although (a) and (b) are all right, too. It's largely a personal decision. However, most mothers remove wedding rings to increase their chances of finding nice, new fathers.

9. (a) is correct, but (c) is acceptable, although it is better to have brought the gift with you when you visited.

10. (b) Yes. When your host enters the room to greet you for the first time since your arrival—rise graciously, gracefully!

11. All are correct! (a)—for formal correspondence; (b)—for informal letters (most pastels are acceptable, except for pink, lavender, turquoise), or, you can use your formal white or ivory; and (c) is popular and fine for informal notes and letters. If you seldom write formal notes (most girls write one only *occasionally*), go ahead and buy the stationery that appeals aesthetically to you.

12. (c) Something like "I'd like you to meet Bobbie and Susie" is more comfortable for everyone. People will assume they're your children or, if they know the situation, will let it go at that. Children usually don't like to be different. If they're old enough, you might ask them which introduction they prefer.

13. If you want to play with the office folks—here's how: *Hold* the drink but don't drink. Drink gingerale—no one will ask if it's plain or mixed! If anyone comments, just say you're slow but steady. After they have two or three, they won't notice.

14. (c) Take pen in hand; *never* type.

15. (c) Let your escort know what you want—he gives your order to the waiter before giving his own.

16. (b) It's *different* from the American style, but perfectly acceptable.

17. Surprise!—(c) No acknowledgement is necessary.

18. (b) Elbows on the table between courses is all right; it doesn't interfere with anyone's eating.

19. (c) You may kiss men/women anyplace you like that they don't mind.

20. (a&b) are acceptable as a one-time situation—but don't let the brother "date" you several times in a foursome with the married couple.

You've got 18 out of 20 right? You're *au courant*. Twelve right? Good. Nine right? You'll get by. Six right? Read this book twice!

PART THREE
The Libidinal You

1. HOW TO BE A VIRGIN WITH STYLE AND GRACE

When you are fresh, dewy, and *very* young, virginity may come naturally. If you are fiercely religious, you have your faith and the church to support you. A congenital man-hater simply couldn't care less . . . and a sexually constricted woman may be too sick to notice. But if you are a slightly disenchanted aging virgin—twenty-five and still counting—you can't help feeling pressured and persecuted in this era of unleashed libido.

Everyone considers the virgin fair game. Your chastity seems to transform otherwise adorable folk into monsters. To some men you are Mt. Everest. You *must* be conquered. To some women you are a threat. You must be reformed . . . converted . . . persuaded.

Let us assume your chaste state is not a reflection of neglect, holier-than-thou superiority, or psychological paralysis. Perhaps you are simply a staunch disciple of the faith that says: I will go to bed only with the man I marry . . . or even, I will go to bed only with the man I love. . . .

When you were an adolescent, legions of staunch suitors tried to undermine your resistance. But many young men were perfectly willing to make a token assault and then accept your limitations, necking feverishly, petting . . . getting wildly excited and then . . . screeching to a respectful (or resentful) halt.

Well, dear, you've hit the big time now. You're playing with the grown-ups and toying with dynamite if you think you can kiss and fondle, even take off your clothes and climb into bed to cuddle with some dazzling Lochinvar and then call "stop" when you've gone as far as *you* want to.

As a virgin on the love-standard you operate on a short string. Your more *giving* sisters can tease and tantalize with slightly more style. You must function constantly on the defensive.

Are you a True Blue Sweetheart or a Battle-Scarred Villainess? A heroine or a heavy?

The heavy cannot resist: flaunting, smugness, advertisements for "my superiority," coy exhibitionism, overt sexual teasing, proselytizing, lectures, gossip, sour grapes, heavy sighs, recrimination, getting the last word. Here are some typical dramas of extended virginity, played both ways. Useful too, for the nonvirgin who just wants to play cool a while.

A. First date. Good night at the door.

    He: Hey, aren't you going to invite me in?

The Heavy: I'm a virgin.

The Heroine: It's an hour past my bedtime and my roommate is probably asleep on the daybed . . . next time. (Strangers and brand-new men in your life are not entitled to the whole philosophical dissertation five minutes after you've met . . . unless you feel like it).

B. Marvelous new man in your life. Fun to be with, talk to, kiss . . .

    He: (Unbuttoning your buttons): Why not?

The Heavy: Do you love me?

The Heroine: Abstinence is part of my meditation course . . . no, really. I'm climbing toward nirvana. Hey, I want you to taste some homemade peach ice cream. (As long as you can keep it light and distract him, amuse him, delight him . . . you postpone the pressure a little longer. Your nonvirginal competition doesn't *necessarily* hop into bed at the libido's first faint call.)

C. A bit annoyed now and crotchety over your continued evasiveness.

    He: I never take a girl out more than twice unless we go to bed.

The Heavy: I think I'm worth more than two cheeseburgers and a double bill of old Sonny Tufts flicks.

The Heroine: I'm going to try awfully hard to change your pattern. (Make it clear you're *deeply* interested in him.)

D. He knows the truth now . . . that you are a virgin.

    He: What are you waiting for, you poor deluded waif?

The Heavy: A four-karat solitaire and my Mrs. "degree."

The Heroine: Love. It's that simple. I've just never been in love . . . I guess I was never really ready for love . . . before. (It's not a noose you're swinging. You are honest and hopeful.)

E. After a particularly torrid scene.

    He: It just isn't healthy. For you. Or for me.

The Heavy: That's *your* problem. *I* feel fine. I could neck like this indefinitely.

The Heroine: Oh, sweetheart. Do you feel as shaky as I do? It's scary. I want so much to know you better. (There's a limit to how far you can go and then draw back without insult and trauma. You want to be concerned about his needs as well as your own.)

F.   *He:* Have you tried psychoanalysis?

  The Heavy: I think *you're* the one who's sick.

The Heroine: My analyst says there's nothing wrong with me that love won't cure. (You're healthy.)

G.   *He:* Don't you ever melt?

  The Heavy: Not to that tired old routine.

The Heroine: I can hardly control myself right this very minute. My built-in discipline never failed me before . . . now . . . (You're as sexy as he is.)

H. Things are getting a little bit desperate.

          He: Well, let me just spend the night. I won't try anything, I promise.

  The Heavy: Well . . . O.K. (Lights out . . . the struggle begins.) Don't you realize when I say no I mean no?

The Heroine: I would love to be with you. . . . But I don't trust myself. Not yet. (Don't say yes when you really mean no.)

You are a normal, healthy, wholesome, functioning female with just this one old-fashioned "eccentricity." Everything you do is designed to reflect your sense, your warmth, your sincerity. You are not a manipulative machine. You are not trading your body for a 30-year mortgage and split-level security. You are reasonable, passionate, even, ultimately, seducible. And you want him to hang around.

In the course of every adult relationship there comes a time for intimate involvement or . . . the end of the static "affair." Do you find yourself drifting constantly from one quite marvelous man to the next? Is that fear that keeps you denying your love? If you feel yourself wanting to take the step of commitment, struggling habitually and losing . . . you definitely need professional help. Don't waste any time. Find a good psychologist or psychiatrist . . . make sure either has been trained in psychotherapy however. Not all are . . . even those with big names.

2. SEXUAL EXPERTISE AND HOW TO GET IT

No one expects you to slide behind the wheel of a car for the first time and drive on to win the Indianapolis 500. And no one expects you to come on like a courtesan or a stand-in for the sensuous woman the first time fate and your libido place you in the proper position.

If you're still a virgin—or relatively inexperienced in bed, some men will find your innocence positively exciting. And you may have the good fortune to be seduced by a man who was born to be your Pygmalion. At any rate, there's no need *ever* to apologize for real naïveté or lack of how-to information.

There are several suitable academies for sexual learning.

1. A willing lover.

2. Movies—above ground and the most primitive pornography.

3. Literature—you can learn a good deal from nonfiction best sellers like J's *The Sensuous Woman*, and Dr. David Reuben's candid tome can tell you "everything you've always wanted to know. . . ." You wouldn't attempt to make Beef Wellington without a cookbook, would you? Two *excellent* books: *The ABZ of Sex*, and *The XYZ of Love*—both authored by Inge and Sten Hegeler. COSMOPOLITAN magazine is another source for practical, psychological, emotional self-help information.

4. Marriage manuals are written for lovers—married or otherwise. Buy several. Read them. Try.

If your lover wants you to do something you don't want to do, a simple refusal without venom is sufficient. Just "No, I don't want to . . ." or "No, I can't do that" . . . "I don't want to discuss it now" . . . should be sufficient. Later the two of you can talk about it . . . perhaps you'll change your mind. There is nothing that can happen between two adults in bed that is wrong as long as they both want it.

Sex is a "best-thing-in-life"—less than love but sometimes *more*. It is an art that can transform you—it can liberate your body, feed your intelligence, and intoxicate your spirit.

3. HOW I TURN A MAN ON

I am terribly thrilled to be a girl. I feel feminine through and through all the time. I like men. I expect them to find me attractive and they do. When I meet some particular man—at a party, in a business group, on a plane—whom I want to attract, I concentrate on letting him know that I'm interested, that I'm *available*, at least for a date.

I am very conscious of my own body, and I enjoy it. I take the most expensive care of it. My body is always slender, soft, and fragrant; I put soft, beautiful things on it. As someone once wrote, "The body of man is capable of infinite pleasure," and I think of my body that way. Because I think of my body as capable of giving and receiving pleasure, a man will often think of it that way, too. I expect him to. I can look at a man across a room and know that I am capable of infinite pleasure and that he is, too.

He gets the message.

If I'm with a man I want to turn on, I try to pretend we have all the time in the world to get acquainted . . . even if we're only going to be together a few moments. Jitters, jumpiness, darting looks around the room—any movement that is nonlanguorous is out.

I wait on a man—yes, even if we *just* met—because it is the exact opposite of what is *supposed* to happen at parties (i.e., men are there to wait on girls). I light *his* cigarette. This takes a little finesse but it can be done femininely and appealingly. I may even take the matches out of his hand. I will try not to let his glass become totally empty. We can stop our conversation long enough to catch the waiter's eye, or I may go with him to the bar for a refill.

If I want to turn a man on, I let him know as soon as I can that I like him, that I find him charming and attractive. I find *something* to admire about him . . . his cuff links, his tan, his eyebrows. If you look a man

227

over, you can always find *something*. Often, instead of making conversation, I think of what I genuinely want to know that he could tell me. Then I listen when he does so.

Sometimes I don't wear a girdle, and sometimes not even a bra. The movement of the breasts and buttocks under the kind of soft, graceful clothes I wear speaks a language that almost all men understand. And when a man can feel the natural softness of your body, in dancing, or as you brush past him, it turns him on.

I listen to a man very carefully. I stand closer to him than is necessary, and once in a while I touch him, as if accidentally. I pick out some little thing he says that shows an attitude or an opinion and I question him about it, then compliment him on his insight and perceptiveness. I remember things he said and quote them back to him most effectively.

I ask men to help me . . . everywhere . . . under all circumstances. They adore it!

I ask men for advice, to explain things to me.

I am enthusiastic with men, eager. I show pleasure in their company. I am natural, relaxed.

I behave toward each man as if he were the only man alive. (But I let him know, very subtly, so as not to make him angry, that there *are* other men in my life.)

I am *soft*—in my manner, my voice, my touch and smile, in the way I walk, I am not a pal or one of the boys. I am many things he is not—I am *feminine!*

I am a woman, and I know it—every single minute. And that is how I turn men on!

4. HOW SEXUALLY GENEROUS A GIRL SHOULD BE

Even in the Permissive Seventies, girls still suffer through the virginity crisis. How many yearning nineteen-year-olds have wrestled with their conventional moral upbringing to agonize: "If he wants me so much and I love him, how can I say no?" (See Part Three, Chapter 1).

But the concept of sexual generosity is losing ground in this Age of Sexual Emancipation. Today's sexually liberated women is not likely to consider her body as that one great ultimate gift reluctantly surrendered in a wave of generosity. Sex, at least *good* sex (which we want or ought to want, unless we're a little loose in the head), implies a *mutual* giving. The greatest gift is love, commitment, and the total acceptance of what each lover offers to the other.

Unfortunately, one unhappy side effect of our new sexual freedom has been a strange distortion of sexual generosity. For some girls, sex has become compulsively commercialized. Sex is no longer joyous giving. It has become calculated trading—bed for insurance of a date next weekend or a dinner at Trader Vic's or a weekend at Stowe. Bed, because she owes it to him ("He spent sixty-five dollars on me tonight") . . . bed, because: "If I make a fuss, we'll wake my roommate" . . . bed, because: "Everybody does it" . . . "I know he'll never call again if I don't" . . . "We've gone this far. How can I say no, now?"

This is not sexual generosity, but sheer profligacy. It's not carefree liberation, it's a dreary slavery of habit. It's not giving, but a colossal waste of a girl's resources. Certainly, the concept of sexual giving is totally absent from the growing acceptance that any casual date must inevitably end in bed—his or hers, it scarcely matters which. Far too many girls have abdicated an active role in the sexual relationship and find themselves drifting aimlessly, almost lustlessly, from bed to bed out of resignation, routine, habit, passive nonresistance. And all this joyless bedding about is accomplished under the guise of sensuality and free love.

Well, it *isn't* love and it isn't lust.

Don't get me wrong. I'm not about to suggest that sex outside of marriage is doomed to despair, or that sex without love should be avoided. Of course, the grand passions are the greatest, but a magnificent love affair need not necessarily lead to marriage, and a lot of less-than-love affairs have a legitimate place in the sexual scheme of things. Sex *is* a form of expression . . . sex *can* bring instant intimacy . . . sex *does* stave off loneliness. A girl can have an absolutely fantastic evening in bed with a fascinating man whose name she might not necessarily know and whose face she may never see again.

But it is pitiful to be deluded.

The "Forced" Affair

My friend Lydia is trying, through sex, to throw herself into a great new romance. A really smashing blonde with a model's figure and walk and a Ph.D. in speech therapy, Lydia at twenty-nine has been trying to patch together her battered dignity after a particularly devastating finale to the great love affair of her life. It has been a year since her photographer friend, Stan, began the final breaking off. Yet, without fail, at least once every four or five weeks, he will appear at Lydia's door, usually unannounced, "to see how you're getting along," to be nursed if he has the flu, to be loved if he's in heat, to be fed if he's hungry. Lydia can't bring herself to say "No." After each such painful interlude, she starts dating madly and is in and out of bed with every guy she sees—in a desperate hunt for involvement. "I know that once I'm involved again, I'll be able to throw Stan out of my life," she explains. "But as long as I'm sitting here being so miserable and on the loose like this, I just can't bring myself to slam the door in his face." It doesn't help to remind Lydia that it took ten years on the Manhattan dating scene to find her great romance, and she can hardly expect to find another, instantly intense and beautiful, in bed with a stranger.

I remember very well the summer she met Stan. Both were dating others at the time. They kept seeing each other at parties and on Fire Island weekends. They'd known each other for months and seen each other day and night for two weeks one hot August, before great affection grew into passion and took them to bed.

No doubt history records a significant number of fulfilling relationships that may have begun in bed. One girl I spoke to insists she can't remember a single man with whom she had an extended affair that she did not go to bed with on the first night they met. And I recall speaking to a recent Northwestern U. graduate and her roommate in Chicago who felt the bed-or-not-to-bed debate in the postgraduate dating scene was so contrived and exhausting. It was better to "get that hassle out of the way by going to bed—then get to know each other afterwards without all that tension."

Still, it must be clear that you can't create rapport out of nothing. And as my friend Lydia is learning, even if it hasn't reached her conscious mind yet, you can't force love to grow out of a perfunctory encounter.

Sex as a balm for loneliness is not to be denied. And sex as a distraction from a broken heart can be delightful. But two coldly uninvolved bodies in bed do not create real warmth. You can be lonelier in bed with a disinterested stranger than alone with a tuna-fish sandwich and a fat, juicy novel.

There is, I am convinced, a flaw in the concept of total sexual freedom—a flaw for both men and women. Perhaps you recall from your high school economics course that old law: Bad money drives out good. My friend, Dr. Harold Greenwald, the psychologist, who wrote *The Call Girl*, has a similar theory about sex: "Bad sex drives out good." Going to bed out of passivity, habit, obsession, or nagging insecurity seems to build up a reservoir of sexual and emotional numbness and, in many girls I talked to, feeds both guilt and sexual hostility.

Juggling Men

How, for instance, is a girl to juggle two or three simultaneous affairs, especially if she happens to be very fond of one man and only friendly or physically attracted to the others? Jeannine, a quietly pretty receptionist for a big TV film-producing firm in Los Angeles, has just that problem. She really likes (maybe even loves) her rancher friend from Dallas. He calls daily, talks about getting a divorce, seems serious, and Jeannine dates as always—old friends, ex-lovers, the dreary parade of blind dates dredged up by well-meaning relatives,. When a man appeals to her, she goes to bed with him. And she has been sleeping on and off for several months with Bernie, a man whose company she enjoys but with whom she sees no future. "When Larry comes in from Dallas, I feel almost guilty," Jeannine says. "I feel as if I've been unfaithful. I don't understand it. We have no commitment. Maybe he'll get a divorce and maybe he won't. You know how those things go." She shrugs. "The whole scene is doing something to me," she says. "I find myself being bitchy to Larry for no reason at all and loathing Bernie and feeling a little bit decadent when I happen to wind up in bed with some fabulous guy I've just met."

Is this what Dr. Greenwald means when he talks about bad sex driving out good? I would think so. Certainly, a girl can get so caught up in less-than-great sexual adventures that she is less likely to be ready to recognize or accept anything better.

Many girls seemed unsettled, some highly disturbed, by their own sexual behavior. "I do worry that I go to bed too easily," confided Carla, secretary to a lawyer I know. "I wonder, can any girl really be attracted to that many men in one lifetime? When things don't work out or the guy I thought was so groovy turns out to be a bastard, I try to abstain for two weeks or a month. To prove something, I suppose." Prove what? "That I'm still a nice girl, and not some kind of nymph, I guess."

The Breakfast Test

Less anxious but still obviously concerned was Annie, a lively brunette newspaper reporter whose day is crowded with predatory males. "I remember when I used to tell myself, you don't go to bed with a man unless it's love. Now I say, not unless you like him . . . I mean, *really* like him. Breakfast is the big test. I may have liked him well enough the night before, but if I can't stand him at breakfast, I know it was a mistake." Even so, Annie's regret is not particularly debilitating or inhibiting. "You learn to discrimnate better," she says. "You get so that you are less likely to make the mistakes."

What rescues many girls from the potential disaster of compulsive and meaningless sexuality is just that: You *do* learn. Though it's hard to believe when you look at her now, Kristan, a lean bundle of chicly arranged bones, was a plump, unfashionable, and incredibly naïve farmgirl when she first came to New York nine years ago. Now, she is a top-paid model and sometime actress. But then: "I was so insecure, I used to think I really had nothing to offer a man but my body. I used to think, the way New York is, if you don't go to bed with a man by the third date, you've had it.

"One day, it just came to me . . . if a man is really coming back just because of *that*, who wants *him?* Maybe that was the beginning of growing up. I'm a woman and I don't need to play children's sex games any more."

As for owing a man your company in bed because he's invested $25 or $50 or $100 in an evening—Kristan is vehement. "What am I? Woolworth's? Is sex some kind of commodity to trade on the market? Forget it. I don't care what you look like or where he has taken you or how much he spent, you don't owe a man anything but your charming companionship—and if you're not willing to be a charming companion, then don't accept the date."

Between Affairs

Of course, it is easy enough for Kristan to turn down dates. She has a dozen men waiting in the wings to take her out. Not only is she great to look at, but she's fun, bright, and clearly likes men. There is no sexual dueling on a date with Kristan, and, as she says, no childish sex games. But what about a girl who doesn't have would-be escorts hopefully lined up? What about the girl between affairs and out of the dating whirl after a relationship that was great but somehow didn't work out?

Under the old repressive moral codes, a nice girl knew the answer was always no. But now we are a new breed of women. We are free to express ourselves sexually. We have The Pill and a growing belief that each of us must determine for herself what is right, moral, comfortable, fulfilling, fun.

Yet, today, with so much candor and the all-pervading emphasis on unrepressed sexuality, many women are pressured into behavior they *cannot* handle and aren't any good at. And some of us have the mistaken idea that hopping in and out of bed is sexy.

"I'm just a very lusty girl," my occasional research assistant, Joyce, assured me, explaining that her sex life is so demanding she can't always be available when I need her. "Some girls are just sexier than others," she added, with a self-satisfied sigh. Joyce is a plump, aggressive, rather dominating girl, who may be trying to prove how sexy (i.e., attractive) and feminine she is, but the message she conveys is that of desperate uncertainty. Casual and indiscriminate sex is, after all, no measure of a woman's sexiness. Better *one* good, satisfying orgasm and all that. If anything, preoccupation with one's sexiness is a dead giveaway that something female is lacking somewhere. Constant promiscuity is a pattern of nymphomania. And psychologists agree that the true nymphomaniac is a most unsexy, driven, and unfulfilled creature, pathetically unsure of her own femininity.

It takes courage, a measure of self-understanding, and maturity to draw the fine line between wholesome hedonism (now and then good) and compulsive promiscuity (bad). A permissive, nonpromiscuous code still leaves considerable room for experiment, mistakes, and kicks. (Don't knock kicks!)

The danger here, of course, is that a once-in-a-lifetime adventure may be written off as harmless, kooky, fey, or even amusing, but as a style of life, it is obsessive and unwholesome. The first time my wealthy sculptor friend, Betsey, picked up a construction worker on the streets of Boston and asked him to pose for her, it must have seemed like a lark. And it was still a lark when they wound up the afternoon in bed. He was handsome, virile, even eager to see Betsey again, but she was not really interested. Now, Betsey is thirty-three, no better a sculptor, still stalking the streets. A tall, exotic brunette, she has little difficulty persuading most men to "pose" for her. Posing sessions invariably wind up in bed. Once or twice these affairs last a few days or even a week. But pickups have beome a compulsive pattern for Betsey. She seems incapable of any other kind of sexual relationship and sees no reason why she should abandon her "hobby."

Fortunately, most girls do not slip into this kind of obsessive behavior. Routinized, meaningless sex is ultimately so unrewarding that most girls abandon it. It helps to know that many men, especially the more sexually experienced, also find "just sex" can be meaningless and a bore.

Mutual Giving

Well, we all have our bad days when we look like Elsa Lanchester playing *The Bride of Frankenstein*. But, do you really feel sex is all you have to offer? For heaven's sake, work up some other act. Are you jealous because the girl next door just came back from Atlantic City, "where he kept ordering champagne and we never left the hotel all weekend"? Surely, three days in a hotel room with the *wrong* man is worse than a month confined to quarters—I don't care if it's vintage champagne. And with the *right* man? Well, it's only *one* of life's thrills.

Be a giver, not a trader. There are many levels of giving. You can be as giving, in a charitable way, as a doormat or a punching bag. But what are you . . . the Ford Foundation? Genuine giving requires equal generosity in the acceptance. It is impossible to give when the recipient neither needs nor wants nor accepts what you offer. If you are caught in the embrace of a man for whom yours is just the most convenient bed, hasn't all meaning been lost? Is that giving? Or are you being taken? There comes a time when kicks and adventure and sexy interludes grow into something fulfilling. Then, sexual generosity begins and the games end.

5. HOW TO COMMUNICATE IN BED

Lea, a voluptuous sunny blonde, sexier now at thirty than in her freckle-faced bouncy cheerleader teens, knows more about men and marvelous things to do in bed than most people who write best-selling books on the subject. And her husband, Hans, is no innocent either. But almost from the day they were married these two have had disturbing problems in bed. Hans is a nonstop talker, a homey philosopher type, and Lea is a verbal whiz, flip and sardonic but sensitive too. And yet these two bright, hip, sexually liberated worldlings cannot or will not confront their frustrating communication gap: each is absolutely unable to talk about his sexual desires to the other.

Talk you *must*. Knowing all the intercourse positions just isn't enough. And yet we often mumble or groan or suffer in silence or else blunder and blurt, saying all the wrong things at the wrong time. Sex *is* communication. The act of making love is the ultimate communication. It says, "I am me. I am a woman. I adore you. I need you. You turn me inside out . . . I want to devour you." All the unspoken messages we transmit with bedroom body-language.

Subliminal communication is *not* enough. You have to talk to your man. Breathes there a man (or woman) with sexual prowess so notorious he is tired of hearing what a fabulous lover he is? I doubt it. Men are insecure. Kings and presidents are insecure. Great beauties are insecure. We're all insecure. There isn't anyone who doesn't need to be reminded he is brilliant, clever, talented, intuitive, understanding, handsome, loved and, especially . . . fantastic in bed.

It is more precarious than ever to be a man today . . . because women are not sheltered innocents anymore. The man who comes to your bed wonders how he rates against the performance of his predecessor. Reassure him. The confident lover is a better lover. cosmo's male voice, Bill Manville, recommends . . . kissing. "Kissing," writes Bill, "is active, encouraging, arousing . . . a feminine form of courtship that doesn't impinge on masculine initiative."

Sexual *complaints* take tact and timing.

Never assume that he knows . . . he *must* know . . . if he loves me he would *surely* know! The reality: he hasn't a clue. Lovers are not necessarily mind readers. Tell him.

Not: "Why aren't you sexy anymore?"

Better: "Why do you think we aren't making love very often these days?"

Not: "For God's sake, don't come so fast."

Better: "Wait. Wait for me."

Not: "I'm bored with being on the bottom all the time."

Better: "I'm the queen and you're my slave."

Serious potency problems and orgasm mismatches should never be discussed five or six minutes after a slightly unhappy mating. Or in the middle of rising enthusiasm. Save it . . . for tomorrow morning at breakfast . . . or tomorrow night in front of the fire during a less emotionally charged moment in your lives.

Sexual troubles desperately need to be worked out. Try to analyze what's bothering you . . . fight, scream, and weep if you must . . . but weep over what's bothering you. Don't invent smoke screens. If he's upset about the garbage overflowing, solve the garbage problem . . . don't let him punish you in bed. If you're furious because he came home smelling of Arpege (and you wear Femme), talk about it.

If you smell sweet and look positively esculent in your see-through brown chiffon nightshirt, the message is: I want to make love.

If you haven't had a shower for two days and appear in your frowzy old granny gown, the message is equally clear.

Why doesn't he please you?

You know what turns you on. Tell him. Show him.

Once in a while forget about him as a person. Pretend you're in bed with a super pleasure machine. Don't be concerned with his pleasure at all . . . just let yourself give in to your senses. Your intense sensuality, your rare selfishness excites him. If you get too frantic about your performance—what *does* he want?—you won't be able to give him what he wants desperately—an aroused, contented, satiated you.

It may be a bit of a drag if he is never happier than when you come to bed in a black lace garter belt . . . learn to love it.

What Not to Say While Making Love

"Oh hell, I forgot to send in the income tax payment."

"You're doing it wrong again."

"The baby is crying."

"Gee, you've put on weight over the holidays."

"You forgot to brush your teeth . . . don't kiss me."

"Let's finish this. I'm getting bored."

And I'm sure you have some special ones of your own. Stop!

The Etiquette of the Orgasm

Call girls fake it. That's their business. But a history of faking orgasm is a distress signal.

Faking orgasm is right, proper, considerate, prudent . . . if making love and orgasm mean absolutely nothing to *you*, but you love this man and want to keep *him* happy. Faking it is proper, kind, considerate, the first time you go to bed with a man . . . on an anniversary . . . after a spectacular display of sexuality on his part . . . on a day he is noticeably depressed and desperately needs an ego boost. Perhaps you aren't really in the mood . . . or it all happened too fast . . . or the doorbell distracted you . . . or the timing was just a bit off. He needs all the encouragement he can get . . . you give it.

However, faking it is wrong, cruel, self-defeating . . . if it becomes a habit. No need to live a lie . . . confide, talk it over, work it out, seek professional advice. Do you need a lock on the door . . . more intense prologues . . . a tranquilizer : . . encouragement . . . a drink. Are you constantly distracted by anxiety and the most ridiculous household problems? To chase the specters that haunt you (and give you insomnia), concentrate on black. Imagine a big black square in the middle of your head. Concentrate on the deep black nothingness. Now, lightly distracted, let your senses take over.

6. TWENTY-FIVE THOUGHTFUL THINGS TO DO FOR A MAN IN THE BEDROOM

1. Bring him breakfast in bed . . . fresh-squeezed orange juice or the extract of a fresh apple, bananas au rhum . . . caviar-and-sour-cream omelette . . . coffee cake you baked yourself . . . a croissant. Something he can't get at the corner cafeteria. Dinner in bed is fun too.

2. Give him a really great back rub, a serious massage with your heart in it. No groans or moans. No sighing how tired you are (that's like giving a gift with the price tag still on it). If you don't *know* what a good back rub is, go to a masseur and find out. The Y.W.C.A. often has a class on massage.

3. Smell good . . . not a perfume cover-up, but a fresh start, clean all over and then a big cloud of your favorite scent—your trademark because it precedes and follows wherever you go.

4. Don't let long leisurely tub soaks turn into such an indulgence that when you appear all pink and rosy and ready, you find him bored into sound sleep.

5. Surround him with a neat bedroom. Maybe it's just a temporary little clutter to you, but it's a depressing *mess* to him.

6. Is he sick? Treat him as if he were a lot sicker than he really is. Men usually don't coddle their ills the way women do. Persuade him just this once to surrender . . . do the whole Nurse Jane bit (*sexy Nurse Jane*) with rice pudding and poached eggs and tea with lemon and honey, pulse counts, alcohol back rubs.

7. Learn to make a bed with him in it.

8. Wear a fresh, flattering filmy nightgown . . . nothing is sweeter than a pouf of see-through yellow chiffon or black satin at the foot of the bed next morning.

9. Tell him you're too tired to move . . . ask him to undress you. Men love to undress women. Somewhere in the middle you will probably feel much less tired.

10. Never mention your backache or your headache after 7:30 P.M. You may not *mean* it as anything more than a request for two aspirin or a little sympathy, but a sensitive lad may think you are hinting you're not up to lovemaking.

11. Be more aggressive. My psychiatrist friend says even today's liberated sexpots still wait for the man to make the *first* move. Every now and then . . . attack.

12. Squirt him here and there with Redi-Whip and lick it off (the psychiatrist's wife came up with that thought). A bit fattening, though!

13. Kiss his toes.

14. Do not let mundane rituals interfere with passion. If he wants you now *now* now! . . . at once! . . . for heaven's sake, forget about brushing your teeth.

15. Lick and kiss him somewhere you *never* have before. Even if you've been climbing into beds together for ten years, there *must* be a quarter inch of skin you've somehow missed. Tell him what you're up to . . . so he'll know it's a sexy thought and not just a kooky idea.

16. Rearrange the lighting to flatter you . . . choose soft pink bulbs. Try candles only.

17. Rum raisin ice cream in bed by candlelight. Or an elegant crystal goblet of Madeira.

18. Love your body . . . walk tall. And naked, in your maribou boa.

19. Never stop telling him how attractive he is . . . how sexy his small flaws are . . . even the most confident narcissist hunk of male beauty *likes* to hear it.

20. Kiss him a lot . . . in a dozen different, teasing ways . . . and tell him how sensitive he is . . . how extraordinary a lover. He will be inspired to even greater performance.

21. Play games . . . dress up . . . dress him up. Act out a fantasy.

22. Buy him pornographic movies; watch them while both of you are in bed naked.

23. Of all these thoughtful things . . . which pleased him most? Do it again.

24. And again.

25. Twice on his birthday.

THINGS THAT ARE TACKY

Greasy cream stuff . . . you're supposed to be silky, dear, not slippery.

Hair rollers (surely *everybody* knows about not being seen in plastic rollers, but just in case . . .).

White-nighty-turned-gray (if you can't get it white again, dye it red).

The unmade bed.
Rotting apple cores, cigarette butts in dirty ashtrays.
Ice-cold feet.
Apathy.
Perpetual passivity.
Forgetting your pill.
Dirty sheets.

It would be the maddest arrogance to suggest all these inspirations drifted out of one single brain—even mine. Clever geisha that I am, I shared the fantasy of this project with . . . men. Sex seemed to be about the sixth item on their minds—after breakfast in bed, super back rubs, clean sheets, and smelling good. Consider that!

7. THINGS TO DO WITH YOUR HANDS THAT MEN LIKE

Fluff his pillow.

Section his grapefruit.

Pat his stomach.

Massage the backs of his legs (when he's standing *up*).

Give him a manicure.

Light a candle next to the bed.

Write his thank-you notes.

Sew on his wobbly buttons.

Hold his one *big* hand in your two little ones at the movies.

Do needlepoint.

Put your fingertips across his mouth (sexy).

Put your fingers *in* his mouth (*sexier*).

Take his temperature (fingertips to brow) when he's feverish or just *thinks* he's feverish. Take his pulse (even if you don't know how).

Rearrange his tie after you've both mussed it.

Hold your wineglass toward him; say a lovely toast and look in his eyes.

Put his evening studs in.

Clip the back of his neck when his new hairstyle is a little *too* long.

Give him a pedicure.

Turn off the lights.

Twist a lemon on the rim of his glass.

Plant a tree with him.

Take off your bra.

Smash his goblet in the fireplace.

Polish his leather seat covers. (Ask the hardware-store man for advice on materials and do it before seats get a cakey texture.)

Sock it to him (playfully) with a pillow.

Brush him lightly all over with your face-blusher brush.

Give his knees an unexpected knead.

Take the phone out of his hand when he's making one more call.

Trace his ear with your fingertips.

Let your hair down every night . . . or afternoon.

Always give him your hand to help you from the car.

Unkink his tense neck muscles with massage.

Polish and sort his cuff links.

Rub baby oil into his entire body after a shower.

Write on his back with your finger.

Dangle grapes over his mouth. Feed him one at a time.

Put your hands on his naked waist and stare at him.

Tuck your scented handkerchief under his pillow.

Count his ribs.

Hand his orange juice to him while he's toweling after the shower.

Give him some more ice.

Pamper his doggy or pussycat.

Tuck your hand in his overcoat pocket.

Take your phone off the hook.

Tie him up and tickle him.

Take something great off your plate and feed it to him . . . before *you've* begun.

Offer to drive when he's sleepy.

Reach for him in the pool.

Make him an ice-cream cone.

Give him an egg shampoo, and use the massage brush.

Read his palm.

Direct-dial his number.

Hold his *arm* with your two hands.

Take a letter (like his secretary).

Caress his legs underwater.

Smooth on suntan lotion.

Polish his ring. (Toothpaste is a good gleamer.)

Build him a sand castle.

Toy with his belt.

Lead him to a sofa after a hard day's work. Put cushions under his head and feet. Bring him a Vodka gimlet.

Bring his daily vitamin pill to him with water in a crystal glass.

Massage each part of him from top down or bottom up . . . when he's lying down.

Shake hands with his ex-wife.

Unpack his bags after a trip.

Immerse him in a warm tub in the middle of Sunday afternoon and play geisha.

Lie on his stomach and stroke his sides.

Pull your midiskirt off your supersinuous frame slow and easy.

Make a sandwich out of him and two pillows. Your feast.

Study all the nooks and crannies of his anatomy with your two hands.

Bring him a tumbler of jelly beans or a glass of cold white wine when he's reading.

Hold his hand when he lights your cigarette.

Frolic in his chest hairs.

Try his ring on all your fingers.

Pumice his calluses.

Give him an alcohol rub.

Feel his muscles.

Type him a love letter.

Treat his feet as sacred from time to time. Massage. Rub in oil. Powder between the toes.

Guarantee that his body couldn't ask for anything more.

8. A PHILOSOPHY OF CONSIDERATE ADULTERY

As a single girl you juggled the ethical conflicts of going out (and staying home) with a married man. Now *you* are a married woman and the glue that holds together the fortress of your emotional and intellectual commitment to fidelity is under attack. You are climbing into bed with a man who doesn't happen to be married to you. The moral and psychological acrobatics that bring you here are your own. Some will argue that adultery and etiquette simply cannot coexist, that no "lady" is ever an unfaithful wife. We could debate the semantics endlessly. However, *observation* indicates that some highly civilized women do now and then, and sometimes habitually, stray. Frankly, the best etiquette, that is, the most thoughtful thing, is *not* to do it. But infidelity can be handled in a thoughtful, considerate manner.

The unbreakable rule is . . . discretion.

For centuries wives have accepted and rationalized the infidelities of errant mates most effectively when the wives' noses are not rubbed in the news. It's supportable and bearable if no one else knows and no one tells and the wife doesn't read about it in the gossip columns. Society is amused and tolerant with the wayward husband. But the persisting double standard is not quite so permissive with the unfaithful wife. And her mate is threatened—his masculinity as defined by Western tradition is under siege.

The wife who strays would be kindest and most prudent if her lover is *not* her husband's best friend, his brother, his executive assistant, his boss, his poker crony, or an old school pal.

The ideal extramarital adventure—in terms of potential for discretion—is the visiting author-lecturer who is leaving next week or the man from Omaha you met during a convention. Or a cabana boy at a club to which you don't belong. Or your minister or analyst—someone with *more* to lose from exposure than you. Alas, lust is not always thoughtfully disciplined or disciplinable. Then only the strongest determination and tact can preserve discretion.

Never involve your children as accomplices or covers. Never talk to your lover on the telephone if *anyone* is present, even a two-year-old.

If asked, lie.

If caught, lie. Never admit anything. Never accept exposure. Lie, embroider, improvise, deny. Be convincing.

Never bring your lover home to your own double bed. Indulging in this kind of danger turns some women on. If such games are the *only* turn-on that arouses you, you are in big trouble and ought to work it out with your analyst.

Gifts from your lover should be tasteful, inexpensive things you might buy yourself. Diamond chokers and sable berets are impossible to explain unless you are already well-established in the diamond-and-sable league. Funky joke gifts and obscene mementos are not easily explained either.

Do not spend your husband's money for your lover's gifts. It's also crass to snitch a husband's smuggled Havana cigars for your lover.

If you love your husband and hope to keep him, you'll want him to benefit from your revived lust . . . your beautiful new confidence . . . and new sexual expertise. Be subtle and understated about the latter, though. Bring it home to bed with a kind of ad-lib spirit . . . as if you just thought it up. Or read it in a book. Your husband is *not* a dummy!

The husband deserves to share in all the rediscovered pleasures inspired by your occasional adventure: the new perfumes, sexier underwear, cream-silked flesh, and scented powder dustings. Don't save just for your lover.

Another thought about adultery and suspicion.

Perhaps it seems polite to pretend you don't recognize your boss's wife, Jenny, sitting fourth row center at the theatre with a young man holding her hand. You pretend you don't notice your best friend's husband perched in the corner of the Pump Room with that tall, striking blonde in the Saint Laurent knickers . . . and hope he won't notice you.

By your embarrassed reaction, the ducked head, the averted eye, the nervous giggle, and your pointed rudeness in not shaking hands and saying hello, you are clearly saying you suspect the worst.

There are hundreds of reasons why a man or woman might be seen about town—on the street, in the shadowy recesses of a rooftop bar, at the movies, in Saks' fur department—with a mysterious unknown companion of the opposite sex.

He may be her furrier, her brother, a client, her broker. Just because the giggly creature with old Teddy is slightly tipsy and only half-wrapped in slinky mauve Banlon doesn't mean she couldn't be his sister-in-law (wife Lottie is down with a virus), or an out-of-town client.

Say hello. Shake hands. Your friend will introduce her companion. With or without a simple, not too self-conscious, explanation. Don't stand around; don't leer. Say hello and leave.

9. THE ETIQUETTE OF NOT GETTING PREGNANT

Nothing is ruder—more cruel and careless—than an unwanted pregnancy. Accidental pregnancy or pointed threats of imminent motherhood—real, imagined, or invented—may seem like a legitimate weapon in the husband-trapping arsenal, but only to sickies and kooks. That's why contraception is not only good manners . . . it's an expression of your wholesome life-style.

The frail innocent who loves to make love but can't bother her fluffy head about anything so clinical or calculated as birth control went out of style along with obligatory white gloves and cast-iron girdle.

Where do you go for birth-control information? There are several possibilities:

First you can sound out a sophisticated friend, but don't act on her advice alone. She's *knowledgeable* but not a doctor.

Buy a book. Several top-notch surveys of contraceptive information are available. Here are four:

1. Calderone, Mary S., ed. *Manual of Contraceptive Practice.* 2nd ed., Williams and Wilkins, $14.50.

2. Consumer Reports Editors. *Consumers Union Report on Family Planning.* Doubleday, $1.75.

3. Guttmacher, Alan F. and others. *Complete Book of Birth Control.* Ballantine, paperback $0.50.

4. Neubardt, Selig. *Contraception.* Pocket Books, paperback $0.95.

Call your local Planned Parenthood office. They don't care whether you're married or about to be or hope to be . . . someday. But if you feel more relaxed pretending to be engaged, pretend . . . it doesn't harm anyone.

See a gynecologist. Get names from girl friends, or call your county Medical Society (see telephone book for listing) or a local hospital . . .

they will give you a choice. The public library has medical directories.

If you live in a small town or a suburb with a small-town attitude, you may prefer to slip anonymously into the nearest big city; try the campus health center if you are at college.

There is no one "best" or "most thoughtful" contraceptive. You, your doctor, your anatomy, and your emotional or spiritual make-up will determine what is best or most workable for you—the pill, a diaphragm with contraceptive jelly or cream, contraceptive foam, an intrauterine device. The rhythm method of abstinence during the fertile period is another possibility, but not without some justification has it sometimes been referred to as Vatican Roulette. If rhythm is your choice, you owe it to yourself, your man, and your future to learn *all* its intricacies. It has a high risk rate. The pill has the lowest risk rate, but there has been considerable controversy about possible dangers. The gynecologists Cosmo consults are definitely *for* the pill, but it is for each girl and her doctor to decide what is safest for her individual chemistry.

Living with the Pill

The Pill is the Ultimate in Gracious Sexual Living . . . taken every day as automatically as you brush your teeth. The action is blissfully isolated from the act of love. How thoughtful. How considerate. How discreet. This is what etiquette is about.

Now . . . suppose you need a reminder until you get used to the pill routine. A note on the refrigerator is perfectly proper, or on the bathroom mirror . . . perhaps a string tied around the bedpost. Three-foot-long red arrows over the medicine chest and a fire alarm should *not* be necessary.

How clever you are to carry a few *extra* pills in your evening bag. Now you don't have to drag yourself through the deserted streets at 3:00 A.M. when you'd much prefer snuggling deeper under the covers of your temporary bed across town.

If the gang should suddenly decide to drive up to Vermont for the weekend or fly off to San Francisco for dinner and you've no pill along, you needn't get hysterical with the rituals of your gynecological obligations. In an emergency, most druggists, given a credible reason, will sell you a *single* pill or a handful of your brand without a prescription. You are prepared for all eventualities!

If you *forget* one pill, there is also no need to dissolve in fits or alert the National Guard. Take one as soon as you discover the lapse and take your regular pill for that day at the usual time. If you miss two days in a row, you need a backup system for the rest of the month—diaphragm, gel, foam, or abstinence. Don't take my word for it. Check with your doctor.

Other Devices

Why not treat your diaphragm almost as casually and automatically as you do your comb or lipstick? Use it *whenever* you go out. Even if you have no thought of needing it that night, if there is even the tiniest *possibility* that you will, then you're ready. Preparedness doesn't mean you fall into bed with the nearest amiable male; you are as discriminating and demanding as always, but you have managed to make your diaphragm *unobtrusive*. My friend Nancy has been handling her contraceptive armor this way for years. She's married now and she still uses it automatically, every night without fail, even if her husband has a temperature of 105. He knows that should he be seized with a feverish fit of passion, Nancy is . . . ready. Neither of them thinks any more about it.

You may find this "always prepared" attitude too Girl Scouty for you, and now here you are wrapped around each other on your living room sofa—how do you extricate yourself to tend to this practical matter without dampening the mood? (He's a new man in your life and you didn't expect things to happen quite so fast.) Don't wait till you're both simmering and tearing at each other's clothes before ducking out. Excuse yourself at some early tentative moment, or, if that moment thundered by twenty minutes ago . . . *now!* "I'll be back in a minute . . . don't you dare go away," you'll say. Never say . . . "Oh hell, I forgot the blankety-blank diaphragm, blast it." Sure, it's a drag for you . . . but don't make him suffer too. If he says, "That's all right . . . I'll take care of it," you may assent or refuse . . . "No, I'd rather do it by myself. . . ." And off to the bathroom. Spare him the specter of the clinical implements and details.

If you're in his lair and your essential equipment is five miles across town, then the man uses his prophylactic or else, alas, you abstain.

10. ACCIDENTAL PREGNANCY COUNTDOWN

I have just pored through half a dozen fat, thorough books of contemporary etiquette and not one seems to confront reality on certain subjects. They all sail through the formal ceremonies of life, but none offers a single clue to the ironies of the pregnant bride! Actually there *are* "right" and "wrong," i.e., sensible and considerate vs. cruel and thoughtless, ways to confront an unwanted pregnancy and particularly the ceremony of abortion.

Unwanted pregnancy can be a devastating, shattering event. The ethics and morality of resolving the crisis are, after all, a life-and-death decision. No one can provide an *ideal* answer. Even with skilled, professional guidance, ready help from friends, family, and the man in your life, the decision about what to do is never easy and sometimes tinged with trauma and guilt. What *etiquette can* do is merely provide suggestions for behavior or attitudes that might make this trauma period smoother, easier, less painful—to you and the other people involved.

Countdown: Stage One

A. I think I'm pregnant.
Some girls are "absolutely sure" they are pregnant twelve times a year. Guilt? Anxiety? Wishful thinking? Only an analyst could say. If you send too many false alarms, no one is going to believe you or express concern for you when you *really* need it. (A tiny suspicion magnified to test the man's reaction is childish, cruel, and unwise. He may say something you don't want to hear . . . brinkmanship can quickly kill a relationship.) Suggestion: Don't say "I think" if you only have an awful feeling. Find out! See your doctor, or a *new* doctor if you want to keep the news exclusive. Stifle your urge to babble, weep, and speculate with your lover and with friends until you know for sure . . . you'll have saved considerable embarrassment.

Countdown: Stage Two

B. *I am pregnant—a real doctor, a real frog, an actual pregnancy test confirm it.*

ALTERNATIVE I

You both want to marry. Honest. Neither of you is practicing emotional blackmail on the other. You have put off marriage for no good reason . . . or even for very good reason. Now this crisis makes you realize marriage is right. O.K. . . .

1. Tell anyone you know will be pleased to hear the news.

2. Omit certain details with parents, elderly aunts, old schoolteachers, uptight office gossips, absolutely *anyone* who would be offended, hurt, panicked . . . or give you a hard time. This group can count on its fingers later and say whatever it pleases.

3. If the bride's pregnancy is not visible, she may wear white, satin, lace, heirloom veils . . . ivory, blue, cranberry, brown velvet, go barefoot, wind daisies through her hair . . . whatever she pleases. Have the wedding of your childhood daydreams with tiered cake dripping with candy roses and triumphal trumpets . . . or an earth ceremony in country cotton to the music of Dylan and words of e.e. cummings. Munch Alice B. Toklas fudge brownies!

4. The visibly pregnant bride will feel not only silly but enormous in white satin . . . and may prefer a small private ceremony . . . or even to wait until after the baby's delivery to get married. Fine. But, if the bride and groom are unrestrainedly happy and feel they can gracefully handle a wild blast of a wedding party, that's fine too. Those who thought they'd feel like weeping may decide, intoxicated by the punch and the good cheer of the bridal couple, it's really all for the best.

ALTERNATIVE II

You (or he) want to marry. But the partner says no.

This can be a tragic emotional impasse—or it may just be that he wants to be persuaded. Are you being wantonly obstinate? Do you *know* this is wrong but are letting the pressure get to you? Try not to panic but quietly decide what is best for you both—not just you alone. Get professional advice if you need it. Once you have decided, if the answer is to *marry* . . . apply the same rules as Alternative I.

ALTERNATIVE III

You want to have the baby and

    A. Raise it yourself.

    B. Give it up for adoption.

Both choices contain many hidden dangers. Telling you mere etiquette here is not enough . . . you need practical help and professional advice. Consult a psychotherapist promptly.

ALTERNATIVE IV

You want an abortion.

The growing acceptance of legalized abortion has begun to change all the rules of behavior about a ritual of life that was *already* more common than society even admitted. A long-sought-after right is finally ours—the right to choose—legally—*not* to bear an already conceived child.

Now that abortion has emerged from criminal back rooms, in some states at least, and Blue Cross has agreed to pay the bills, abortion, which was never a *carefree* act, although a relatively simple operation, is becoming more civilized. (As of July, 1970, New York became the one state in the Union with the most liberal abortion law.) Even with this fresh air of candor and reality, being pregnant inadvertently calls for enormous restraint and reserve of character if you're to resist the need to strike back at others in this time when you feel so vulnerable. You need *help*. Friends, doctors, a clergyman, a friend of a friend who just had an abortion can give information. Try Planned Parenthood, Family Planning Information Service, the Clergy Consultation Services (currently in twenty-eight cities in twenty-two states); try to contact the nearest Women's Liberation group. If they don't have the latest, best information . . . they'll know who has. Or call Z.P.G., Los Altos, Calif. They have an Abortion Information Data Bank which now lists about 500 abortion sources. They will send you a list of the eight or ten doctors and clinics nearest you with fees and other facts. The charge: a $5 donation if you can afford it.

The man you love, the man you loved, the man who loves you, the men who are fond of you (one or none may be the father of this unborn child) may want to know and help. Even the casual lover may feel protective although he may not feel at all *obligated*. You may tell or not. Consider your motivation for confiding . . . are you asking for help and support? Or are you getting revenge, rationalizing hurt, manipulating?

Most parents are cooler then they used to be. Nobody throws rocks at Vanessa Redgrave or boycotts her movies just because she hasn't gotten around to marrying the father of her baby. Still, some girls involve their parents in an unwanted pregnancy as a subliminal kind of test or punishment. Interviewing college girls for a study of campus sexual attitudes, I talked with one girl who said, "I'd never tell my mom . . . she'd have a heart attack if she knew." But then she *did* tell mom after finding herself in a pregnancy bind. Most of us can gauge the flexibility and resources of our parents. But pregnancy is a grown-up complication, best handled in a grown-up, independent way. If possible, it is probably kindest to leave your parents out of it.

Countdown: Stage Three

Who pays for what? There are community pregnancies—in a college dorm, for instance, where the crowd rallies to raise money for Ginger's abortion . . . selling suede vests to each other or pawning precious jewelry. Most pregnancies will be your own responsibility, however.

If the pregnancy is no one participant's fault, both are financially obligated. If you lied saying, "Yes, I took my pill," when you had been skipping it for months . . . the financial burden is rightly yours. If he lied about being sterile—or insisted when you said no—it is his. If you made some miscalculation out of aesthetic, romantic, or poetic illusion or sheer laziness, the fault is yours. Still he may wish to assume all or half the bill. Or he may refuse all help. Or you may refuse his offer.

There is no polite way to make a man pay. You can threaten to tell his wife . . . or his boss . . . or his mother. You can write letters or telephone at 2:00 A.M. or stand on the street corner across from his office and scream at the top of your lungs. It *might* get a bundle of bills pressed into your sweaty palm. But it *guarantees* hysteria for you, is a vengeful and manipulative act, degrading to you both. Try reasoning with him. A mutual friend can plead your case. Convince your lover of your calm, your discretion, your absolute determination to protect his name and his reputation, as well as yours. If the answer is still no—*give up*. Why not borrow from the bank? Ask for a vacation loan.

If you don't know who the father is . . . you might take up a collection from all the possibles. This calls for a light, slightly playful manner . . . heavyweight drama is terribly old-fashioned for a girl like you.

If an uninvolved friend offers a loan, of course you can accept but don't postpone paying it back.

Your parents may want to pay the bills. If it's no hardship, accept. If it is, pay them back later.

11. ILLICIT TOGETHERNESS

It's ex-officio official. You are a two, a couple, a ménage, a togetherness. It happened by schedule and plan, quite by passion, or by gentle aimless drift. You are living together. The morality or pragmatics of your single togetherness is not our concern here. Rather let us be brown-paper bag practical in a delightful situation on which Emily Post has never commented. Yes, today an adventuress *can* be a lady . . . even the adulteress can be thoughtful, considerate, sensible . . . positively a contemporary heroine.

Where You Live

HIS APARTMENT OR YOURS? The place doesn't matter . . . unless it does. He may feel more in control of your liaison if he moves semigingerly into your place . . . where he can storm out the first time you pout. Or you may feel less Scarlet Woman if you live out your fantasies a few blocks from where everyone knows you. Which apartment is coziest and roomier? Whose roommate can be least painfully excised? Is it hopeless to think you can turn out Escoffier dinners in his broom-closet kitchen? Is he pitifully attached to his stereo, caved-in mattress, and wall-to-wall view of the San Francisco Bay? Consider all. Talk together. Agree.

DO YOU KEEP THE VACATED APARTMENT, SUBLET, OR ABANDON IT FOREVER? That vacant pad is a beautiful escape . . . the perfect retreat for trial separations. Freedom is the joy, the thrill, and the danger of illicit housekeeping . . . this standby apartment (temporarily sublet to some amiable chum) is a symbol of your freedom. Why not hang on to it?

WHY NOT A FRESH START IN A NEW FLAT? What a beautiful thought! Sit down with the classified ads and circle your dream apartments, then go hunting together. It's fun, but prepare your story for the landlord before venturing forth. The average building owner of a big city is not concerned about last names not matching. He figures he's lucky if you don't keep pet gorillas or manufacture LSD in the pullman kitchen. What he wants to know is . . . can you pay the rent? Still . . . the sub-average and small-town landlord may be a bundle of repressions and intolerance. Hedge. Couples often shop for a flat before the wedding . . . you two are simply being farsighted . . . no need to mention *how* far off and indefinite wedding plans actually are. Of course you still use your single name. Doesn't Sophia Loren and Bendel's president Geraldine Stutz?

Who signs the lease? Your lover does. Unless you are the Big Breadwinner and Are Keeping Him. (It can happen. See below.)

WHO PAYS FOR WHAT? Avoid disaster, mistrust, recrimination. . . . Work out the fiscal arrangements in *advance*. The rules are flexible, depending upon who is the tycoon and who the heiress, or who the struggling actor and who an old-fashioned male chauvinist.

YOU HAVE A TWO-INCOME LIAISON

Here are three possible life-styles in sharing:
1. The Kitty: Both pool salaries after taxes, insurance, and pre-determined savings, then share *all* living expenses (each pays for his own car, clothes, medical, dental, cosmetic bills).
2. Proportioned Chip-In (depending on income): Each contributes a *percentage* of net income for housekeeping and entertainment expenses; each pays his own *personal* expenses.
3. Male-Ego Supportive Plan: He pays rent, utilities, phone bills, car, outside entertainment, and his own personal expenses. You pay for food, home entertainment, laundry, cleaning, the once-a-week cleaning lady, and *your* personal needs.

YOU HAVE TWO INCOMES BUT CHIVALRY PREVAILS.

He wants to support you in that sweet, marvelous, emeralds-and-caviar style, but he also finds your career fascinating . . . wouldn't *dream* of asking you to give it up, and suggests you save your pay for that Lindner watercolor you crave or a summer in Amalfi. In that case, our prince pays all household expenses, finances, entertainment, and vacations . . . even your appendicitis if he insists (of course you have Blue Cross, but he wants you to have a private room with a river view). There is a *hint* of decadence, of course, in accepting even your pocket money from him and charging pantyhose and tweezers to his account. You now have almost more money than you know what to do with! . . . spend some on mad luxuries for *him*—eighteen-carat monogrammed cigar clipper, lapis lazuli cuff links, a letter signed by George Washington.

HE INSISTS YOU GIVE UP YOUR INCOME AND
OLD-FASHIONED MALE CHAUVINISM TRIUMPHS.

He wants to *keep* you . . . insists you quit your job and devote yourself to him, his houses, wine cellar, and Russian wolfhounds. The M.C. pays for *everything* . . . and if he doesn't dig shopping, you'll be given a blank check and sent off to buy the sable wrap *yourself*. This is a perfectly proper and acceptable relationship . . . not unlike being a wife. You should not have to depend on cash handouts, however. Have your own checking account, which he refills.

THERE IS ONE INCOME AND IT'S YOURS.

He is poor, unemployed . . . a student, perhaps, or a struggling artist . . . maybe he's that beautiful naïf you rescued from a macrobiotic commune. At any rate, you've taken him into your nest and are paying for *everything* while he casts *objets d' estime* in Lucite, auditions, or stirs up seaweed soup. It is easy to emasculate the most virile man in this situation! You, as the sorcerer's apprentice, must brew all kinds of magic to make him feel *he* is firmly in charge. If you can't pay the bills graciously, don't get *into* a philanthropic entanglement. If you're already in such a relationship, stifle basic bossiness . . . those martyred sighs . . . all hints of resentment, exasperation, recriminations. Never say, "I knock myself out all week to keep you in sirloin and you can't even remember to pick up the laundry" . . . or . . . "Is that why I paid the orthodontist $500 . . . so you could act in a pornographic movie?" Do not load your beloved boarder with menial household errands or make him ask for handouts. Give him his checking account and deposit a nice monthly allowance to cover cigarettes, beer, bus fare, soybeans and sesame seed oil, his subscription to *Evergreen Review* and an occasional hero sandwich . . . enough so he can take you to the movies, too.

More Helpful Hints

DO YOU MERGE AT THE BANK? A joint housekeeping checking account is convenient. Otherwise each hangs on to his own savings, stocks, mutual funds, bonds, broker, and piggy bank.

WHO'S AT HOME? Both names go on the mailbox and door buzzer (unless for community or professional reasons you are pretending to be married). His name first (I'm so old-fashioned!), yours second. Use first-name initials *only* (it's subtle, and female names on door buzzers can give burglars and rapists ideas). So—R. Montague

J. Capulet

For visits from folks who don't know (your mother, his great Aunt Clarissa, his boss) you have substitute buzzer and mailbox labels. With a flick of the card, the buzzer reads: "R. Montague" alone . . . or "J.

Capulet." Other solutions: Montague and/or Capulet. Montague and Capulet, Inc. (or Ltd.)

WHOM DO YOU TELL? Everyone who will be pleased and delighted by your happy merger. You can predict fairly accurately . . . though you may make a few miscalculations. Your boss is so worldly, so playful . . . such a rogue himself . . . you never thought he'd turn into a jealous monster. Or your mother, so contemporary and sexually adventurous herself since the face-lift, may prove to be weepily sentimental. But probably you *know* who will be pleased and cheered, and who will feel threatened.

HEDGE WITH:

Superintendent
Lady next door
Exterminator
Delicatessen that delivers
Mailman
United Parcel Man (why shouldn't you shop at Saks under your career-girl name)

DO NOT LIE TO:

Analyst
Gynecologist
Sensory-awareness group
Abandoned ex-beaux (they deserve the truth)
Librarian
Bartenders (they'll understand your problems better if you tell the truth)
Lawyer
Broker
Internal Revenue Service
Passport Office

Concerning those with whom you hedge; certain lies can only trap you in layers of confusion. When a little camouflage *is* necessary, never claim you're married if you are not. It is better to lie by denying you're living together.

WHAT SHALL I SAY TO MOTHER? The truth will probably hurt her; lie. I don't care if you are the President of the Society Against Hypocrisy, hypocrisy is golden if you sense that parents (his or yours) and elderly relatives or prissy friends from out-of-town honestly prefer to be spared the details of your delicious infamy. You will be astonished what mother can overlook if she is determined not to see what's going on—size 13 sneakers under the bed, your new subscription to *Sports Il-lustrated*, and his moustache box in the medicine chest. It is kinder to rearrange the incriminating evidence before she arrives. If yours (or his) is an out-of-town mother, encourage short, happy, *intense* visits and put your mate up at a friend's for the duration. A stiff, unyielding, nonconvertible sofa may encourage brevity . . . or send Mom off to a hotel.

WELL, NOW SHE KNOWS . . . WHAT CAN I SAY?

He to his Mom: "You're always nagging me to settle down. Look how settled I am."

You to yours: "I haven't had hives *once* since he moved in."

Mom the Ostrich was simple; parents who *know* are something else. Your folks are afraid he'll never marry you, his are petrified he *will!* Watch for sabotage, pressure, and loaded missiles from both quarters. Jolly them along. Tell them good news: he bought you a gold love-knot ring for your birthday. Spare them the bad: it doesn't fit *that* finger. Be polite to parental saboteurs if it kills you.

WHAT ABOUT THE CLEANING LADY? Keep yours, not his. Cleaning ladies can be more hysterical and jealous than mothers. You want her on your side. Her life probably is so dull, your slightly sinful state can't help but intrigue her.

WHO GETS THE KEYS? All three of you, I hope. Him, you and the cleaning lady. If the apartment is yours, denying him a key is tense and rude. What could be warmer and more affectionate than giving him a fourteen-karat gold key from Tiffany's . . . of course, it's sad and weepy when you have to ask for it back (or change the lock), but if you paralyze yourself by anticipating tragic endings, you'll never have your share of glorious beginnings.

WHAT ABOUT THE TELEPHONE? Two phones and two separate numbers are ideal and avoid assorted crises. But one phone—listed under both names—need not be a booby trap. If you've an answering service, they know all your darkest secrets anyway . . . no point in lying. They answer with the number—Butterfield 8-2267—rather than your name or his . . . nicely noncommittal. If your boss, your dad, or anyone who doesn't know calls and *he* answers, the explanation is short and casual; you were next door borrowing a lemon and your date picked up the phone . . . or your Russian tutor . . . or the piano tuner. At 2:00 A.M., of course, you are not likely to be next door borrowing lemons; in that case it was your tax accountant . . . you were out in the kitchen brewing coffee. Or it *could* be the wrong number. When the phone rings again, *you* answer. Similarly, *you* were: the girl next door, his interior decorator, the Avon lady. Ex-flames, surprised to hear a male voice, are told: "That's Danny . . . we're together most of the time."

WHAT TO DO WITH ABANDONED MISTRESSES AND SLIGHTED LOVERS?
1. Be truthful.
2. Invite them to your parties.
3. Meet them for lunch.

Ex-beaux may continue to send flowers, candy, love letters (bitter, seductive, hopeful . . . riddled with shreds of poetry). His ex-inamorata may send chocolate-chip cookies, bake birthday cakes, and rust-out your mailbox with tear-sodden notes. Any of these offerings—calculated or innocent—should be dismissed casually but with *sympathy*. You and he may eat the cake and cookies, drink the Dom Perignon. Pile the four dozen long-stemmed yellow roses into the champagne cooler (it would be *criminal* to toss living yellow roses down the incinerator). *But* the hand-knit sweater from her dear hands should be stuffed into the deepest recesses of the closet (too cruel for him to return it), to be kept as you might keep old love letters, photographs, or pressed corsages. (Does anyone still press gardenias?) Aging momentos should never be destroyed, not even when you marry or your *children* marry. They feed the ego with remembered pleasures.

DATING . . . DARE WE? How can you even think of it? If yours is nothing but a cold-blooded share-the-rent arrangement, I suppose you do go out with other men. But if this is love, extramural activity is the grossest gluttony. A lady might (for very good reason) be unfaithful to her husband, but *never* to her lover.

WHAT ABOUT WELL-MEANING FRIENDS WHO TRY TO FIX YOU UP? Don't be crudely candid: "Didn't you know I'm living with Fred." Or coy: "My roommate won't let me." Try honest understatement: "I'm sort of involved with Karl."

Matchmaking hostesses who invite you to meet a bachelor brother-in-law or to be the scintillating single to a gaggle or extra men should be told: "I'm sorry . . . I can't come because I'm only seeing George" . . . or "going steady" or "not dating anyone but . . ." Your hostess then has the choice of inviting you both or finding herself another free-lance lovely. Don't put her on the spot with: "I'd love to come but I must bring Fred." She may already have fourteen extra male bodies on her hands. (How nice for *her!*)

If it's a command-performance where one of you is needed or wanted in your singleness—his boss or yours, a client's daughter to be escorted to the theatre, a business-linked cocktail party, even a weekend in Palm Springs—then you or he must go, solo. Unless you are a professional call girl or a paid gigolo, all that is expected of you is charm, wit, and spirit.

HOW DO WE SIGN OUR CHRISTMAS CARDS? Letters and cards to mutual close friends are signed with both your first names. Cards or letters to business friends or an old school crony who never heard of you are signed simply by him.

Letters you address to a couple with a liaison like yours are not written:

Romeo Montague and friend
Romeo Montague and family
Romeo Montague and roommate

Mr. and Mrs. R. Montague (unless that is their announced fiction) but rather both names appear as below:

Mr. R. Montague

Ms J. Capulet

or— Montague and Capulet, Inc.

It's not Emily Post. It's contemporary COSMOPOLITAN and it's right! If you don't want to lie but you can't quite face the truth in black and white, avoid *sending* cards.

WHAT IS THE BIGGEST, MOST GRUESOME THREAT TO YOUR UNWED BLISS? Garbage. Some of your most shattering battles are going to be over hair in the sink, wet pantyhose hanging half-mast on the shower rail, and garbage soaked through the bag. Being neat may not be congenital, but it *is* thoughtful, aesthetically creative, and sometimes positively crucial. Women can be awesome pigs and men, though not always scrupulously neat, have a much lower tolerance for clutter than we. If you are a secret slob, closet slob, or outright *total* slob . . . fight it, hide it, deny it! Fold, sweep, wipe, vacuum, replace the cap . . . no—under the bed is *not* a place to store the overflow. His mother, my dear, was a paragon of Clean.

Yes, I know . . . for ten years you have been divinely content to use brown-paper grocery bags in the garbage can, leak what may. His mother uses tear-off pull-up plastic garbage bags . . . now you do, too. And don't wait for garbage to spill over the top before you dispose of it.

WHY DOES HE KEEP SCREAMING AT ME? Are you nearsighted? (You paint your face with your nose an inch from the bathroom mirror, then dash blindly "beautiful" into the bedroom). Put on your *glasses*, Scheherezade, and peek at that bathroom sink. Eeeccckk! Ha. Never saw it before . . . not really. Clean it up . . . look for "spiders"—fake eyelashes that always end on the floor! Medicine-chest chaos is *another* ground for divorce . . . even when you're not married. Why not hang a second medicine chest so he'll have his very own? And know that someday he is going to reach into *yours* for the hair spray and sixty-seven partly used eye shadow sticks are going to roll out at his feet. Be merciless. Organize. Scour the rust off and camouflage with pretty paper.

HIS FRONT CLOSET IS A SWAMP AND HE SEEMS TO LOVE IT THAT WAY. Good Lord. Don't move a single moldy thing. Respect his warrens. Allow his eccentricities and concede your own . . . beg him to ignore them. It is not necessarily a chink in your perfect love if he grows livid because you used his toothbrush. People are different: he needs privacy in the bathroom, you want someone to soap you all over. You can't put two words together before 10:00 A.M.; he's a conversational demon at 7:00 A.M. He never uses a towel more than once; yours are makeup smudged. You cannot function without a peppermill; he hates spices. So be it.

Listen more.

Are you fighting about what's really bugging you, or covering up?

A sweet thought is sweeter spoken . . . *never* repress a compliment. Try to say yes more often.

Accept his fictions . . . whenever possible. If he thinks his *risotto* is extraordinary or his voice is transformed in the shower or his toes are aristocratic . . . it accomplishes nothing to expose the lie, unless you want him to go away *permanently.* In that case tell him so . . . don't hurt him needlessly by pecking him to pieces.

SHALL I TELL HIM EVERYTHING? Let your antennae guide you. Some men really don't want to know. Others are deeply fascinated with everything that has shaped your personality. And a few lightly disguised sadists just want ammunition to torture you . . . or themselves.

It's marvelous to know that this is a man to whom you can say anything, absolutely anything. But not everything. Especially those hateful truths that come in the height of rage. If you have the one revelation that can really destroy him . . . file it. Also, would you trust him with all your secrets should you part?

HOW CAN I BE OPEN AND HONEST AND PRESERVE THE MYSTERY? Don't worry there is *always* mystery. He knows now that your hair isn't naturally beige and that you talk in your sleep and eat peanut butter with a spoon, but you are *still* a fascinating, unpredictable creature. There is always a vast area of the unstated and unknown in each of us . . . the very *nature* of Homo sapiens. Be mostly truthful and don't worry.

HOW ELEGANT SHOULD WE BE? Very. Use your grandmother's heirloom silver, previously kept tucked away in a hope chest. Life together should be as beautiful and luxurious as you can afford. What is the heirloom silver *waiting* for?

SHOULD I GIVE AWAY THE EXTRA IRON AND TOASTER? I'm superstitious. If you remember your umbrella it never rains. Why not keep the duplicates . . . store them away somewhere. Knowing about them enhances your sense of freedom . . . and danger. Should you *never* part, they'll be nice for your beach house.

SOME OF OUR FRIENDS ACT SO STRANGE. Friends are ambivalent, married friends especially. Vicariously, they share in your slightly wicked freedom, but they are envious too and perhaps a little threatened. Your carefree singlehood seems much too attractive. Girl friends are happy for you (and jealous!) but they also can't resist hanging around and flirting with *him.* Your cousin Joni says he is not the ogre she thought he'd be, but why should he marry you when he's already got everything he wants. You know *that* thinking went out with the wind-up Victrola, but you sort of cluck along with her. His best friend can't resist cataloging the parade of your lissome predecessors in his love nest. Listen and learn. *Don't let any of their hangups become yours.*

Your lover *is* going to *loathe* some of your friends, and you a few of his. Compromise and tolerance are called for . . . if you have to be with people you don't like, surround them with people you *do* . . . as a buffer.

Do entertain. If you cook like Julia and look like Raquel, you both want to show you off. Master the art of the near-effortless dinner party . . . or the shared-effort Sunday brunch. For friends and relatives who are innocently unaware of your togetherness—try a super picnic for fresh-air gourmets. If he must entertain his boss or client and home is too touchy an exposure, take them to a favorite restaurant. Order a fabulous Greek supper or a Chinese banquet. But don't underestimate the flexibility of the old folks . . . they might be tickled to sip champagne in a cozy den of iniquity.

THINGS THAT ARE TACKY

Reading his mail.
Telling terrible stories about the man you used to live with (your current mate gets premonitions for the future).
Forgetting to take the pill.
Discussing his frailties with your girl friend.
Describing his sexual prowess or eccentricities with *anyone* (except your shrink).
Not brushing teeth till late in the afternoon or Sunday.
Forgetting *twice* that he loathes eggplant.
Losing his place in the book you're both reading.
Listening in on the extension.
Wearing something you know he hates.
Criticizing him in front of . . . anyone.
Crumbs in bed.
An aging douche bag swinging from the shower head.
Chocolates with one bite gone replaced in the box.
Forgetting to buy vermouth, stamps, shaving cream (he asked you twice).
Martyrdom.
Rubbing his nose in your sacrifices.
I-told-you-so's.
Your silky hairpiece on a chair post . . . some men are shaken by disembodied beauty aids.
Serious cosmetic make-over in his presence . . . like bleaching your moustache.
High-power flirting with his friends. You are a vital, lusty female, but not at all predatory.

Index

Abortion, 251–252
See also Pregnancy, accidental

Adultery, 243–245
See also Sex

Affairs
See Sex

Apologies, 210–214

Beauty, 5–12
See also Body

Birth control, 246–248
devices, 247–248
information sources, 246–247
pill, 247
See also Pregnancy, accidental

Boats
behavior on, 178–184
nautical glossary, 183–184
what to wear on, 179–180

Body, 5–12
beauty-aid survival kits, 9–10
exercise, 7, 50
hair, 7
hands, 10, 241–242
perfume, 10
posture, 7, 50
skin, 8
skin, effect of sun on, 8
survival kit, his, 11
survival kit, home, 9
survival kit, office, 10
survival kit, traveling, 10
See also Hairdresser's; Makeup;
Teeth and gums

Body language, 6
in the bedroom, 235

Books, recommended
birth control, 246
cooking, 133, 139
sex, 226
Women's lib, 216

Brown, Helen Gurley, 1–2, 10, 133

Chanel, Gabrielle ("Coco"), 6, 16, 119

Charge accounts, 193–194
See also Money

Class, 35–41
U and non-U speech, 51–56
with friends, 38
with men, 37–38
with money, 35–37
with possessions, 39
with public property, 38–39

Cleaning women, 151–155
how to find one, 151–152
how to fire her, 154–155
how to interview her, 152–153
how to keep her, 153–154

Clothes
See Dress

Cocktail parties
See Entertaining; Parties

Compliments
from men you know, 75–76
from women, 76
street variety, 75–79

Consciousness-raising groups, 215–216

Contraception
See Birth control

Conversation, starting one, 57–61
in familiar surroundings, 59–61
in semi-impersonal situations, 59–61
in totally impersonal situations, 59–61
See also Speech

Cookbooks, 133, 139

Cosmetics
See Makeup

Cosmopolitan, 8, 20, 42, 226

Credit cards, 193–194
See also Money

Dating, 95–101
  being a great date, 97–101
  inexpensive fun, 95–97

Dining out
  French, 102–109
  Italian, 110–116
  menu terms, French, 107–109
  menu terms, Italian, 115–116
  taking a man to lunch, 194–196
  See also Tipping

Dinner parties
  See Entertaining

Dress, 16–20
  boating wear, 179–180
  choosing right clothes, 18–19
  fashion slavery, 17
  handbags, 19
  hats, 19
  men, dressing to please them, 16
  midis, 17
  rules, how they've changed, 16, 19
  shoes, 17
  special occasions, 19
  wardrobe, keeping it in shape, 17–18
  See also Fashion experts; Tacky,
    things that are

Drinks
  See Entertaining

Entertaining, 129–150
  away from home, 143–144
  bar, all-purpose, 138
  breakfast guest, unexpected, 144–145
  budget, 199
  cocktail parties, 131–138, 166–167
  dinner parties, 138–143
  drinks, how to mix, 134–138
  foreign guests, feeding of, 147–150
  parties, kinds to give, 130–131
  table settings, 140–142
  See also Cookbooks; Houseguests;
    Tacky, things that are

Etiquette
  defined for today, 1–2
  quickie quiz, 217–220
  See also individual listings

Etiquette no-no's
  See Tacky, things that are

Exercise, 7, 50
  See also Body

Fashion
  See Dress

Fashion experts, advice from, 21–25
  Beene, Geoffrey, 23–24
  Blass, Bill, 21–22
  Brooks, Donald, 22
  Gernreich, Rudi, 22–23
  Klein, Anne, 17, 24–25
  Nassarre, Tom, 23

Food
  See Dining out; Entertaining

Friends
  finding them, 73–74
  use and abuse of, 70–72

Generosity, 205–209
  sexual, 229–234

Gifts, 122–128
  for girl friends, 126
  for men, 125–126
  for rich friends, 123–124
  for your boss, 126
  for your hostess, 117, 125
  from men, 126–127
  homemade, 199–200
  of money, 124
  thank-you notes, 127
  See also Tacky, things that are

Greetings, 44–47
  cheeks, 45
  handshakes, 45
  kisses, 44–45
  what to use when, 46–47

Grooming
  See Body; Tacky, things that are

Gums
  See Teeth and gums

Hair
  See Body; Hairdresser's

Hairdresser's, 7–8
tipping, 203

Handshakes
See Greetings

Hostess gifts, 117, 125

Hotels
See Tipping; Traveling

Houseguests
being one, 156–159
having them, 146–147

Household help
See Cleaning women

Investing money
See Money

Kinesis
See Body language

Kisses
See Greetings

Language
See Speech

Living with a man, 253–261
apartment, his or yours, 253
apartment, keeping yours, 253
names on mailbox, 255–256
nitty-gritty things, 259–260
separate bank accounts, 255
telephone listing, 257
who pays for what, 254–255
who to lie to, 256
See also Tacky, things that are

Love letters, 65–69
gimmicks, 68
ten simple rules, 66–69

Lovers
See Living with a man; Men; Sex;
Traveling

Lying, 86–94
brutal truths, 91–92
campaign lie, 89
careless lie, 91
gentle truths, 92–94
loving lie, 90–91
mannerly lie, 88–89

Makeup
at the hospital, 27
essentials, 27–28
false eyelashes, 9
for daytime, 8
for night, 8
for sports, 28
fresh-scrubbed look, 29–31
in bed, 29
in the shower, 29
See also Body

Manners
defined for today, 1–2
See also individual listings

Marriage
See Pregnancy, accidental

Men
bed, things to do for them in, 238–239
boat, how to act on his, 178–184
class with, 37–38
compliments on the street, 75–79
dating, 95–101
dressing for, 16
foreign variety, 189–192
gifts for, 125–126
gifts from, 126–127
grooming aids for, 11
hands, things to do with your, 241–242
kissing his hand, 45
makeup, how they feel about, 29–31
making breakfast for, 144–145
male ego, care and feeding of, 83
meeting his mother, 117–118
meeting at a party, 161
meeting while traveling, 184–192
mixing drinks for, 134–138
starting a conversation with, 57–61
taking one to lunch, 194–196
telling the bachelor from the husband, 162
traveling with, 168–170
turning them on, 227–228
See also Birth control; Living with a man; Love letters; Office romances; Pregnancy, accidental; Sex

Money, 193–204
  being broke with style, 196–197
  budget dating, 95–97
  budget entertaining, 199
  charge accounts, 193–194
  credit cards, 193–194
  gifts of, 124
  investing, 194
  paying for an abortion, 252
  slobby spending, 205–209
  stock market, 194
  taking a man to lunch, 194–196
  when you live with a man, 254–255
  See also Class; Shopping; Tipping

Nakedness, 20
  See also Body language; Sex

Names, how to remember them, 62–63

Office romances, 119–121

Orgasm, faking of, 237
  See also Sex

Parties
  how to cope while there, 159–165
  See also Entertaining

Perfume, 10

Pill, the
  See Birth control

Post, Emily, 1, 19, 253

Posture, 7, 50
  See also Body

Pregnancy, accidental, 249–252
  abortion, 251–252
  abortion, paying for, 252
  having the baby without marrying, 250
  marrying, 250
  See also Birth control

Restaurants
  See Dining out; Tipping

Servants
  See Cleaning women

Sex, 221–261
  adultery, 243–245
  basic how-to's, 226
  body language in bed, 235
  books, 226
  communicating in bed, 235–237
  for the liberated woman, 229–234
  hand language, 241–242
  meaningless sexuality, 232
  orgasm, faking of, 237
  simultaneous affairs, 231–232
  things not to say in bed, 236–237
  things to do for a man in bed, 238–239
  troubles, sexual, 236
  turning a man on, 227–228
  virginity, 223–225
  See also Birth control; Office romances; Pregnancy, accidental; Tacky, things that are

Shopping on a budget, 197–199
  off-season buying, 198–199

Skin, 8
  See also Body; Makeup

Speech, 42–43, 48–56
  dirty jokes, 43
  four-letter words, 42–43
  tired words to avoid, 55–56
  U and non-U speech, 51–56
  voice faults, 49
  voice, improving your, 49–51
  See also Conversation

Stinginess, 205–209

Stock market, 194

Swearing, 42–43

Table settings, 140–142

Tacky, things that are
  entertaining, 143
  fashion, 20
  gifts, 127–128
  grooming, 11–12
  living with a man, 261
  office romances, 121
  sex, 239–240
  traveling, 171

Tact, how to have, 80–85
  in social situations, 84
  when to be blunt, 84–85
  with men, 83

Teeth and gums, care of, 13–15
  brushing, 13–14
  inflammation, 13
  Periodontitis, 15
  Stim-U-Dents, 14
  Water Pik, 14

Tipping, 200–204
  airplanes, 202
  apartment personnel, 201–202
  bars, 203
  cleaning women, 203
  delivery boys, 201
  hairdresser, 203
  hotels, 202
  moving men, 202
  parking lots, 202–203
  porters, 202
  restaurants, 203
  taxis, 202
  trains, 202

Traveling, 168–192
  airplane romance, 171–178
  foreign men, understanding, 189–192

hotel check-in, 169–170
meeting men abroad, 184–192
service personnel, 171
survival kit, 10
with a lover, 168–170
See also Boats; Tacky, things that are;
  Tipping

Undressing, 20
  See also Body language; Sex

Vanderbilt, Amy, 1, 19

Virginity, 223–225
  See also Sex

Visiting
  meeting his mother, 117–118
  See also Houseguests

Voice
  See Speech

Women's lib, 215–216